BASIC SPANISH GRAMMAR

SIXTH EDITION

BASIC SPANISH GRAMMAR

Ana C. Jarvis
Chandler-Gilbert Community College

Raquel Lebredo
California Baptist University

Francisco Mena-Ayllón
University of Redlands

Houghton Mifflin Company
Boston   New York

Director, Modern Language Programs: E. Kristina Baer
Development Manager: Beth Kramer
Associate Sponsoring Editor: Amy Baron
Associate Development Editor: Rafael Burgos-Mirabal
Associate Project Editor: Amy Johnson
Senior Production/Design Coordinator: Jennifer Waddell
Senior Manufacturing Coordinator: Florence Cadran
Marketing Manager: Patricia Fossi
Cover Design: Rebecca Fagan
Cover Image: "Ocean Park #72" Richard Diebenkorn, 1975
(Philadelphia Museum of Art)

Photo Credits: p. 1, Beryl Goldberg; p. 13, Ulrike Welsch; p. 25, Mark Antman/The Image Works; p. 41, Robert Fried; p. 53, DDB Stock Photo; p. 65, Beryl Goldberg; p. 79, Peter Menzel; p. 99, Robert Frerck/Odyssey/Chicago; p. 111, Peter Menzel; p. 123, Ulrike Welsch; p. 137, Ulrike Welsch; p. 153, Beryl Goldberg; p. 175, Grant le Duc/Monkmeyer Press; p. 187, Beryl Goldberg; p. 199, Ulrike Welsch; p. 209, David Simson/Stock Boston; p. 219, Inga Spence/ DDB Stock Photo; p. 241, Peter Menzel; p. 253, Ulrike Welsch; p. 263, Chip & Rosa Maria Peterson; p. 273, K. McGlynn/ The ImageWorks; p. 283, Beryl Goldberg

Printed in the U.S.A.

Student Text ISBN: 0-395-96297-8

Instructor's Edition ISBN: 0-395-96298-6

Library of Congress Catalog Card Number: 99-71967

789-QW/F-07 06 05 04 03

Contents

Lección 2

1. Agreement of articles, nouns, and adjectives   43
2. The present indicative of regular **-er** and **-ir** verbs   44
3. Possession with **de**   45
4. Possessive adjectives   46
5. The personal **a**   48
   En el laboratorio   49

Lección 3

1. The irregular verbs **ir, dar,** and **estar**   55
2. **Ir a** + infinitive   56
3. Uses of the verbs **ser** and **estar**   57
4. Contractions   59
   En el laboratorio   61

Lección 4

1. The irregular verbs **tener** and **venir**   67
2. Expressions with **tener**   68
3. Comparative forms   71
4. Irregular comparative forms   73
   En el laboratorio   75

Lección 5

Lección 6

Lección 7

Lección 8

Lección 9

1. Possessive pronouns   139
2. Reflexive constructions   141
3. Command forms: **Ud.** and **Uds.**   144
4. Uses of object pronouns with command forms   146

   En el laboratorio   150

Lección 10

1. The preterit of regular verbs   154
2. The preterit of **ser, ir,** and **dar**   156
3. Uses of **por** and **para**   158
4. Seasons of the year and weather expressions   160

   En el laboratorio   163

   ¿Cuánto sabe usted ahora?
   Lecciones 6–10   166

Lección 11

1. Time expressions with **hacer**   177
2. Irregular preterits   178
3. The preterit of stem-changing verbs (**e:i** and **o:u**)   180
4. Command forms (**tú**)   182

   En el laboratorio   185

Lección 12

1. **En** and **a** as equivalents of *at*   189
2. The imperfect tense   190
3. The past progressive   192
4. The preterit contrasted with the imperfect   193

   En el laboratorio   196

Lección 13

Lección 14

Lección 15

Lección 16

Lección 17

Lección 18

Lección 19

Lección 20

Appendices/Vocabularies

Preface

Basic Spanish Grammar, Sixth Edition, presents the essential points of Spanish grammar to students or professionals seeking a working knowledge of Spanish. Grammatical structures and high-frequency vocabulary that are indispensable for communication are presented clearly and concisely and reinforced through a variety of practice exercises.

The Student's Edition

The organization of this central component of the *Basic Spanish Grammar* program reflects its emphasis on the acquisition of Spanish fundamentals for practical use. The Student's Edition consists of two preliminary lessons, twenty regular lessons, and four self-tests, organized as follows:

◆ The preliminary lessons enable students to communicate in Spanish using basic, high-frequency language from the outset of the course.

◆ The twenty regular lessons contain the features listed below.

A core vocabulary list of essential words and expressions, organized by parts of speech. Since this vocabulary is used in the lesson's grammar explanations and activities, students should familiarize themselves with these terms before proceeding. A vocabulary activity, *Palabras y más palabras*, reviews the vocabulary introduced in the lesson.

Three to six grammar structures per lesson, explained clearly and concisely in English so that the explanations may be used independently as an out-of-class reference. All explanations are followed by numerous examples of their practical use in natural Spanish. After each explanation, the *Práctica* offers immediate reinforcement of new concepts through a variety of structured and open-ended activities.

En el laboratorio exercises to be completed in conjunction with the Audio Program. Signalled by a cassette icon, the laboratory exercises include *Vocabulario* and *Práctica* (grammar) sections, as well as a *Para escuchar y entender* (listening comprehension) section.

◆ *¿Cuánto sabe usted ahora?* self-tests after Lessons 5, 10, 15, and 20 allow students to review the structures and vocabulary of the five preceding lessons. Organized by lesson and by grammar structure, the self-tests enáble students to determine quickly what material they have mastered and which concepts to target for further review. An answer key is provided in Appendix D for immediate verification.

◆ Reference Materials: The following sections provide students with useful reference tools throughout the course:

Maps: Up-to-date maps of the Spanish-speaking world appear at the front of the textbook for quick reference.

Appendices: Appendix A summarizes the sounds and key pronunciation features of the Spanish language, with abundant examples. Conjugations of high-frequency regular, stem-changing, and irregular Spanish verbs constitute Appendix B. Appendix C provides a list of the Spanish names of more than 100 professions and occupations to facilitate personalized classroom discussion. Appendix D is the answer key to the *¿Cuánto sabe usted ahora?* self-tests.

Vocabularies: Spanish-English and English-Spanish glossaries list all active vocabulary introduced in the *Vocabulario* lists and in the grammar explanations. Each word or expression is followed by the number of the lesson in which it becomes active.

Audio Program

The complete Audio Program to accompany *Basic Spanish Grammar,* Sixth Edition, is available on audio CDs or audiocassettes for student purchase. Recorded by native speakers, it contains the vocabulary lists and laboratory activities from *Basic Spanish Grammar.* Vocabulary and grammar exercises, plus two or three listening comprehension passages, accompany each student text lesson.

Other Components of the Basic Spanish Grammar Program

The *Basic Spanish Grammar* program features a full range of components designed to meet the needs of students who wish to learn Spanish for specific purposes. To maximize students' exposure to natural spoken Spanish, each of the seven companion manuals is accompanied by its own audio program.

Companion Manuals

Students studying Spanish for professional reasons have specific needs and limited study time. In response to these issues, all components of the *Basic Spanish Grammar* program have been designed to facilitate individualized instruction and independent study. Seven manuals develop practical communication skills for both general and professional use. All may be used in conjunction with the core text in introductory Spanish classes or as stand-alone texts in a one-semester course for students who have had at least one year of Spanish. In each lesson, realistic dialogues and activities present and reinforce vocabulary specific to particular situations or professions and provide practical applications of the grammatical structures introduced in the corresponding lesson of *Basic Spanish Grammar,* Sixth Edition.

Getting Along in Spanish, Fifth Edition
This communication manual develops practical vocabulary for everyday situations by emphasizing common themes such as travel, eating in a restaurant, shopping, running errands, and going to the doctor. Realistic dialogues, personalized questions, situational role-plays, and realia-based activities prepare students to carry out normal daily interactions in Spanish.

Spanish for Communication, Fourth Edition
Spanish for Communication covers the same themes as *Getting Along in Spanish*, but at a more advanced level.

Spanish for Business and Finance, Sixth Edition
Spanish for Business and Finance presents and practices business and finance vocabulary in realistic contexts. Tax preparation, banking operations, real estate, and insurance are among the topics addressed, along with the essentials of business travel such as renting a car, staying in a hotel, and ordering meals. *Suplemento* sections after every few lessons introduce the basics of commercial correspondence and provide both models and practice activities.

Spanish for Law Enforcement, Sixth Edition
Designed specifically for law enforcement personnel, *Spanish for Law Enforcement* introduces and reinforces vocabulary and communicative functions essential to police officers, firefighters, court clerks, and other professionals who interact with the Spanish-speaking community.

Spanish for Medical Personnel, Sixth Edition
Spanish for Medical Personnel presents situations and vocabulary that medical personnel encounter in the course of their daily work. The updated *Notas culturales* highlight Hispanic customs and traditions relevant to health care, as well as information on medical conditions and concerns affecting Hispanics in the United States. Supplementary readings on illnesses such as diabetes, cancer, heart disease,

and AIDS reflect some of the most urgent concerns of the medical community.

Spanish for Social Services, Sixth Edition

Extensive in its coverage of vocabulary and themes requisite to social services professionals or those who are planning a career in the field, *Spanish for Social Services* develops and reinforces communication skills within a context of cultural sensitivity, preparing students for such tasks as explaining available services and eligibility requirements, conducting home visits, and taking family histories.

Spanish for Teachers, Fifth Edition

Spanish for Teachers prepares current and prospective elementary and secondary school teachers, including ESL teachers, to communicate effectively with Spanish-speaking students and their parents. Key vocabulary related to a full range of subject areas and administrative duties is presented.

Audio Programs

Each companion manual of the *Basic Spanish Grammar* program has its own Audio Program, available for student purchase. The audio programs include an introduction to Spanish sounds followed by the dialogues (paused and unpaused versions) and vocabulary lists for each lesson, and the *Práctica oral* questions from the four *Repaso* sections. The readings in the *Lectura* sections of *Spanish for Law Enforcement*, *Spanish for Medical Personnel*, *Spanish for Social Services*, and *Spanish for Teachers* are recorded in their respective audio programs.

Supplementary Materials for the Instructor

Instructor's Edition

The Introduction to the Instructor's Edition provides a detailed description of the entire *Basic Spanish Grammar* program, suggestions for its implementation in the classroom, and a complete answer key to textbook exercises with discrete answers.

Testing Program/Transparency Masters

Completely revised, this supplement includes twenty quizzes (one for each regular lesson), two in-class midterms, two take-home midterms, and two final exams for *Basic Spanish Grammar*. It also contains vocabulary quizzes for all of the regular lessons in each career manual and in *Getting Along in Spanish*, along with a sample vocabulary quiz for *Spanish for Communication*. Also included are comprehensive final exams for *Getting Along in Spanish*, the career manuals, and *Spanish for Communication*. Suggestions for grading and scheduling quizzes and tests complete the program. For vocabulary review, a set of twenty transparency masters containing art from *Getting Along in Spanish* and five transparency masters with diagrams of the human body from *Spanish for Medical Personnel* are bound with the *Testing Program.*

Audioscripts
Complete transcripts for the audio programs to accompany *Basic Spanish Grammar, Getting Along in Spanish,* the career manuals, and *Spanish for Communication* are bound together in one volume.

We would like to hear your comments on and reactions to the sixth edition of the *Basic Spanish Grammar* program. Reports on your experiences using this program would be of great interest and value to us. Please write us in care of Houghton Mifflin Company, College Division, 222 Berkeley Street, Boston, MA 02116-3764.

Acknowledgments

We wish to thank our colleagues who have used previous editions of *Basic Spanish Grammar* for their many constructive comments and recommendations. We especially appreciate the valuable suggestions of the following reviewers of *Basic Spanish Grammar,* Fifth Edition:

Melania Aguirre-Rabon, *Wake Technical College*
Elaine d'Entremont Graybill, *Tyler Junior College*
Mary Ellen Kohn, *Mount Mary College*
Lina Llerena, *Fullerton College*
Norma Lomboy, *New York University*
Suzanne McLaughlin, *Chemeketa Community College*
Germán Pavía, *University of Miami at Coral Gables*
Carmen Sobrino, *Wichita Friends University*

We also extend our sincere appreciation to the Modern Languages Staff of Houghton Mifflin Company, College Division: E. Kristina Baer, Director; Beth Kramer, Development Manager; Amy Baron, Associate Sponsoring Editor; Rafael Burgos-Mirabal, Associate Development Editor; and Amy Johnson, Associate Project Editor.

Ana C. Jarvis
Raquel Lebredo
Francisco Mena-Ayllón

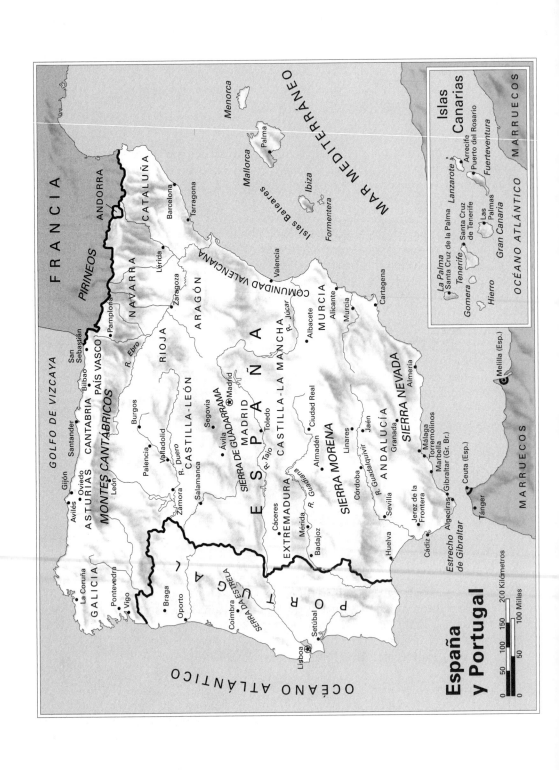

España y Portugal

OCÉANO ATLÁNTICO

FRANCIA

GOLFO DE VIZCAYA

PIRINEOS

ANDORRA

San Sebastián
Pamplona
NAVARRA
R. Ebro
Bilbao
Santander
PAÍS VASCO
Gijón
Oviedo
Avilés
ASTURIAS
CANTABRIA
MONTES CANTÁBRICOS
La Coruña
Pontevedra
Vigo
GALICIA
León
Palencia
Burgos
RIOJA
ARAGÓN
Zaragoza
Lérida
CATALUÑA
Barcelona
Tarragona
Valladolid
Zamora
R. Duero
CASTILLA-LEÓN
Salamanca
Braga
Oporto
Coimbra
SERRA DA ESTRELA
SEGOVIA
Ávila
SIERRA DE GUADARRAMA
MADRID
Madrid
Toledo
R. Tajo
CASTILLA-LA MANCHA
Ciudad Real
COMUNIDAD VALENCIANA
Valencia
R. Júcar
Albacete
MURCIA
Alicante
Murcia
Cartagena
EXTREMADURA
Cáceres
Mérida
Badajoz
R. Guadiana
Almadén
SIERRA MORENA
Linares
Jaén
Córdoba
R. Guadalquivir
Granada
ANDALUCÍA
SIERRA NEVADA
Almería
Sevilla
Huelva
Jerez de la Frontera
Cádiz
Algeciras
Estrecho de Gibraltar
Gibraltar (Gr. Br.)
Ceuta (Esp.)
Tánger
Málaga
Torremolinos
Marbella
Melilla (Esp.)
MARRUECOS

E S P A Ñ A

P O R T U G A L

Lisboa
Setúbal

MAR MEDITERRÁNEO

Menorca
Palma
Mallorca
Ibiza
Formentera
Islas Baleares

Islas Canarias

La Palma
Santa Cruz de la Palma
Gomera
Hierro
Tenerife
Santa Cruz de Tenerife
Lanzarote
Arrecife
Puerto del Rosario
Fuerteventura
Las Palmas
Gran Canaria

OCÉANO ATLÁNTICO

MARRUECOS

0 50 100 150 200 Kilómetros
0   50   100 Millas

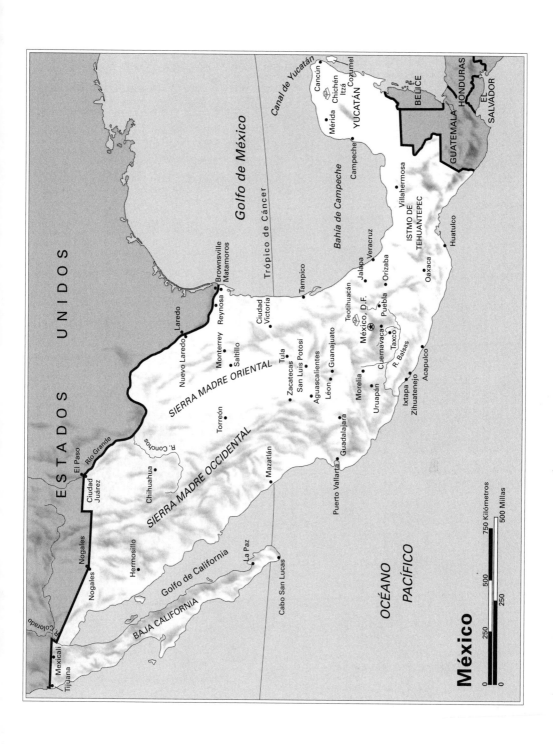

México

ESTADOS UNIDOS

Golfo de México

Bahía de Campeche

Canal de Yucatán

Trópico de Cáncer

OCÉANO PACÍFICO

Golfo de California

BAJA CALIFORNIA

SIERRA MADRE OCCIDENTAL

SIERRA MADRE ORIENTAL

ISTMO DE TEHUANTEPEC

Colorado

Río Grande

R. Conchos

R. Balsas

Tijuana
Mexicali
Nogales
Nogales
Hermosillo
Ciudad Juárez
El Paso
Chihuahua
La Paz
Cabo San Lucas
Mazatlán
Torreón
Saltillo
Monterrey
Nuevo Laredo
Laredo
Reynosa
Matamoros
Brownsville
Ciudad Victoria
Tampico
Zacatecas
San Luis Potosí
Aguascalientes
Léon
Guanajuato
Tula
Puerto Vallarta
Guadalajara
Morelia
Uruapán
Teotihuacán
México, D.F.
Cuernavaca
Taxco
Ixtapa
Zihuatenejo
Acapulco
Puebla
Orizaba
Veracruz
Jalapa
Oaxaca
Huatulco
Villahermosa
Campeche
Mérida
Chichén Itzá
Cancún
Cozumel
YUCATÁN
BELICE
GUATEMALA
HONDURAS
EL SALVADOR

750 Kilómetros
500 Millas
500
250
250
0
0

250

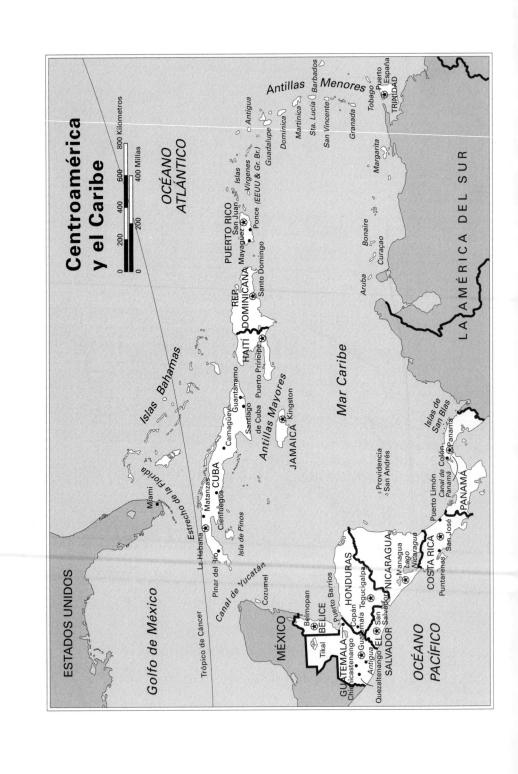

Centroamérica
y el Caribe

ESTADOS UNIDOS

Golfo de México

OCÉANO
ATLÁNTICO

Trópico de Cáncer

Miami

Estrecho de la Florida

Islas Bahamas

Canal de Yucatán

Cozumel

Pinar del Río

Le Habana

Matanzas

CUBA

Cienfuegos

Isla de Pinos

Camagüey

Santiago
de Cuba

Guantánamo

Antillas Mayores

JAMAICA   Kingston

Puerto Príncipe

HAITÍ

REP.
DOMINICANA

Santo Domingo

PUERTO RICO

San Juan

Mayagüez   Ponce (EEUU & Gr. Br.)

Islas
Vírgenes

Guadalupe

Dominica

Martinica

Sta. Lucía

San Vincente

Antigua

Barbados

Granada

Tobago

TRINIDAD

Puerto
España

Antillas Menores

Mar Caribe

Margarita

Bonaire

Curaçao

Aruba

Providencia
San Andrés

MÉXICO

Tikal
Belmopan
BELICE
Puerto Barrios
Copán
HONDURAS
GUATEMALA   Tegucigalpa
Chichicastenango
Quezaltenango
Antigua   Guatemala
EL   San
SALVADOR   Salvador
NICARAGUA
Managua
Lago
Nicaragua
Lago
COSTA RICA
Puntarenas
San José
Puerto Limón

OCÉANO
PACÍFICO

Islas de
San Blas

Canal de Colón
Panamá

Panamá

PANAMÁ

LA AMÉRICA DEL SUR

800 Kilómetros
400 Millas
0   200   400   600
0   200

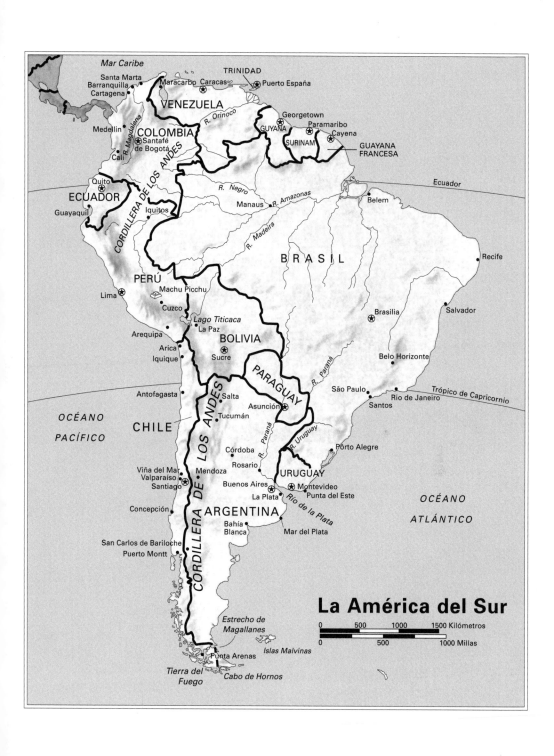

La América del Sur

Lección preliminar

1 Greetings and farewells
Saludos y despedidas

—Buenos días, doctor Rivas.
¿Cómo está usted?
"Good morning, Doctor Rivas. How are you?"

—Muy bien, gracias. ¿Y usted?
"Very well, thank you. And you?"

—Bien, gracias. Hasta luego.
"Fine, thank you. See you later."

—Adiós.
"Good-bye."

—Buenas tardes, señora.
"Good afternoon, madam."

—Buenas tardes, señor.
"Good afternoon, sir."

—Pase y tome asiento, por favor.
"Come in and sit down, please."

—Gracias.
"Thank you."

—Buenas noches, señorita.
¿Cómo está usted?
"Good evening, miss. How are you?"

—No muy bien.
"Not very well."

—Lo siento. Hasta mañana.
"I'm sorry. I'll see you tomorrow."

—Hola, César. ¿Qué tal?
"Hi, César. How's it going?"

—Bien, gracias. ¿Y tú?
"Fine, thank you. And you?"

—Muy bien.
"Just fine."

—Muchas gracias, señor.
"Thank you very much, sir."

—De nada, señora. Adiós.
"You're very welcome, madam. Good-bye."

—Mucho gusto, profesor Vera.
"Pleased to meet you, Professor Vera."

—El gusto es mío, señorita Reyes.
"The pleasure is mine, Miss Reyes."

Vocabulario: Saludos y despedidas

SALUDOS Y DESPEDIDAS

Buenos días.	*Good morning. (Good day.)*
Buenas tardes.	*Good afternoon.*
Buenas noches.	*Good evening. (Good night.)*
Hola.	*Hi. (Hello.)*
Hasta luego.	*I'll see you later.* (lit., *until later*)
Hasta mañana.	*I'll see you tomorrow.*
Adiós.	*Good-bye.*

TÍTULOS

doctor (Dr.)[1]	*doctor* (masc.)
doctora (Dra.)	*doctor* (fem.)
profesor	*professor, teacher, instructor* (masc.)
profesora	*professor, teacher, instructor* (fem.)
señor (Sr.)	*Mr., sir, gentleman*
señora (Sra.)	*Mrs., madam, lady*
señorita (Srta.)	*Miss, young lady* (unmarried)

EXPRESIONES ÚTILES

¿Cómo está usted?	*How are you?*
Muy bien, ¿y usted?	*Very well, and you?*
¿Qué tal?	*How's it going?*
Bien, ¿y tú?	*Fine (Well), and you?*
No muy bien.	*Not very well.*
Lo siento.	*I'm sorry.*
Mucho gusto.	*It's a pleasure to meet you.*
El gusto es mío.	*The pleasure is mine.*
Pase.	*Come in.*
Por favor.	*Please.*
Tome asiento.	*Have a seat.*
Gracias.	*Thank you.*
Muchas gracias.	*Thank you very much.*
De nada.	*You're welcome.*

ATENCIÓN: Use the **tú** form when addressing a friend, a relative, or a very young person.

Práctica

A. Familiarize yourself with each of the dialogues on page 2, and then act them out with another student.

B. What would you say in the following situations?

1. You meet Mr. García in the morning and ask him how he is.
2. You thank Miss Vera for a favor and tell her you will see her tomorrow.
3. You greet Mrs. Nieto in the afternoon and ask her to come in and sit down.
4. A young woman is introduced to you.
5. Someone thanks you for a favor.
6. Someone asks you how you are and you are not feeling well.
7. You say "hi" to a friend and ask how it's going for him/her.

[1] Notice that in Spanish, titles are not capitalized except when they are abbreviated.

2 Cardinal numbers 0–39
Los números cardinales 0–39

0	cero	21	veintiuno[1,2]
1	uno[1]	22	veintidós
2	dos	23	veintitrés
3	tres	24	veinticuatro
4	cuatro	25	veinticinco
5	cinco	26	veintiséis
6	seis	27	veintisiete
7	siete	28	veintiocho
8	ocho	29	veintinueve
9	nueve	30	treinta
10	diez	31	treinta y uno
11	once	32	treinta y dos
12	doce	33	treinta y tres
13	trece	34	treinta y cuatro
14	catorce	35	treinta y cinco
15	quince	36	treinta y seis
16	dieciséis[2]	37	treinta y siete
17	diecisiete	38	treinta y ocho
18	dieciocho	39	treinta y nueve
19	diecinueve		
20	veinte		

Práctica

A. Read the following numbers aloud in Spanish.

0	10	9	31	25	19	7	33
15	37	16	11	21	20	29	17
28	14	13	8	4	12	30	22

B. Read the following telephone numbers in Spanish. Say each number one by one.

383–5079	254–2675	792–5136	689–0275
985–0746	765–1032	985–7340	872–0695

C. Find out the phone number of three classmates. Ask: **¿Cuál es tu número de teléfono?** (*What is your phone number?*)

---

[1] **Uno** changes to **un** before a masculine singular noun: **un libro** (*one book*.). **Uno** changes to **una** before a feminine singular noun: **una silla** (*one chair*). All other numbers ending in **-uno** or **-una** follow the same pattern: **veintiún libros** (*twenty-one books*), **veintiuna sillas** (*twenty-one chairs*).

[2] The numbers 16 to 29 may also be written as separate words: **diez y seis, veinte y uno,** and so on. The most common spelling, however, is the single word form used in this text.

3 The alphabet
El alfabeto

Letter	Name	Letter	Name	Letter	Name	Letter	Name
a	a	h	hache	ñ	eñe	t	te
b	be	i	i	o	o	u	u
c	ce	j	jota	p	pe	v	ve
d	de	k	ka	q	cu	w	doble ve
e	e	l	ele	r	ere	x	equis
f	efe	m	eme	rr	erre	y	i griega
g	ge	n	ene	s	ese	z	zeta

Práctica

A. Read the following in Spanish.

    FBI   MIT   IBM   NFL   NBA   NHL

B. A Spanish-speaking person may not know how to spell your name. He or she may ask: **¿Cómo se escribe?** (*How do you spell it?*) Learn how to spell your name in Spanish and ask other members of the class how to spell theirs.

4 Personal information
Información personal

—**¿Nombre y apellido?**   *"Name and surname?"*
—**María Valdés.**   *"María Valdés."*

—**¿Estado civil?**   *"Marital status?"*
—**Casada.**   *"Married."*

—**¿Apellido de soltera?**[1]   *"Maiden name?"*
—**Rivas.**   *"Rivas."*

—**¿Nacionalidad?**   *"Nationality (citizenship)?"*
—**Norteamericana.**[2]   *"North American (U.S.)."*

—**¿Lugar de nacimiento?**   *"Place of birth?"*
—**La Habana, Cuba.**   *"Havana, Cuba."*

—**¿Edad?**   *"Age?"*
—**Veintinueve años.**   *"Twenty-nine years (old)."*

---

[1] The preposition **de** + *noun* in Spanish is the equivalent of two nouns used together in English. Notice that the first noun functions as an adjective in English.
[2] Native Spanish speakers use **norteamericano(a)** or **americano(a)** to refer to people from the United States.

—¿Ocupación?[3]	*"Occupation?"*
—Enfermera.	*"Nurse."*
—¿Lugar donde trabaja?	*"Place of work?"*
—Hospital Municipal.	*"Municipal Hospital."*
—¿Dirección?	*"Address?"*
—Calle Magnolia,[4] número veintitrés.	*"Number twenty-three Magnolia Street."*
—¿Ciudad?	*"City?"*
—Riverside.	*"Riverside."*
—¿Número de teléfono?	*"Phone number?"*
—682–7530.	*"682–7530."*
—¿Número de seguro social?	*"Social Security number?"*
—566–14–9023.	*"566–14–9023."*

Vocabulario: Información personal

el nombre   *name*
el apellido   *surname*
el apellido de soltera   *maiden name*
el estado civil   *marital status*
  soltero(a)   *single*
  casado(a)   *married*
  separado(a)   *separated*
  divorciado(a)   *divorced*
  viudo(a)   *widowed*
la nacionalidad   *nationality*
  norteamericano(a)   *North American (from the U.S.)*
el lugar de nacimiento   *place of birth*
la edad   *age*
el año, los años   *year(s)*
la fecha de nacimiento   *date of birth*
la ocupación   *occupation*
el (la) enfermero(a)   *nurse*
el lugar donde trabaja   *place of work*
la dirección, el domicilio   *address*
la calle   *street*
la ciudad   *city*
el número   *number*
el número de teléfono   *phone number*
el número de seguro social   *Social Security number*

---

[3] See Appendix C for a list of occupations.
[4] In Spanish, the name of the street is placed before the number.

el número de la licencia *driver's license number*
  para conducir (manejar)
el sexo *sex*
  femenino *feminine*
  masculino *masculine*

Práctica

Interview a classmate, using the following questions. When you have finished, switch roles.

1. ¿Nombre y apellido?
2. ¿Estado civil?
3. ¿Apellido de soltera? *(If you are talking to a married woman)*
4. ¿Nacionalidad?
5. ¿Lugar de nacimiento?
6. ¿Ocupación?
7. ¿Lugar donde trabaja?
8. ¿Dirección? (¿Domicilio?)
9. ¿Ciudad?
10. ¿Número de teléfono?
11. ¿Número de seguro social?
12. ¿Número de la licencia para conducir?

5 Days of the week
Los días de la semana

—¿Qué día es hoy?   "What day is it today?"
—Hoy es lunes.   "Today is Monday."

—Hoy es martes, ¿no?   "Today is Tuesday, isn't it?"
—No, hoy es miércoles.   "No, today is Wednesday."

—¿Qué día es hoy?   "What day is it today?
  ¿Jueves?   Thursday?"
—No, hoy es viernes.   "No, today is Friday."

—Hoy es... sábado...   "Today is . . . Saturday
  ¡no! domingo...   . . . no! Sunday . . ."
—Sí, hoy es domingo.   "Yes, today is Sunday."

Los días de la semana

lunes	*Monday*	**viernes**	*Friday*
martes	*Tuesday*	**sábado**	*Saturday*
miércoles	*Wednesday*	**domingo**	*Sunday*
jueves	*Thursday*		

ATENCIÓN: The days of the week are not capitalized in Spanish, and in Spanish-speaking countries, the week begins on Monday. **El** and **los** are frequently used with the days of the week to express *on*: **el lunes** *(on Monday)*, **los martes** *(on Tuesdays)*, etc.

Práctica

The people asking the following questions are always a day ahead. Tell them the correct day.

Modelo: —Hoy es lunes, ¿no?
       —**No, hoy es domingo.**

1. Hoy es miércoles, ¿no?
2. Hoy es domingo, ¿no?
3. Hoy es viernes, ¿no?
4. Hoy es martes, ¿no?
5. Hoy es sábado, ¿no?
6. Hoy es jueves, ¿no?

6 Months of the year

Los meses del año

enero	*January*	**julio**	*July*
febrero	*February*	**agosto**	*August*
marzo	*March*	**septiembre**	*September*
abril	*April*	**octubre**	*October*
mayo	*May*	**noviembre**	*November*
junio	*June*	**diciembre**	*December*

ATENCIÓN: The names of the months are not capitalized in Spanish.

♦ To talk about the date, use the following expressions.

—¿Qué fecha es hoy?   *"What's the date today?"*
—**Hoy es el quince de**   *"Today is January fifteenth."*
enero.

—¿Hoy es el primero de   *"Is today May first?"*
mayo?
—**No, hoy es el dos de**   *"No, today is May second."*
mayo.

ATENCIÓN: Spanish uses cardinal numbers to refer to dates. The only exception is **primero** *(first).*

♦ When telling the date, always begin with the expression **Hoy es el...**

Hoy es el veinte de mayo.   *Today is May twentieth.*

◆ Complete the expression by saying the number followed by the preposition **de** (*of*), and then the month.

el **quince de mayo** *May 15th*
el **diez de septiembre** *September 10th*
el **doce de octubre** *October 12th*

ATENCIÓN: Notice that the day precedes the month. Thus, 3–6–96 means June 3rd, 1996. In Spanish, the article (**el**) is usually included when giving the date orally, although it is sometimes omitted in writing.

Práctica

The following are important dates to remember. Say them in Spanish.

1. the 4th of July
2. the 31st of October
3. March 21st
4. April 1st
5. the first of January
6. February 14th
7. December 25th
8. May 5th
9. your birthday
10. today's date

7 Colors
Los colores

amarillo *yellow*
anaranjado *orange*
azul *blue*
blanco *white*
gris *gray*
marrón (café) *brown*
morado *purple*
negro *black*
rojo *red*
rosado *pink*
verde *green*

Práctica

To ask a classmate whether he or she likes something, you say: **¿Te gusta... ?**[1] To say that you like something, say: **Me gusta...**

---

[1] When addressing someone as **usted**, use, **¿Le gusta... ?**

Conduct a survey of your classmates to find out which color is the most popular in class, following the model.

Modelo: —¿Qué color te gusta?
—**Me gusta el color rojo.**

Información personal

Provide the information requested.

Apellido y nombres

_____

Dirección

_____

Ciudad

_____

Teléfono

_____

Estado civil	Sexo	Edad
1. _____ soltero(a)	Masculino _____	_____
2. _____ casado(a)	Femenino _____	
3. _____ separado(a)		
4. _____ divorciado(a)		
5. _____ viudo(a)		

Nacionalidad _____ _____

Ocupación[1] _____

Lugar donde trabaja _____

Número de seguro social _____

Número de la licencia para conducir _____

---

[1] See Appendix C for a list of occupations.

En el laboratorio

The following material is to be used with the tape or audio CD in the language laboratory.

I. Vocabulario

Repeat each word or phrase after the speaker.

SALUDOS Y DESPEDIDAS:	Buenos días. Buenas tardes. Buenas noches. Hola. Hasta luego. Hasta mañana. Adiós.
TÍTULOS:	doctor profesor señor señora señorita
EXPRESIONES ÚTILES:	¿Cómo está usted? Muy bien, ¿y usted? ¿Qué tal? Bien, ¿y tú? No muy bien. Lo siento. Mucho gusto. El gusto es mío. Pase. Por favor. Tome asiento. Gracias. Muchas gracias. De nada.
INFORMACIÓN PERSONAL:	nombre apellido apellido de soltera estado civil soltero casado separado divorciado viudo nacionalidad norteamericano lugar de nacimiento edad año fecha de nacimiento ocupación enfermero lugar donde trabaja dirección domicilio calle ciudad número número de teléfono número de seguro social número de la licencia para conducir sexo femenino masculino
LOS DÍAS DE LA SEMANA:	lunes martes miércoles jueves viernes sábado domingo
LOS MESES:	enero febrero marzo abril mayo junio julio agosto septiembre octubre noviembre diciembre

II. Práctica

A. You find yourself in the following situations. What would you say? Repeat the correct answer after the speaker's confirmation. Listen to the model.

Modelo: You meet Mr. Vega in the morning.
Buenos días, señor Vega.

B. Answer each of the addition problems you hear in Spanish. Repeat the correct answer after the speaker's confirmation. Listen to the model.

Modelo: tres y dos
cinco

C. Say each of the acronyms you hear in Spanish. Repeat the correct answer after the speaker's confirmation. Listen to the model.

Modelo: USA
u-ese-a

D. The speaker will tell you what day of the week today is. Respond by saying what day tomorrow will be. Repeat the correct answer after the speaker's confirmation. Listen to the model.

Modelo: Hoy es lunes
Mañana es martes.

E. The speaker will name several holidays. Name the date on which each holiday falls. Repeat the correct answer after the speaker's confirmation. Listen to the model.

Modelo: Flag Day
el catorce de junio

F. The speaker will name several familiar objects. State the color or colors of each object in Spanish. Repeat the correct answer after the speaker's confirmation. Listen to the model.

Modelo: a violet
morado

Lección preliminar

1. Gender and number

2. The definite and indefinite articles

3. Subject pronouns

4. The present indicative of **ser**

5. Uses of **hay**

6. Cardinal numbers 40–299

Vocabulario

COGNADOS[1]

la **conversación** conversation	el **progreso** progress
la **decisión** decision	el (la) **secretario(a)**
la **idea** idea	secretary
la **lección** lesson	el **sistema** system
la **libertad** liberty	el **teléfono** telephone
el **poema** poem	la **televisión** television
el **problema** problem	la **universidad** university
el **programa** program	

NOMBRES
la **amistad** friendship
la **casa** house
el **clima** climate
el **día** day
el **dinero** money
el **español** Spanish
  (*language*)
el **hombre** man
el **idioma**, la **lengua**
  language
la **lámpara** lamp
el **lápiz** pencil
el **libro** book
la **luz** light
la **mano** hand

el (la) **médico(a)**, **doctor(a)**
  M.D., doctor
la **mesa** table
la **mujer** woman
la **pluma** pen
la **puerta** door
la **silla** chair

VERBO
  ser to be

**OTRAS PALABRAS Y
EXPRESIONES**
  de of, from
  de dónde from where
  dónde where

1 Gender and number

Género y número

Género

Gender the classification of nouns, pronouns, and adjectives as masculine or feminine

In Spanish, all nouns, including abstract nouns and those denoting nonliving things, are either masculine or feminine.

---

[1] Cognates are words that resemble one another and have similar meanings in Spanish and English. Note that English cognates often have different spellings and always have different pronunciations than their Spanish counterparts.

masculine	*feminine*
año	puerta
señor	señora
teléfono	lámpara
progreso	idea

Here are some practical rules to use to determine the gender of Spanish nouns.

♦ Nouns denoting females and most nouns ending in **-a** are feminine. Nouns referring to males and most nouns ending in **-o** are masculine.

masculine	*feminine*
hombre	mujer
teléfon**o**	sill**a**
diner**o**	cas**a**
libr**o**	mes**a**

ATENCIÓN: Two important exceptions to this rule are **día** (*day*), which is masculine, and **mano** (*hand*), which is feminine.

♦ Some nouns that end in **-a** are masculine. These nouns are of Greek origin and have kept the gender they had in that language.

problem**a**	sistem**a**
program**a**	poem**a**
idiom**a**	clim**a**

♦ Nouns ending in **-sión, -ción, -tad,** and **-dad** are feminine.

televi**sión**	lec**ción**
deci**sión**	conversa**ción**
liber**tad**	universi**dad**
amis**tad**	ciu**dad**

♦ The gender of some nouns must be learned.

masculine	*feminine*
español	calle

♦ Many masculine nouns ending in **-o** that refer to people have a corresponding feminine form ending in **-a.**

masculine	*feminine*
enfermer**o**	enfermer**a**
secretari**o**	secretari**a**

♦ Certain masculine nouns ending in a consonant add **-a** to form the corresponding feminine noun.

masculine	*feminine*
profesor	profesor**a**
doctor	doctor**a**

♦ Colors, numbers, days of the week, and months of the year are masculine.

Práctica

Are the following nouns feminine (**femenino**) or masculine (**masculino**)?

1. teléfono
2. día
3. televisión
4. enfermera
5. problema
6. calle
7. mesa
8. universidad
9. dinero
10. idioma
11. silla
12. amistad
13. mano
14. ciudad
15. lección
16. progreso
17. señor
18. profesora
19. programa
20. clima

Número

Number   a term that identifies words as singular or plural: chair, chairs

Nouns are made plural in Spanish by adding **-s** to those ending in a vowel and **-es** to those ending in a consonant. Nouns ending in **-z** are made plural by changing the **z** to **c** and adding **-es**.

teléfon**o**	teléfono**s**	lápi**z**	lápi**ces**
mes**a**	mesa**s**	lu**z**	lu**ces**
profesor	profesor**es**	lección	leccion**es**

ATENCIÓN: Accent marks that fall on the last syllable of singular words are omitted in the plural form: **lección, lecciones.**

Práctica

What are the plural forms of the following nouns?

1. silla	9. clima
2. libro	10. conversación
3. lápiz	11. profesor
4. universidad	12. luz
5. telegrama	13. decisión
6. ciudad	14. doctor
7. lección	15. amistad
8. señor	16. lámpara

2 The definite and indefinite articles
Los artículos definido e indefinido

El artículo definido

> **Definite article**   a word used before a noun to indicate a definite person or thing: **the** woman, **the** money

Spanish has four forms that are equivalent to the English definite article *the*.

	Masculine	Feminine
Singular	el	la
Plural	los	las

el profesor	**la** profesora
los profesores	**las** profesoras
el lápiz	**la** lámpara
los lápices	**las** lámparas

ATENCIÓN: Learning each noun's definite article will help you to remember the noun's gender.

Práctica

What are the definite articles for the following nouns?

1. universidades
2. problema
3. profesor
4. doctor
5. señora
6. señores
7. día
8. televisión
9. silla
10. mujeres
11. dinero
12. profesores
13. idea
14. sistema
15. libertad

El artículo indefinido

> **Indefinite article**   a word used before a noun to indicate an indefinite person or object: **a** child, **an** apple, **some** students

The indefinite article in Spanish has four forms; they are equivalent to *a*, *an*, and *some*.

	Masculine	Feminine
Singular	un	una
Plural	unos	unas

un profesor   **una** profesora
unos profesores   **unas** profesoras
un lápiz   **una** pluma
unos lápices   **unas** plumas

Práctica

How would you name the following items in Spanish?

1. a pen
2. a man
3. some days
4. some chairs
5. a problem
6. a house
7. a light
8. a program
9. some pencils
10. a lesson
11. a friendship
12. a decision

3 Subject pronouns
Pronombres usados como sujetos

Subject person or thing about which something is said in
a sentence or phrase: **Mary** works. **The car** is new.
Pronoun a word that replaces a noun: **she, them, us, it**
Subject pronoun a personal pronoun that is used as a
subject: **They** work. **It** is small.

Singular		*Plural*[1]	
yo	I	{ **nosotros** we (*masculine*)	
		{ **nosotras** we (*feminine*)	
tú	you (*familiar*)	**ustedes**[3] you	
usted[2]	you (*formal*)		
él	he	{ **ellos**	they (*masculine*)
ella	she	{ **ellas**	they (*feminine*)

◆ The masculine plural pronoun may refer to the masculine
  gender alone or to both genders together.

  Juan y Roberto: **ellos**   *Juan and Roberto:* ***they***
  Juan y María: **ellos**   *Juan and María:* ***they***

◆ Use the **tú** form as the equivalent of *you* when addressing a close
  friend, a relative, or a child. Use the **usted** form in all other instances. Notice that **ustedes** is used for both familiar and polite
  plural.

Práctica

Complete the following sentences with the appropriate subject
pronoun.

Modelo: You refer to Mr. Gómez as . . . **él.**

1. You point to yourself and say . . .
2. You refer to Mrs. Gómez as . . .

[1] The second-person plural subject pronoun **vosotros,** used only in Spain, is not taught
in this text. In all other Spanish-speaking countries, **ustedes** is used for both the familiar and the formal plural form of *you.*
[2] Abbreviated **Ud.**
[3] Abbreviated **Uds.**

3. You are talking to a little boy and you call him . . .
4. You are talking to a woman you've just met and you call her . . .
5. Your mother refers to herself and her sister as . . .
6. Your father refers to himself and his sister as . . .
7. You are talking to a few people and you call them . . .
8. You refer to Mr. Gómez and his daughter as . . .
9. You refer to Mrs. Gómez and her daughter as . . .
10. You refer to Mr. and Mrs. Gómez as . . .
11. You are talking with one of your professors and you call him . . .
12. You are talking with one of your friends and you call her . . .

4 The present indicative of ser
El presente de indicativo del verbo ser

The verb **ser** (*to be*) is an irregular verb. It is one of the most frequently used verbs in the Spanish language. Learning its forms and the corresponding subject pronouns will help you express occupation, nationality, day and date, as well as many other useful facts.

ser (*to be*)		
yo	**soy**	I am
tú	**eres**	you are (*familiar*)
Ud.		you are (*formal*)
él	**es**	he is
ella		she is
nosotros	**somos**	we are
Uds.		you are
ellos	**son**	they are (*masculine*)
ellas		they are (*feminine*)

—¿De dónde **son** Uds.?   *"Where are you from?"*
—Yo **soy** de México y   *"I'm from Mexico and Graciela*
    Graciela **es** de Cuba.   *is from Cuba. Where are you*
    ¿De dónde **eres** tú?   *from?"*
—Yo **soy** de Perú.   *"I'm from Peru."*

—¿**Son** Uds.   *"Are you North American?"*
   norteamericanos?
—Sí, nosotros **somos**   *"Yes, we are North American."*
   norteamericanos.

—¿Hoy **es** miércoles?   *"Is today Wednesday?"*
—No, hoy **es** martes.   *"No, today is Tuesday."*

Práctica

A. Use the verb **ser** to complete the following conversations. Then act them out with a partner.

  1. —¿De dónde _____ tú, Anita?
    —Yo _____ de Buenos Aires. ¿De dónde _____ Ud., señora?
    —Yo _____ de Montevideo.
  2. —¿Uds. _____ norteamericanos?
    —Sí, nosotros _____ de California.
  3. —¿Elsa _____ profesora?
    —No, ella _____ enfermera.
  4. —¿Qué día _____ hoy?
    —Hoy _____ viernes.

B. Answer the following questions using complete sentences.

  1. ¿Qué fecha es hoy?
  2. ¿Qué día es hoy?
  3. ¿Uds. son norteamericanos?
  4. ¿De dónde es Ud.?
  5. ¿De dónde es el profesor (la profesora) de español?

5   Uses of hay
Usos de hay

The form **hay** means *there is* or *there are*. It has no subject and must not be confused with **es** (*it is*) and **son** (*they are*).

Hay un lápiz en la mesa.   ***There is** a pencil on the table.*
Hay diez libros en la mesa.   ***There are** ten books on the table.*

Práctica

Say how many of the following items there are in the classroom, using **hay**.

1. profesor(a)
2. hombres
3. mujeres
4. sillas
5. mesas
6. puertas

6 Cardinal numbers 40–299
Números cardinales 40–299

40	cuarenta	90	noventa
41	cuarenta y uno...	100	cien (ciento)
50	cincuenta	101	ciento uno... [1]
60	sesenta	150	ciento cincuenta
70	setenta	200	doscientos
80	ochenta	250	doscientos cincuenta...

ATENCIÓN: **Ciento** becomes **cien** before a noun.

cien días
cien casas

Remember that **uno** becomes **un** before a masculine noun and **una** before a feminine noun, even in compound numbers.

ciento **un** libros
ciento **una** sillas

Práctica

Read the following numbers aloud in Spanish.

86	48	57	123	42	69	74	214
80	91	100	65	111	234	200	261
197	136	115	175	169	185	101	299

En el laboratorio

The following material is to be used with the tape or audio CD in the language laboratory.

---

[1] Notice that the word **y** (*and*) is not used after hundreds: **ciento uno, ciento dos, doscientos veinte,** and so on.

I. *Vocabulario*

Repeat each word after the speaker. When repeating words that are cognates, notice the difference in pronunciation between English and Spanish.

COGNADOS:	la conversación la decisión la idea la lección la libertad el poema el problema el programa el progreso el secretario el sistema el teléfono la televisión la universidad
NOMBRES:	la amistad la casa el clima el día el dinero el español el hombre el idioma la lengua la lámpara el lápiz el libro la luz la mano el médico la mesa la mujer la pluma la puerta la silla
VERBO:	ser
OTRAS PALABRAS Y EXPRESIONES:	de de dónde dónde

II. *Práctica*

A. You will hear some nouns. Repeat each noun, adding the appropriate singular or plural definite article. Repeat the correct answer after the speaker's confirmation. Listen to the model.

Modelo: silla
   la silla

B. You will hear several singular nouns, each preceded by an indefinite article. Make the nouns and the articles plural. Repeat the correct answer after the speaker's confirmation. Listen to the model.

Modelo: un alumno
   unos alumnos

C. Answer the questions, always using the second choice. Repeat the correct answer after the speaker's confirmation. Listen to the model.

Modelo: —¿Tú eres de Argentina o de los Estados Unidos?
   —Yo soy de los Estados Unidos.

D. Say the numbers you hear in Spanish. Repeat the correct answer after the speaker's confirmation. Listen to the model.

Modelo: 157
   ciento cincuenta y siete

1. The present indicative of regular **-ar** verbs

2. Interrogative and negative sentences

3. Forms and position of adjectives

4. Telling time

5. Cardinal numbers 300–1,000

Vocabulario

COGNADOS

la cafetería cafeteria	**el italiano** Italian (*language*)
el champán champagne	**mexicano(a)** Mexican
inteligente intelligent	**el restaurante** restaurant

NOMBRES
la cerveza beer
la comida meal, food
la cuchara spoon
la cuenta bill, check
el francés French
 (*language*)
el inglés English
 (*language*)
el mantel tablecloth
la mañana morning
la muchacha, la chica girl,
 young woman
el muchacho, el chico boy,
 young man
la noche evening
el refresco soft drink, soda
la servilleta napkin
la tarde afternoon
el tenedor fork
el vino wine
el vino tinto red wine

VERBOS
 desear to want, to wish
 estudiar to study
 hablar to speak, to talk
 necesitar to need
 pagar to pay (for)

tomar to drink
trabajar to work

ADJETIVOS
 alemán (alemana)[1]
 German
 español(a) Spanish
 feliz happy
 francés (francesa)
 French
 grande big, large
 guapo(a) handsome,
 attractive
 inglés (inglesa) English

**OTRAS PALABRAS Y
EXPRESIONES**
 ¿a qué hora? at what
 time?
 ¿cuántos(as)? how
 many?
 en in, at
 mucho(a) a lot, very
 much
 pero but
 ¿qué? what?
 ¿Qué hora es? What
 time is it?
 sí yes
 solamente, sólo only

---

[1] Names of languages and nationalities are not capitalized in Spanish.

1 The present indicative of regular -ar verbs

El presente de indicativo de los verbos regulares terminados en -ar

> **Verb**   a word that expresses an action or a state: We **sleep.**
> The baby **is** sick.
> **Infinitive**   the form of a verb showing no subject or number, preceded in English by the word *to*: **to do, to bring**

The infinitive of all Spanish verbs consists of a stem (such as **habl-**) and an ending (such as **-ar**). When looking up a verb in the dictionary, you will always find it listed under the infinitive (*e.g.*, **hablar:** *to speak*). Spanish verbs are classified according to their endings. There are three conjugations: **-ar, -er,** and **-ir.** The stem of regular verbs does not change; the endings change to agree with the subjects. Regular verbs ending in **-ar** are conjugated like **hablar,** as shown.

hablar *(to speak)*		
Singular		
Stem	*Ending*	
yo	habl-**o**	Yo **hablo** español.
tú	habl-**as**	Tú **hablas** español.
Ud.	habl-**a**	Ud. **habla** español.
él	habl-**a**	Juan **habla** español. Él **habla** español.
ella	habl-**a**	Ana **habla** español. Ella **habla** español.
Plural		
nosotros	habl-**amos**	Nosotros **hablamos** español.
Uds.	habl-**an**	Uds. **hablan** español.
ellos	habl-**an**	Ellos **hablan** español.
ellas	habl-**an**	Ellas **hablan** español.

◆ The present tense in Spanish is equivalent to three forms in English.

Yo **hablo** italiano.
$$\begin{cases} \textit{I speak Italian.} \\ \textit{I do speak Italian.} \\ \textit{I am speaking Italian.} \end{cases}$$

◆ Since the verb endings indicate who the speaker is, the subject pronouns are frequently omitted.

—**Hablas** inglés, ¿no?   *"You (familiar) speak English, don't you?"*

—Sí, **hablo** inglés.   *"Yes, I speak English."*

However, subject pronouns may be used for emphasis or clarification.

—**Ellos hablan** inglés, ¿no?   *"They speak English, don't they?"*

—**Ella habla** inglés. **Él habla**   *"She speaks English. He speaks
español.   Spanish."*

◆ Some common verbs that follow the regular **-ar** pattern are:

desear	to want, to wish	**pagar**	to pay
estudiar	to study	**tomar**	to drink
necesitar	to need	**trabajar**	to work

—Ud. **desea** una cerveza, ¿no?   *"You want a beer, don't you?"*

—Sí, y ella **desea** tomar[1] un   *"Yes, and she wants to drink a
refresco. Yo pago la   soda. I'm paying the bill."*
cuenta.

—Ud. **necesita** el mantel,   *"You need the tablecloth,
¿no?   don't you?"*

—Sí, **necesito** el mantel y   *"Yes, I need the tablecloth
las servilletas.   and the napkins."*

—Uds. **estudian** francés en   *"You study French at the
la universidad, ¿no?   university, don't you?"*

—No, pero **estudiamos**   *"No, but we study English."*
inglés.

—El Sr. Paz **trabaja** en   *"Mr. Paz works at a
una cafetería, ¿no?   cafeteria, doesn't he?"*

—No, él **trabaja** en un   *"No, he works at a
restaurante.   restaurant."*

ATENCIÓN: When speaking about a third person (indirect address) and using a title with the last name, the definite article is placed before the title. (*El Sr.* **Paz habla español.**) It is not used when speaking directly to someone (**Buenos días,** *Sr.* **Paz.**).

---

[1] When two verbs are used together, the second verb is in the infinitive.

Práctica

A. Form sentences that tell where these people work, what they study, what they need, and what they want.

1. **trabajar:**   yo / un restaurante
   Anita / la cafetería
   tú / Los Ángeles
   nosotros / la universidad

2. **estudiar:**   Uds. / francés
   Carlos / italiano
   Ud. / la lección dos
   él y yo / español

3. **necesitar:**   Ana y Rosa / dinero
   nosotras / una mesa
   yo / pagar la cuenta
   tú / una servilleta

4. **desear:**   ellos / cerveza
   nosotros / un refresco
   yo / tomar Coca-Cola
   Elsa / estudiar inglés

B. Provide the missing information about yourself and other people.

1. Ella trabaja en Los Ángeles y yo...
2. Tú y yo trabajamos en la cafetería y ellos...
3. Carlos estudia italiano y nosotros...
4. Yo deseo estudiar francés y ellos...
5. Nosotros hablamos inglés y el profesor...
6. Ellos hablan francés y yo...
7. Yo necesito una pluma y tú...
8. María necesita sillas y nosotros...
9. Tú tomas refrescos y yo...
10. Ella toma cerveza y Uds...

2 Interrogative and negative sentences
Oraciones interrogativas y negativas

Interrogative sentences

There are three ways of asking a question in Spanish to elicit a yes / no answer. These three questions ask for the same information and have the same meaning.

1. ¿**Uds.** necesitan el mantel?
2. ¿Necesitan **Uds.** el mantel?   } Sí, nosotros necesita-
3. ¿Necesitan el mantel **Uds.**?   mos el mantel.

◆ Example 1 is a declarative sentence that is made interrogative by a change in intonation.

Uds. necesitan el mantel.   ¿Uds. necesitan el mantel?

◆ Example 2 is an interrogative sentence formed by placing the subject (**Uds.**) after the verb.

◆ Example 3, another interrogative sentence, is formed by placing the subject (**Uds.**) at the end of the sentence.

ATENCIÓN: An auxiliary verb such as *do* or *does* is not used in Spanish to form an interrogative sentence.

   ¿Uds.   toman   vino?
(Do)   *you*   *drink*   *wine?*

Notice that, in Spanish, interrogative sentences have a question mark at the end and an inverted question mark at the beginning.

Práctica

Ask the following questions in two other ways, using the model as an example.

Modelo: ¿**Elena** trabaja en Buenos Aires?
    ¿Trabaja **Elena** en Buenos Aires?
    ¿Trabaja en Buenos Aires **Elena**?

1. ¿Tú tomas vino?   4. ¿Pedro necesita el mantel?
2. ¿Ella estudia inglés?   5. ¿Tú pagas la cuenta?
3. ¿Uds. hablan español?   6. ¿Ud. desea tomar un refresco?

Negative sentences

To make a sentence negative, simply place the word **no** in front of the verb.

Ella   habla inglés.   *She   speaks English.*
Ella **no** habla inglés.   *She **doesn't** speak English.*

ATENCIÓN: Spanish does not use an auxiliary verb such as the English *do* or *does* in a negative sentence.

◆ If the answer to a question is negative, the word **no** appears
twice: at the beginning of the sentence, as in English, and also
in front of the verb.

—¿Necesitas las cucharas?   *"Do you need the spoons?"*
—**No,** (yo) **no** necesito las   *"No, I don't need the spoons,*
    cucharas, pero necesito   *but I need the forks."*
    los tenedores.

ATENCIÓN: The subject pronoun need not appear in the answer because the verb ending identifies the speaker.

Práctica

Answer the following questions in the negative, using the information provided in parentheses. Then create two original questions to ask a classmate.

Modelo: —¿Ud. trabaja en un restaurante? (cafetería)
          —**No, (yo) no trabajo en un restaurante; trabajo**
          en una cafetería.

1. ¿Uds. necesitan los tenedores? (cucharas)
2. ¿Ellos necesitan el mantel? (servilletas)
3. ¿Tú deseas tomar cerveza? (un refresco)
4. ¿Uds. toman Pepsi? (Sprite)
5. ¿Tú pagas la cerveza? (vino)

3 Forms and position of adjectives

Formas y posición de los adjetivos

Formas

Adjective   a word that modifies a noun or a pronoun: **tall**
girl, **difficult** lesson

Adjectives whose masculine singular form ends in **-o** have four
forms, ending in **-o, -a, -os, -as.** Most other adjectives have
only two forms, a singular and a plural. Like nouns, adjectives
are made plural by adding **-s, -es,** or by changing **z** to **c** and
adding **-es.**

Singular		Plural	
Masculine	*Feminine*	*Masculine*	*Feminine*
negro	negra	negros	negras
inteligente	inteligente	inteligentes	inteligentes
feliz	feliz	felices	felices
azul	azul	azules	azules

◆ Adjectives of nationality that end in a consonant are made feminine by adding **-a** to the masculine singular form.

español	española
alemán	alemana
inglés	inglesa
francés	francesa

—¿Dónde trabaja Elsa?   *"Where does Elsa work?"*
—Trabaja en un   *"She works at a*
  restaurante **alemán**.   *German restaurant."*

—¿Hay comida **española**?   *"Is there Spanish food?"*
—No, hay comida   *"No, there is French food."*
  francesa.

—¿Te gusta el champán   *"Do you like French*
  francés?   *champagne?"*
—Sí, me gusta mucho.   *"Yes, I like it a lot."*

Posición

◆ Descriptive adjectives (such as adjectives of color, size, etc.) generally follow the noun in Spanish.

el mantel **rojo**	*the red tablecloth*
la casa **grande**	*the big house*
los muchachos **guapos**	*the handsome young men*
el hombre **soltero**	*the single man*

◆ Adjectives denoting nationality always follow the noun.

el chico **español**   *the Spanish young man*

◆ Other kinds of adjectives (possessive, demonstrative, numerical, etc.) precede the noun, as in English.

tres refrescos   *three sodas*   **mi** servilleta   *my napkin*

—¿Cuántos tenedores   *"How many forks do you need?"*
  necesitas?
—Necesito solamente   *"I need only one fork."*
  un tenedor.

—¿Uds. toman vino **tinto**?   *"Do you drink red wine?"*
—No, tomamos vino **blanco**.   *"No, we drink white wine."*

Práctica

A. Supply the three missing forms of the following adjectives.

1. blanco _____ _____ _____
2. _____ _____ amarillos _____
3. _____ guapa _____ _____
4. _____ _____ _____ alemanas
5. feliz _____ _____ _____

B. Match the nouns in column A with the adjectives in column B.

A	B
1. hombre _____	a. rojo
2. mesa _____	b. inteligentes
3. chicas _____	c. feliz
4. libros _____	d. tinto
5. muchachos _____	e. mexicana
6. lápiz _____	f. verdes
7. vino _____	g. negra
8. comida _____	h. guapos

C. How would you say the following in Spanish?

1. three married women
2. a handsome man
3. a big restaurant
4. a French girl
5. my spoon
6. twenty-five napkins
7. five German girls

4 Telling time
La hora

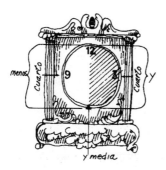

Here are some important points to remember when telling time in Spanish.

◆ **Es** is used with **una** and **son** is used with all the other hours.

Es la **una** y cuarto.   *It is a quarter after one.*
Son las **cinco** y diez.   *It is ten after five.*

◆ The feminine definite article is always used before the hour, since it refers to **la hora.**

Es **la** una y veinte.   *It is twenty after one.*
Son **las** cuatro y media.   *It is four-thirty.*

◆ The hour is given first, then the minutes.

Son las **cuatro** y **diez.**   *It is ten after four* (lit., *four and ten*).

◆ The equivalent of *past* or *after* is **y.**

Son las doce **y** cinco.   *It's five after twelve.*

◆ The equivalent of *to* or *till* is **menos.**

Son las ocho **menos** veinte.   *It's twenty to eight.*

◆ When telling time, follow this order.

    a. Es or **Son**
    b. la or **las**
    c. the hour
    d. y or **menos**
    e. the minutes

Es
la
una       Son
y   las
veinte.   cinco
         menos
         diez.

◆ The equivalent of *at + time* is **a + las + time.**

A la una.   *At one o'clock.*
A las tres y media.   *At three-thirty.*

◆ While both **por la** and **de la** mean *in the* when used with time, they are used differently and are not interchangeable. When a specific time is mentioned, **de la (mañana, tarde, noche)** should be used.

Yo estudio a las dos   *I study at two in the afternoon.*
  de la tarde.

◆   When a specific time is *not* mentioned, **por la (mañana, tarde, noche)** should be used.

Yo estudio **por la** mañana.   *I study in the morning.*

—¿A qué hora estudias tú?   *"At what time do you study?"*
—Yo estudio a las dos   *"I study at two in the after-*
  de la tarde.   *noon."*

—¿Trabajas **por la** noche?   *"Do you work in the evening?"*
—No, yo trabajo **por la**   *"No, I work in the morning."*
  mañana.

Práctica

A. ¿Qué hora es?   (*What time is it?*)   Say the time given on the following clocks, and then write the times in Spanish.

1.   2.   3.   4.

5.   6.   7.   8.

B. With a partner, act out the following dialogues in Spanish.

1. "What time is it?"

   "It's a quarter to six."

2. "At what time does he work?"

   "He works at two-thirty in the afternoon."

3. "Do you study in the morning or in the afternoon?"

   "We study in the evening."

4. "Is it one-thirty?"

   "No, it's twenty-five to two."

C. Interview a classmate to find out the time of day at which he or she does the following things. When you have finished, switch roles.

1. studies
2. works
3. speaks Spanish

5 Cardinal numbers 300–1,000
Números cardinales 300–1.000

300 trescientos	700 setecientos
400 cuatrocientos	800 ochocientos
500 quinientos	900 novecientos
600 seiscientos	1.000 mil[1]

In Spanish, one does not count in hundreds beyond 1,000; thus, 1,100 is expressed as **mil cien.** Note that a period is used instead of a comma to indicate thousands.

1.999	**mil novecientos noventa y nueve**
32.418	**treinta y dos mil cuatrocientos dieciocho**

Práctica

Read the following numbers aloud in Spanish.

896	380	519	937	722
1.305	451	978	643	504
1.000	15.893	11.906	27.567	565.736

Palabras y más palabras

Match the questions in column **A** with the answers in column **B**.

---

[1] Notice that the indefinite article is not used before the word **mil.**

A	**B**
1. ¿Dónde trabaja Luis?	a. Vino tinto.
2. ¿Estudias por la mañana?	b. No, el Sr. Vargas.
3. ¿Qué desean tomar?	c. Los tenedores.
4. ¿Necesitas el mantel?	d. A las cinco de la tarde.
5. ¿Tú pagas la cuenta?	e. No, las servilletas.
6. ¿Qué estudian los chicos?	f. Solamente dos.
7. ¿Qué necesitas?	g. Son las dos.
8. ¿Los manteles son rojos?	h. No, española.
9. ¿A qué hora estudiamos?	i. En un restaurante.
10. ¿Cuántas cucharas necesitas?	j. No, azules.
11. ¿Ana es mexicana?	k. Inglés y español.
12. ¿Qué hora es?	l. No, por la tarde.

En el laboratorio

The following material is to be used with the tape or audio CD in the language laboratory.

I. Vocabulario

Repeat each word after the speaker. When repeating words that are cognates, notice the difference in pronunciation between English and Spanish.

COGNADOS:	la cafetería el champán inteligente el italiano mexicano el restaurante
NOMBRES:	la cerveza la comida la cuchara la cuenta el francés el inglés el mantel la mañana la muchacha la chica el muchacho el chico la noche el refresco la servilleta la tarde el tenedor el vino el vino tinto
VERBOS:	desear estudiar hablar necesitar pagar tomar trabajar
ADJETIVOS:	alemán español feliz francés grande guapo inglés
OTRAS PALABRAS Y EXPRESIONES:	¿a qué hora? ¿cuántos? en mucho pero ¿qué? ¿Qué hora es? sí solamente sólo

II. Práctica

A. Repeat each sentence, then substitute the new subject given by the speaker. Be sure the verb agrees with the new subject. Repeat the correct answer after the speaker's confirmation. Listen to the model.

Modelo: Yo estudio español. (nosotros)
   Nosotros estudiamos español.

1. Yo estudio español. (nosotros / Ud. / ellos)
2. Ella trabaja en la cafetería. (yo / Uds. / tú)
3. Tú necesitas dinero. (él / nosotros / ellas)
4. Nosotros tomamos refrescos. (tú / Elsa / yo)
5. Él paga la cuenta. (nosotros / tú / Uds.)

B. Answer the questions in the negative. Repeat the correct answer after the speaker's confirmation. Listen to the model.

Modelo: ¿Tú necesitas dinero?
   No, no necesito dinero.

C. Change each phrase you hear according to the new cue. Repeat the correct answer after the speaker's confirmation. Listen to the model.

Modelo: señor español (señorita)
   señorita española

1. (manteles)
2. (servilletas)
3. (señora)
4. (mujeres)
5. (chicos)
6. (profesora)
7. (muchacho)
8. (comida)

D. Read the following numbers in Spanish. Repeat the correct answer after the speaker's confirmation. Listen to the model.

Modelo: 1.581
   Mil quinientos ochenta y uno.

1. 322
2. 430
3. 547
4. 659
5. 761
6. 878
7. 985
8. 1.000
9. 543
10. 2.715
11. 5.873
12. 9.108
13. 12.920
14. 15.008
15. 23.192

III. Para escuchar y entender

1. The speaker will make some statements. Circle **L** (**lógico**) if the statement is logical and **I** (**ilógico**) if it is illogical. The speaker will verify your response.

1. L I   4. L I
2. L I   5. L I
3. L I   6. L I

2. Listen carefully to the dialogue. It will be read twice.

   (*Diálogo 1*)

   Now the speaker will make some statements about the dialogue
   you just heard. Tell whether each statement is true (**verdadero**)
   or false (**falso**). The speaker will confirm the correct answer.

3. Listen carefully to the dialogue. It will be read twice.

   (*Diálogo 2*)

   Now the speaker will ask you some questions about the dialogue
   you just heard. Answer each question, omitting the subject. The
   speaker will confirm the correct answer. Repeat the correct
   answer.

1. Agreement of articles, nouns, and adjectives

2. The present indicative of regular **-er** and **-ir** verbs

3. Possession with **de**

4. Possessive adjectives

5. The personal **a**

Vocabulario

COGNADOS

el chocolate chocolate	**el taxi** taxi
el menú menu	**el té** tea
el museo museum	

NOMBRES
el (la) amigo(a) friend
la bebida drink
la botella bottle
el café coffee
la fiesta party
el (la) hijo(a) son, daughter
los hijos children
el huevo egg
la leche milk
el mozo, el (la) camarero(a), (*Méx., Esp.*) waiter, waitress
el ómnibus, el autobús bus
la papa, la patata (*Esp.*) potato
el pastel[1] pie
el pescado fish
el pollo chicken

VERBOS
abrir to open
aprender to learn
beber to drink
comer to eat
deber (+ *inf.*) must, to have to, should
decidir to decide
escribir to write
leer to read

llamar to call
llevar to take (*something or someone someplace*)
recibir to receive
tomar to take (*i.e., the bus*)
visitar to visit
vivir to live

ADJETIVOS
asado(a) roasted, baked
bueno(a) good
caliente hot
frío(a) cold
frito(a) fried
malo(a) bad

OTRAS PALABRAS Y EXPRESIONES
a menudo often
¿a quién? to whom?
aquí here
¿de quién? whose?
con with
¿con quién? with whom?
o or
¿quién(es)? who?, whom?
siempre always
tarde late
temprano early

---

[1] In Mexico, **pastel** is more commonly used for *cake* than for *pie*.

1 Agreement of articles, nouns, and adjectives

Concordancia de artículos, nombres y adjetivos

Agreement   the correspondence in number and gender between an article, a noun, and the adjective that modifies the noun

In Spanish, the article, the noun, and the adjective agree in number and gender.

la papa asad**a**	*the baked potato*
el poll**o** asad**o**	*the roasted chicken*
las papa**s** asad**as**	*the baked potatoes*
los poll**os** asad**os**	*the roasted chickens*

—¿Deseas huev**os** frit**os**
o pescad**o** frit**o**?
—Pescad**o** frit**o** y **una** botella
de vin**o** tint**o**.

*"Do you want fried eggs or
fried fish?"*
*"Fried fish and a bottle of
white wine."*

—¿**La** camarera es mexicana?
—No, es español**a**.

"Is the waitress Mexican?"
"No, she is Spanish."

—¿**La** comida es buena aquí?
—No, es muy mal**a**.

"Is the food good here?"
"No, it's very bad."

Práctica

Make the adjectives agree with the nouns in the list and add the corresponding definite article.

1. _____ pollo frito
   _____ papas _____
2. _____ servilletas blancas
   _____ vino _____
3. _____ muchacho alemán
   _____ mujeres _____
4. _____ champán francés
   _____ vinos _____

5. _____ mozos mexicanos
   _____ comida _____
6. _____ restaurante italiano
   _____ muchachas _____
7. _____ hombre feliz
   _____ camareras _____
8. _____ manteles azules
   _____ servilleta _____

2 The present indicative of regular -er and -ir verbs

El presente de indicativo de los verbos regulares terminados en -er e -ir

Regular verbs ending in **-er** are conjugated like **comer.** Regular verbs ending in **-ir** are conjugated like **vivir.**

comer *(to eat)*		vivir *(to live)*	
yo	com- **o**	yo	viv- **o**
tú	com- **es**	tú	viv- **es**
Ud.		Ud.	
él	com- **e**	él	viv- **e**
ella		ella	
nosotros	com- **emos**	nosotros	viv- **imos**
Uds.		Uds.	
ellos	com- **en**	ellos	viv- **en**
ellas		ellas	

◆ Some other common verbs that follow the same **-er** and **-ir** patterns are:

aprender	to learn	**decidir**	to decide
beber	to drink	**escribir**	to write
leer	to read	**recibir**	to receive
abrir	to open		

—¿Qué **bebes** tú: leche fría, café o té?   *"What do you drink: cold milk, coffee, or tea?"*
—**Bebo** café o chocolate caliente.   *"I drink coffee or hot chocolate."*

—¿**Comen** Uds. temprano?   *"Do you eat early?"*
—No, **comemos** tarde.   *"No, we eat late."*

—¿Dónde **vive** Ud.?   *"Where do you live?"*
—**Vivo** en la calle Unión.   *"I live on Union Street."*

—¿Qué **leen** ellos?   *"What are they reading?"*
—El menú.   *"The menu."*

—¿A qué hora **abren** el restaurante?   *"What time do they open the restaurant?"*
—A las once.   *"At eleven."*

Práctica

A. Provide the missing information about yourself and other people.

1. Nosotros bebemos leche fría y ellos...
2. Yo abro una botella de vino tinto y tú...
3. Elsa come en un restaurante y Uds....
4. Ellos aprenden inglés y yo...
5. Uds. escriben en español y nosotros...
6. Nosotros leemos libros en español y John...

B. Interview a classmate, using the following questions. When you have finished, switch roles.

1. ¿Qué bebes por la mañana: leche, café o chocolate caliente?
2. ¿Qué comes por la noche: pollo asado, pescado o huevos?
3. ¿Uds. comen temprano o tarde?
4. ¿En qué calle vives?
5. ¿Cuánto dinero recibes?
6. ¿Lees muchos libros?
7. ¿Aprendemos mucho en la clase (*class*)?
8. ¿Escribes en español o solamente en inglés?

3 Possession with de

El caso posesivo

De + *noun* is used to express possession or relationship. Unlike English, Spanish does not use the apostrophe.

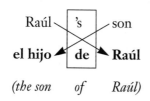

Raúl   's   son

el hijo   **de**   **Raúl**

(the son   of   Raúl)

—¿De **quién** es la casa?	*"Whose house is it?"*
—Es la casa **de** Julio.	*"It is Julio's house."*
—¿Quién es Julio?	*"Who is Julio?"*
—Es el hijo **de** Ana.	*"He is Ana's son."*

Práctica

With a partner, act out the following dialogues in Spanish.

1. "Who is she?"
   "She is Roberto's daughter."
2. "I need Mrs. Prado's address."
   "It's 125 Magnolia Street."
3. "Teresa's last name is Vega?"
   "No, it's not Vega; it's Vera."
4. "Where does María's son live?"
   "He lives at Mrs. Nieto's house."

4 Possessive adjectives
Los adjetivos posesivos

Possessive a word that denotes ownership or possession: **our** house, **their** mother

Forms of the Possessive Adjectives

Singular	Plural	
mi	mis	my
tu	tus	your (*familiar*)
su	sus	his her its your (*formal*) their
nuestro(a)	nuestros(as)	our

Possessive adjectives agree in number with the nouns they modify.

—¿Ud. necesita hablar con **mi** hijo?
"Do you need to speak with my son?"

—No, no necesito hablar con **su** hijo. Necesito hablar con **sus** hijas.
"No, I don't need to speak with your son. I need to speak with your daughters."

—**Mis** hijas no viven aquí.
"My daughters don't live here."

ATENCIÓN: These forms of the possessive adjectives always precede the nouns they introduce and never take an accent.

◆ Since both **su** and **sus** may have different meanings, the form **de él (de ella, de ellos, de ellas, de Ud., de Uds.)** may be substituted to avoid confusion.

el hijo **de Ud. (de Uds.)**

su hijo ⟨ el hijo **de él (de ellos)**

el hijo **de ella (de ellas)**

—¿Ellas son **sus** hijas,   *"Are they your daughters,*
    señora?   *madam?"*
—No, no son **mis** hijas;   *"No, they are not my daughters;*
    son las hijas **de él**.   *they are his daughters."*

◆ **Nuestro** is the only possessive adjective that has the feminine endings **-a, -as.** The others use the same endings for both the masculine and feminine genders.

—¿Con quién debemos   *"With whom should we speak?"*
    hablar?
—Deben hablar con   *"You should speak with our*
    nuestras amigas.   *friends."*

Práctica

A. Fill in the blanks with the appropriate form of the possessive adjective in Spanish. Whenever **su (sus)** is required, give the alternate form with **de**.

Modelo: (*his*) _____ silla
    su silla / la silla **de él**

1. (*my*) _____ amiga
2. (*his*) _____ hija / _____ hija _____ _____
3. (*our*) _____ casa
4. (*her*) _____ idioma / _____ idioma _____ _____
5. (*your—***Ud.**) _____ dinero /
    _____ dinero _____ _____
6. (*my*) _____ hijos
7. (*our*) _____ mantel
8. (*your—***tú**) _____ ocupación
9. (*your—***Uds.**) _____ amigos / _____ amigos _____
    _____
10. (*their—fem.*) _____ lecciones /
    _____ lecciones _____ _____

B. Ask a classmate the following questions. When you have finished, switch roles.

1. ¿Dónde vive tu mejor (*best*) amigo(a)?
2. ¿Cuál es el número de teléfono de tu mejor amigo(a)?
3. ¿De dónde es nuestro(a) profesor(a)?
4. ¿A qué hora es nuestra clase (*class*) de español?
5. ¿Tus otras (*other*) clases son por la mañana?
6. ¿Tú necesitas mi libro?

5 The personal a
La a personal

In Spanish, as in English, a verb has a subject and may require one or more objects. The function of objects is to complete the idea expressed by the verb.

In English, the direct object cannot be separated from the verb by a preposition: *She killed **the burglar**. He sees **the nurse**.* In the preceding sentences, *the burglar* and *the nurse* are direct objects.

In Spanish, the preposition **a** is used before a direct object that refers to a specific person. This preposition is called "the personal **a**" and has no equivalent in English.

Yo visito **a** Carmen.
I visit   Carmen.

♦ The personal **a** is not used when the direct object is not a person.

—¿**A** quién llevas a la fiesta? — *"Whom are you taking to the party?"*
—Llevo **a** mi amiga. — *"I'm taking my friend."*
—¿Ella lleva las bebidas? — *"Is she taking the drinks?"*
—No, lleva los pasteles. — *"No, she is taking the pies."*

—¿Tú visitas **a** tus hijos a menudo? — *"Do you visit your children often?"*
—Sí, yo visito **a** mis hijos los domingos. — *"Yes, I visit my children on Sundays."*

—¿Qué visitan los chicos hoy? — *"What are the boys visiting today?"*
—Visitan el museo. — *"They are visiting the museum."*

—¿**A** quién llama Ud.? — *"Whom are you calling?"*
—Llamo **a** la profesora. — *"I'm calling the professor."*

—¿Desea llamar un taxi?   *"Do you want to call a taxi?"*
—No, siempre tomo el   *"No, I always take the bus."*
ómnibus.

Práctica

With a partner, act out the following dialogues in Spanish.

1. "Do you want to take the bus, Mrs. Peña?"
   "No, I want to call a taxi."
2. "Mr. Ríos, are you taking your friend Teresa to María's party?"
   "No, I'm taking my daughter."
3. "Whom are you calling, Tere?"
   "I'm calling my friend Paco."
4. "Do you visit your son often?"
   "No, but I always call my son on Saturdays."

Palabras y más palabras

Circle the word or phrase that best completes each sentence.

1. Comemos (huevos, café) por la mañana.
2. Bebo chocolate (asado, caliente) en la cafetería.
3. El mozo (abre, decide) una botella de vino.
4. Deseo comer pescado (feliz, frito).
5. Ellos (beben, leen) leche fría.
6. Diego (vive, escribe) en la calle Tercera.
7. Ellos visitan (el pollo, el museo) el sábado.
8. El restaurante Azteca no es bueno; es muy (malo, grande).
9. ¿Uds. comen temprano o (asado, tarde)?
10. Comen papas (asadas, felices).

En el laboratorio

The following material is to be used with the tape or audio CD in the language laboratory.

I. Vocabulario

Repeat each word after the speaker. When repeating words that are cognates, notice the difference in pronunciation between English and Spanish.

COGNADOS: el chocolate   el menú   el museo
el taxi   el té

NOMBRES:	el amigo la bebida la botella el café la fiesta el hijo los hijos el huevo la leche el mozo el camarero el ómnibus el autobús la papa la patata el pastel el pescado el pollo
VERBOS:	abrir aprender beber comer deber decidir escribir leer llamar llevar recibir tomar visitar vivir
ADJETIVOS:	asado bueno caliente frío frito malo
OTRAS PALABRAS Y EXPRESIONES:	a menudo ¿a quién? aquí ¿de quién? con ¿con quién? o ¿quién? ¿quiénes? siempre tarde temprano

II. Práctica

A. Answer the questions, always using the second choice. Omit the subject. Repeat the correct answer after the speaker's confirmation. Listen to the model.

Modelo: —¿Ana vive en la calle Cinco o en la calle Siete?
—**Vive en la calle Siete.**

B. Using the cues provided, say to whom the following items belong. Repeat the correct answer after the speaker's confirmation. Listen to the model.

Modelo: el libro (Susana)
Es el libro de Susana.

1. (Antonio)
2. (mi hijo)
3. (Juan)
4. (la profesora)
5. (Estela)

C. Answer the questions, using the cues provided. Remember to use the personal **a** when needed. Repeat the correct answer after the speaker's confirmation. Listen to the model.

Modelo: —¿A quién visitas? (Rosa)
—**Visito a Rosa.**

1. (el museo)
2. (la Sra. Vega)
3. (el ómnibus)
4. (dinero)
5. (la profesora)

III. Para escuchar y entender

1. The speaker will make some statements. Circle **L** (**lógico**) if the statement is logical and **I** (**ilógico**) if it is illogical. The speaker will verify your response.

   1. L   I   5. L   I
   2. L   I   6. L   I
   3. L   I   7. L   I
   4. L   I   8. L   I

2. Listen carefully to the dialogue. It will be read twice.

   (*Diálogo 1*)

   Now the speaker will make some statements about the dialogue you just heard. Tell whether each statement is true (**verdadero**) or false (**falso**). The speaker will confirm the correct answer.

3. Listen carefully to the dialogue. It will be read twice.

   (*Diálogo 2*)

   Now the speaker will ask you some questions about the dialogue you just heard. Answer each question, omitting the subject. The speaker will confirm the correct answer. Repeat the correct answer.

1. The irregular verbs **ir**, **dar**, and **estar**

2. **Ir a** + infinitive

3. Uses of the verbs **ser** and **estar**

4. Contractions

Vocabulario

COGNADOS

argentino(a) Argentinian	**el hospital** hospital
el club club	**el hotel** hotel
el dólar dollar	**el metal** metal
el (la) estudiante student	**la profesión** profession
la familia family	

NOMBRES
el (la) **abuelo(a)** grandfather, grandmother
el **coche**, el **carro**, el
automóvil, el **auto**
car, automobile
el (la) **cuñado(a)**
brother-in-law,
sister-in-law
los **Estados Unidos**
United States
el (la) **hermano(a)**
brother, sister
la **madera** wood
la **mamá**, la **madre** mom,
mother
el (la) **novio(a)** boyfriend,
girlfriend
los **padres** parents
el **papá**, el **padre** dad,
father
el (la) **primo(a)** cousin
el (la) **sobrino(a)** nephew,
niece
el (la) **suegro(a)** father-
in-law, mother-in-law
el (la) **tío(a)** uncle, aunt

VERBOS
dar to give
esperar to wait (for)
estar to be
ir to go
viajar to travel

ADJETIVOS
alto(a) tall
bonito(a) pretty
cansado(a) tired
enfermo(a) sick

**OTRAS PALABRAS Y
EXPRESIONES**
a to
¿adónde? where (to)?
ahora now
¿cómo? how?
¿Cómo es? What is
he (she, it) like?
¿cuál? what?, which
one?
mañana tomorrow
¿por qué? why?
porque because

1 The irregular verbs ir, dar, and estar

Los verbos irregulares ir, dar y estar

Irregular verbs do not follow the normal pattern of stem changes and endings that regular **-ar, -er,** and **-ir** verbs follow, and therefore must be learned by memory. One irregular verb that you have already learned is **ser.**

	ir *(to go)*	dar *(to give)*	estar *(to be)*
yo	**voy**	**doy**	**estoy**
tú	**vas**	**das**	**estás**
Ud. él ella	**va**	**da**	**está**
nosotros	**vamos**	**damos**	**estamos**
Uds. ellos ellas	**van**	**dan**	**están**

—¿**Vas** a la fiesta que **dan** Rosa y David?   *"Are you going to the party that Rosa and David are giving?"*

—No, no **voy** porque **estoy** muy cansada. ¿Con quién **van** Uds.?   *"No, I'm not going because I'm very tired. With whom are you going?"*

—**Vamos** con Raúl. Él **está** con mi familia ahora.   *"We are going with Raúl. He's with my family now."*

—¿Tú **das** dinero para la fiesta?   *"Are you giving money for the party?"*

—No, yo no **doy** dinero, pero Raúl **da** diez dólares.   *"No, I'm not giving money, but Raúl is giving ten dollars."*

Práctica

A. Complete the following dialogues with the present indicative of **ir, dar,** and **estar.** Then act them out with a partner.

1. —Buenos días, ¿cómo _____ Ud., señora?
   —_____ muy bien, gracias.
   —¿Adónde _____ Ud.?
   —_____ a la fiesta que _____ la Dra. Sánchez.

2. —¿Cuánto dinero _____ Uds. para la fiesta?
   —Nosotros _____ diez dólares. ¿Cuánto _____ tú?
   —Yo _____ solamente cinco dólares.
3. —¿No _____ Uds. a la fiesta?
   —No, no _____ porque _____ muy cansados.
4. —¿Los chicos _____ aquí?
   —No, _____ en el museo.

B. Interview a classmate, using the following questions. When you have finished, switch roles.

1. ¿Dónde estás ahora?
2. ¿Dónde están tus amigos?
3. ¿Dónde está tu familia?
4. ¿Adónde vas los viernes?
5. ¿Con quién vas?
6. ¿Vas a la biblioteca (*library*) los sábados?
7. ¿Van Uds. (tú y tus amigos) a la universidad los domingos?
8. ¿Das tu número de teléfono?

2 Ir a + infinitive
Ir a + infinitivo

The construction **ir a** + *infinitive* is used to express future time. It is equivalent to the English expression *to be going to* + *infinitive*. The "formula" is:

ir	+	**a**	+	*infinitive*	
Yo voy		**a**		**viajar**	con mis abuelos.
I'm going				*to travel*	*with my grandparents.*

—¿Con quién **vas a comer**?   "*With whom are you going to eat?*"
—**Voy a comer** con mi primo.   "*I'm going to eat with my cousin.*"

—¿Uds. **van al** restaurante ahora?   "*Are you going to the restaurant now?*"
—No, primero **vamos a llamar** a mi mamá.   "*No, first we are going to call my mom.*"

—¿Nora **va a viajar** con sus padres?   "*Is Nora going to travel with her parents?*"
—No, con su papá y su hermano.   "*No, with her dad and her brother.*"

Práctica

A. Use your imagination to describe what these people are going to do.

> *Modelo:* yo / mañana por la mañana
> **Yo voy a estudiar mañana por la mañana.**

1. mi hermano / por la noche
2. nosotros / el lunes
3. tú / esta tarde
4. los muchachos / el sábado
5. Ud. / el viernes
6. yo / el miércoles

B. Interview a classmate, using the following questions and two of your own. When you have finished, switch roles.

1. ¿Qué vas a comer en el restaurante?
2. ¿Qué van a beber Uds.?
3. ¿A qué hora vas a estudiar mañana?
4. ¿Qué van a hacer (*to do*) tú y tus amigos el sábado?
5. ¿Adónde vas a viajar en junio?
6. ¿Tus padres van a ir también?

C. With a partner, talk about what you and your friends and relatives are going to do tomorrow.

3 Uses of the verbs ser and estar
Usos de los verbos ser y estar

Although both **ser** and **estar** are equivalent to the English verb *to be*, they are not interchangeable. They are used to indicate the following.

ser	estar
1. Possession or relationship	1. Current condition (usually the product of a change)
2. Profession	2. Location
3. Nationality	
4. Origin	
5. Basic characteristics (color, shape, size, etc.)	
6. Marital status	
7. Expressions of time and dates	
8. Material (metal, wood, glass, etc.)	
9. Events taking place	

—El coche **es** de Pedro,   *"The car is Pedro's, isn't it?"*
¿no?
—No, **es** de mi sobrina.   *"No, it's my niece's."*

—¿Cuál **es** la profesión   *"What is your aunt's*
de tu tía?   *profession?"*
—**Es** profesora.   *"She is a professor."*

—Elena **es** muy inteligente.   *"Elena is very intelligent."*
—Ella **es** de Argentina,   *"She's from Argentina, isn't*
¿no?   *she?"*
—Sí, **es** argentina, pero   *"Yes, she's an Argentinian,*
ahora **está** en los   *but now she's in the*
Estados Unidos.   *United States."*

—¿Cómo **es** tu mamá?   *"What is your mom like?"*
—**Es** alta y muy bonita.   *"She's tall and very pretty."*

—¿**Es** Ud. casada?   *"Are you married?"*
—No, **soy** soltera.   *"No, I am single."*

—¿Qué día **es** hoy?   *"What day is today?"*
—Hoy **es** martes.   *"Today is Tuesday."*

—¿**Es** de madera la mesa?   *"Is the table made of wood?"*
—No, **es** de metal.   *"No, it is made of metal."*

—¿Dónde **es** la fiesta?   *"Where's the party?"*
—**Es** en el hotel Azteca.   *"It's at the Azteca hotel."*

—¿Cómo **está** Ud.?   *"How are you?"*
—**Estoy** bien, gracias.   *"I am fine, thanks."*

—¿Dónde **está** tu novio?   *"Where is your boyfriend?"*
—**Está** en el hospital.   *"He is in the hospital. He is*
Está enfermo.   *sick."*

Práctica

A. Complete the following dialogues with **ser** or **estar**, as appropriate. Then act them out with a partner.

1. —¿Cómo _____ Amelia?
   —_____ muy inteligente y muy bonita.
   —¿De dónde _____ ella?
   —_____ argentina, pero ahora _____ en los Estados Unidos.
   —¿_____ soltera?
   —No, _____ casada.
   —¿Hoy no trabaja?
   —No, porque _____ enferma. _____ en el hospital.

2. —¿Las sillas _____ de metal?
　—No, _____ de madera.
　—¿_____ de tu novia?
　—No, _____ de mi sobrino.
3. —¿Cuál _____ su profesión, Sr. Paz?
　—_____ profesor.
4. —¿Cómo _____ sus hijos?
　—_____ altos y guapos.
5. —¿Qué fecha _____ hoy?
　—Hoy _____ el veinte de mayo.
　—¿_____ lunes?
　—No, hoy _____ martes.
6. —¿Dónde _____ las bebidas?
　—_____ en el auto de Jorge.
7. —¿La fiesta _____ en el hotel México?
　—No, _____ en el hotel Hilton.

B. How would you describe Alberto in Spanish?

Alberto is a very handsome young man. He's not an American; he's from Buenos Aires, but now he's in California. His father is a professor and his mother is a doctor. He's single. Alberto studies at the University of California. Today he's at home (**en casa**); he is very sick.

C. Use **ser** or **estar** to tell a classmate the following information about yourself.

1. nationality and origin
2. profession (student)
3. marital status
4. basic characteristics (i.e., appearance, qualities)
5. state of health
6. location

D. Go to the map of South America on page xxi and say what the capital of each Spanish-speaking country is.

Modelo: **Buenos Aires es la capital de Argentina.**

4 Contractions
Contracciones

Contraction the combination of two or more words into one, with certain sounds or letters missing: **isn't, don't, can't, I'm**

In Spanish there are only two contractions: **al** and **del**.

◆ The preposition **de** (*of, from*) plus the article **el** is contracted to form **del**.

Leen los libros **de + el** profesor.   Leen los libros **del** profesor.

◆ The preposition **a** (*to, toward*) or the personal **a** plus the article **el** is contracted to form **al**.

Esperamos **a + el** profesor.   Esperamos **al** profesor.

ATENCIÓN: None of the other combinations of prepositions and definite articles (**de la, de los, de las, a la, a los, a las**) is contracted.

—¿Llaman Uds. **al** cuñado de Julio?
"*Are you calling Julio's brother-in-law?*"

—No, llamamos a su suegra.
"*No, we're calling his mother-in-law.*"

—¿Adónde vas mañana? **¿A la** fiesta?
"*Where are you going tomorrow? To the party?*"

—No, voy **al** club.
"*No, I'm going to the club.*"

—¿Necesitan ellos el coche **de la** señora Villegas?
"*Do they need Mrs. Villegas's car?*"

—Sí.
"*Yes.*"

Práctica

Complete the following dialogues, using one of the following: **de la, de las, del, de los, a la, a las, al,** or **a los**. Then act them out with a partner.

1. —¿Por qué llamas _____ cuñado de Raúl?
   —Porque él va a llevar _____ hijas _____ Sr. López _____ fiesta _____ club.
2. —¿Uds. van _____ museo o _____ universidad mañana?
   —Vamos _____ restaurante.
3. —¿Dónde están los libros _____ estudiantes (*masc.*)?
   —Están en la casa _____ profesor.
4. —¿A quiénes llevas _____ fiesta? ¿_____ muchachos?
   —No, _____ muchachas.
5. —¿A quién esperan Uds.?
   —_____ profesor.

Palabras y más palabras

Complete the following exchanges, using the vocabulary learned in this lesson.

1. —¿Gerardo es tu primo?
   —Sí, es el hijo de mi _____ Estela.
2. —¿Maribel es tu _____?
   —Sí, es la esposa de mi hermano.
3. —¿_____ vas?
   —Al club.
4. —¿La mesa es de metal?
   —No, es de _____.
5. —¿Aurora _____ en el hospital?
   —Sí, está muy _____.
6. —¿_____ es Alicia?
   —Es alta y bonita.
7. —¿Héctor es de Buenos Aires?
   —Sí, es _____.
8. —¿Uds. van a viajar en ómnibus?
   —No, vamos en mi _____.

En el laboratorio

The following material is to be used with the tape or audio CD in the language laboratory.

I. Vocabulario

Repeat each word after the speaker. When repeating words that are cognates, notice the difference in pronunciation between English and Spanish.

COGNADOS:	argentino el club el dólar el estudiante la familia el hospital el hotel el metal la profesión
NOMBRES:	el abuelo el coche el carro el automóvil el auto el cuñado los Estados Unidos el hermano la madera la mamá la madre el novio los padres el papá el padre el primo el sobrino el suegro el tío

VERBOS:	dar esperar estar ir viajar
ADJETIVOS:	alto bonito cansado enfermo
OTRAS PALABRAS Y EXPRESIONES:	a ¿adónde? ahora ¿cómo? ¿Cómo es? ¿cuál? mañana ¿por qué? porque

II. Práctica

A. Answer the questions, always using the second choice. Omit the subject. Repeat the correct answer after the speaker's confirmation. Listen to the model.

Modelo: —¿Vas a la cafetería o a la universidad?
            —**Voy a la universidad.**

B. Answer the questions, using the cues provided. Repeat the correct answer after the speaker's confirmation. Listen to the model.

Modelo: —¿Con quién vas a ir tú? (con Elena)
            —**Voy a ir con Elena.**

1. (a la universidad)
2. (las bebidas)
3. (a las doce)
4. (la calle Victoria)
5. (con mi primo)
6. (a mi suegro)
7. (con mi hermano)
8. (a la fiesta de Eva)

C. Answer the questions, using the cues provided. Repeat the correct answer after the speaker's confirmation. Listen to the model.

Modelo: —¿Paula es argentina? (sí)
            —**Sí, es argentina.**

1. (no)
2. (de Lima)
3. (alto y guapo)
4. (bien)
5. (en el club)
6. (en el hotel Hilton)
7. (viernes)

D. Answer the questions, using the cues provided. Repeat the correct answer after the speaker's confirmation. Listen to the model.

Modelo: —¿Adónde vas? (club)
            —**Voy al club.**

1. (Sr. López)
2. (profesor Mena)
3. (hijo de Marta)
4. (universidad)
5. (Dr. Barrios)
6. (cuñado de Ana)

III. Para escuchar y entender

1. The speaker will make some statements. Circle **L** (**lógico**) if the statement is logical and **I** (**ilógico**) if it is illogical. The speaker will verify your response.

1. L I	5. L I
2. L I	6. L I
3. L I	7. L I
4. L I	8. L I

2. Listen carefully to the narration. It will be read twice.

   (Narración)

   Now the speaker will make some statements about the narration you just heard. Tell whether each statement is true (**verdadero**) or false (**falso**). The speaker will confirm the correct answer.

3. Listen carefully to the dialogue. It will be read twice.

   (*Diálogo*)

   Now the speaker will ask you some questions about the dialogue you just heard. Answer each question, omitting the subject. The speaker will confirm the correct answer. Repeat the correct answer.

1. The irregular verbs **tener** and **venir**

2. Expressions with **tener**

3. Comparative forms

4. Irregular comparative forms

Vocabulario

COGNADOS

la clase class	**el (la) supervisor(a)** supervisor

NOMBRES
el aire acondicionado   air conditioning
la biblioteca   library
el (la) dueño(a)   owner
la esposa   wife
el esposo   husband
el (la) gerente(a)   manager
el gimnasio   gym
la habitación, el cuarto room
la hora   hour
la llave   key
la maleta, la valija suitcase
el mercado   market
la pensión   boarding house
la piscina, la alberca (*Méx.*) swimming pool
la tienda   store

VERBOS
creer   to think, to believe
llegar   to arrive

tener   to have
venir   to come

ADJETIVOS
barato(a)   inexpensive
caro(a)   expensive
mayor   older; bigger
mejor   better
menor   younger; smaller
peor   worse
pequeño(a)   small, little (*size*)
poco(a)   little (*quantity*)
solo(a)   alone

OTRAS PALABRAS Y EXPRESIONES
mal   badly
más   more
menos   less, fewer
otro(a)   other; another
que   than, that
también   also, too
tan... como   as . . . as
tener que (+ *inf.*) to have to (+ *inf.*)

1 The irregular verbs tener and venir

Los verbos irregulares tener y venir

tener (*to have*)		venir (*to come*)	
yo	**tengo**	yo	**vengo**
tú	**tienes**	tú	**vienes**
Ud. él ella	**tiene**	Ud. él ella	**viene**
nosotros	**tenemos**	nosotros	**venimos**
Uds. ellos ellas	**tienen**	Uds. ellos ellas	**vienen**

—¿El hotel **tiene** piscina?
—Sí, y también **tiene** gimnasio.

"Does the hotel have a pool?"
"Yes, and it also has a gym."

—¿**Tienes** la llave del cuarto?
—Sí.

"Do you have the key to the room?"
"Yes."

—¿Con quién **viene** Ud. a la biblioteca? ¿Con su hijo?
—No, **vengo** sola. Tengo que trabajar.
—¿Cuántas horas **tiene** que trabajar?
—Ocho horas.

"With whom are you coming to the library? With your son?"
"No, I'm coming alone. I have to work."
"How many hours do you have to work?"
"Eight hours."

—¿Cuántos hijos **tiene** Ud.?

"How many children do you have?"

—**Tengo** tres hijos y una hija.

"I have three sons and one daughter."

ATENCIÓN: The personal **a** is not used with the verb **tener**.

—Ana, ¿**tienes** novio?
—No, no **tengo** novio.

"Ana, do you have a boyfriend?"
"No, I don't have a boyfriend."

ATENCIÓN: **Un** and **una** are not used with the verb **tener** when the numerical concept is not emphasized.

No **tengo** novio.

I don't have a boyfriend.

Práctica

A. Complete the dialogues with the present indicative of **tener** and **venir**, as appropriate. Then act them out with a partner.

1. —Teresa, ¿tu hermano _____ a la universidad con su novia?
   —Él no _____ novia.
2. —¿A qué hora _____ Uds. mañana?
   —_____ a las cinco de la tarde. ¿A qué hora _____ Ud.?
   —Yo _____ a las cinco también.
3. —¿Cuántos hijos _____ Uds.?
   —_____ dos hijos. ¿Cuántos hijos _____ tú?
   —Yo _____ un hijo.
4. —¿Cuántas horas _____ que estudiar Uds.?
   —_____ que estudiar tres horas.

B. Interview a classmate, using the following questions. When you have finished, switch roles.

yo voy vendre

1. ¿A qué hora vienes a la universidad?
2. ¿Vienes solo(a)?
3. ¿Cuántas clases tienes?
4. ¿Tienes clases los sábados?
5. ¿Qué días tenemos clase de español?
No voy — 6. ¿Vienes a la universidad los domingos?
7. ¿Tú y tus amigos vienen a la universidad los sábados?
8. ¿La universidad tiene piscina? ¿Tiene gimnasio?

2 **Expressions with** tener
Las expresiones con tener

In Spanish, many useful idiomatic expressions are formed with the verb **tener** and a noun, while English uses *to be* and an adjective.

tener calor *to be hot*	**tener hambre** *to be hungry*
tener frío *to be cold*	**tener sed** *to be thirsty*
tener cuidado *to be careful*	**tener prisa** *to be in a hurry*
tener sueño *to be sleepy*	**tener razón** *to be right*
tener miedo *to be afraid*	
tener... años (de edad) *to be . . . years old*	

◆ The equivalent of *I am very hungry*, for example, is **Tengo mucha hambre.**

—**¿Tienes hambre**, María?   *"Are you hungry, María?"*
—No, pero **tengo** mucha **sed**.   *"No, but I am very thirsty."*

—¿**Tienes calor,** Carlos?   *"Are you hot, Carlos?"*
—Sí, **tengo** mucho **calor.**   *"Yes, I'm very hot."*
—¿El hotel no tiene   *"Doesn't the hotel have*
   aire acondicionado?   *air conditioning?"*
—No.   *"No."*

—¿Cuántos **años tiene**   *"How old is your daughter?"*
   su hija?
—Mi hija **tiene** seis **años.**   *"My daughter is six years old."*

—Deseo hablar con el   *"I wish to speak with the*
   dueño, por favor.   *owner, please."*
—Ahora no, lo siento. Él   *"Not now, I'm sorry. He's in*
   tiene mucha **prisa.**   *a big hurry."*
—**Tiene razón.** Es tarde.   *"You're right. It's late."*

Práctica

A. Tell what is happening in each of the pictures. Follow the model.

Modelo:

Ella...
Ella tiene hambre.

1. Carlos...

2. Él...

3. Yo...

4. Ellas...

5. ¿Ud...?

6. Tú...

7. Nélida...

B. With a partner act out the following dialogues in Spanish.

1. "I'm hungry and I'm also very thirsty."
   "Me too."
2. "Are you cold, Paquito?"
   "No, I'm hot."
3. "How old are you, Anita?"
   "I'm six years old."
4. "Are you in a hurry, Miss Vega?"
   "Yes, it's very late."
5. "You must be careful, Mrs. López."
   "You are right."

C. Interview a classmate, using the following questions. When you have finished, switch roles.

1. ¿Qué bebes cuando tienes sed? ¿Y cuando tienes frío?
2. ¿Qué comes cuando tienes hambre?
3. ¿Cuántos años tienes?
4. ¿Cuántos años tiene tu madre? ¿Y tu padre?
5. En tu familia, ¿quién tiene razón siempre? ¿Y en la clase?
6. ¿Tienes miedo a veces (*sometimes*)?

3 Comparative forms
Las formas comparativas

Comparisons of inequality

◆ In Spanish, the comparative of most adjectives, adverbs, and nouns is formed by placing **más** (*more*) or **menos** (*less*) before the adjective, adverb, or noun and **que** after.

Ella es **más bonita que** Rosa.
She is   prettier   than Rosa.

		adjective		
más		or		
	+	*adverb*	+	**que**
menos		or		
		noun		

In the construction shown in the chart, **que** is equivalent to *than*.

—El hotel Azteca es **barato**.
"The Azteca Hotel is inexpensive."

—Sí, pero creo que es **más caro que** la pensión.
"Yes, but I think it is more expensive than the boarding house."

—Yo tengo muy **poco** dinero.
"I have very little money."

—¡Yo tengo **menos dinero que** tú!
"I have less money than you!"

—¿Quién llega **más tarde:** el gerente o el supervisor?
"Who arrives later? The manager or the supervisor?"

—El supervisor llega **más tarde que** el gerente.
"The supervisor arrives later than the manager."

Comparisons of equality

◆ To form comparisons of equality with adjectives, adverbs, and nouns, use the adverb **tan** or the adjective **tanto, -a, -os, -as** and **como**.

When comparing adjectives or adverbs:	When comparing nouns:
tan (*as*) < bonita / tarde + **como**	**tanto** (*as much*) dinero **tanta** bebida **tantos** (*as many*) libros **tantas** plumas } + **como**

—¿Te gusta el hotel California?
"*Do you like the California Hotel?*"

—Sí, pero no es **tan bonito como** el hotel Victoria.
"*Yes, but it's not as pretty as the Victoria Hotel.*"

—Tu casa es muy grande.
"*Your house is very big.*"

—Sí, pero no tiene **tantas habitaciones como** la casa de tus padres.
"*Yes, but it doesn't have as many rooms as your parents' house.*"

The Superlative

◆ The superlative construction is similar to the comparative. It is formed by placing the definite article before the person or thing being compared.

definite article	+	noun	+	**más** or **menos**	+	adjective	+	**de**

—¿Cuál es **la habitación más grande de** la pensión?
"*Which is the biggest room in the boarding house?*"

—La habitación número 5.
"*Room number 5.*"

ATENCIÓN: After a superlative construction, *in* is expressed by **de** in Spanish. In many instances, the noun may not be expressed in a superlative.

La habitación número 5 es **la más grande.**
Room number 5 is the biggest (one).

Práctica

A. Compare these people, places, or things to each other.

> *Modelo:* Vermont / California (pequeño)
> Vermont **es más pequeño que** California.

1. Texas / Rhode Island (grande)
2. tú / tu amigo (alto)
3. Tom Cruise (Meg Ryan) / tú (guapo/bonita)
4. Chile / Brasil (pequeño)
5. un Rolls Royce / un Ford (caro)
6. el hotel Hilton / el Motel 6 (barato)

B. With a partner take turns asking each other the following questions.

1. ¿Tú eres más alto(a) que tu mejor amigo?
2. ¿Quién es la persona más inteligente de tu familia?
3. ¿Tú tienes tanto dinero como tus padres?
4. ¿Tú trabajas tanto como tu papá?
5. ¿Tú hablas español tan bien como el profesor?
6. ¿Quién crees tú que es más guapo: Leonardo diCaprio o Brad Pitt? ¿Quién es más bonita: Julia Roberts o Meg Ryan?
7. ¿Cuál es el hotel más grande de la ciudad donde tú vives? ¿Y el más caro?
8. ¿Cuál es el motel más barato de la ciudad donde vives?

4 Irregular comparative forms
Las formas comparativas irregulares

Adjectives	*Adverbs*	*Comparative*	*Superlative*
bueno	bien	mejor	el (la) mejor
malo	mal	peor	el (la) peor
grande		mayor	el (la) mayor
pequeño		menor	el (la) menor

◆ When the adjectives **grande** and **pequeño(a)** refer to size, their regular forms are generally used.

| Tu maleta es **más grande** que la de Rita. | *Your suitcase is bigger than Rita's.* |

◆ When these adjectives refer to age, the irregular forms are used.

—¿Felipe es **mayor** que tú?   *"Is Felipe older than you?"*
—No, es **menor** que yo.   *"No, he is younger than I (am)."*

—¿Quién es **mayor**? ¿Ud.   *"Who is older? You or Elsa?"*
  o Elsa?
—Elsa. Ella es **la mayor**   *"Elsa. She is the oldest in the*
  de la clase.   *class."*

—Este hotel es muy malo.   *"This hotel is very bad."*
—Sí, pero el otro es **peor**.   *"Yes, but the other one is worse."*

—¿Su esposo habla   *"Does your husband speak Spanish*
  español tan **bien**   *as well as you do?"*
  como Ud.?
—No, él habla español   *"No, he speaks Spanish much*
  mucho **mejor** que yo.   *better than I."*

—¿El mercado es **más**   *"Is the market bigger than the*
  grande que la tienda?   *store?"*
—No, el mercado es   *"No, the market is smaller than*
  más pequeño que la   *the store."*
  la tienda.

Práctica

A. Answer the following questions.

1. ¿Es Ud. menor o mayor que su mejor amigo o amiga?
2. ¿Tiene Ud. un hermano mayor (un hermano menor)?
3. ¿Cuál es la mejor universidad de los Estados Unidos?
4. ¿Quién habla mejor el español: Ud. o el profesor (la profesora)?
5. ¿Cuál cree Ud. que es el peor restaurante de la ciudad donde Ud. vive? ¿Y el mejor?

B. With a partner, take turns comparing yourselves with other members of your families.

Palabras y más palabras

Match the questions in column A with the answers in column B.

A	B
1. ¿Vas a hablar con el gerente? _____	a. Sí, y también tiene piscina.
	b. No, solo.
2. ¿Qué necesitas? _____	c. No, a la tienda.
3. ¿Necesitas las maletas? _____	d. No, en una pensión.
	e. Sí, porque voy a viajar.

4. ¿El hotel tiene gimnasio?

    _____

5. ¿A qué hora llegan ellos?

    _____

6. ¿Vas al mercado? _____
7. ¿Eres mayor que tu esposo?

    _____

8. ¿Viene con su esposa?

    _____

9. ¿Están en un hotel? _____
10. ¿Dónde estudian Uds.?

    _____

11. ¿La habitación es grande?

    _____

12. ¿Con quién tienes que hablar?

    _____

f. No, es muy pequeña.
g. No, con la dueña.
h. Con el supervisor.
i. A las dos.
j. Sí, él es menor que yo.
k. La llave del cuarto.
l. En la biblioteca.

En el laboratorio

The following material is to be used with the tape or audio CD in the language laboratory.

I. Vocabulario

Repeat each word after the speaker. When repeating words that are cognates, notice the difference in pronunciation between English and Spanish.

Cognados:	la clase el supervisor
Nombres:	el aire acondicionado la biblioteca el dueño la esposa el esposo el gerente el gimnasio la habitación el cuarto la hora la llave la maleta la valija el mercado la pensión la piscina la alberca la tienda
Verbos:	creer llegar tener venir
Adjetivos:	barato caro mayor mejor menor peor pequeño poco solo
Otras palabras y expresiones:	mal · más menos otro que también tan... como tener que

II. Práctica

A. Answer the questions, using the cues provided. Omit the subject. Repeat the correct answer after the speaker's confirmation. Listen to the model.

Modelo: —¿Cuántos hijos tienes? (tres)
—**Tengo tres hijos.**

1. (cuatro)
2. (no)
3. (los martes y los jueves)
4. (no)
5. (sí)
6. (cinco)
7. (los domingos)
8. (hoy)

B. Answer the questions in the affirmative, always using **mucho** or **mucha,** as appropriate. Repeat the correct answer after the speaker's confirmation. Listen to the model.

Modelo: —¿Tienes hambre?
—**Sí tengo mucha hambre.**

C. Answer the questions, always using the second choice. Omit the subject. Repeat the correct answer after the speaker's confirmation. Listen to the model.

Modelo: —¿Quién es más bonita: Rosa o Ana?
—**Ana es más bonita que Rosa.**

III. Para escuchar y entender

1. The speaker will make some statements. Circle L (**lógico**) if the statement is logical and I (**ilógico**) if it is illogical. The speaker will verify your response.

1. L I	5. L I
2. L I	6. L I
3. L I	7. L I
4. L I	8. L I

2. Listen carefully to the dialogue. It will be read twice.

(*Diálogo 1*)

Now the speaker will make some statements about the dialogue you just heard. Tell whether each statement is true (**verdadero**) or false (**falso**). The speaker will confirm the correct answer.

3. Listen carefully to the dialogue. It will be read twice.

(*Diálogo 2*)

Now the speaker will make some statements about the dialogue you just heard. Tell whether each statement is true (**verdadero**) or false (**falso**). The speaker will confirm the correct answer.

4. Listen carefully to the dialogue. It will be read twice.

(*Diálogo 3*)

Now the speaker will make some statements about the dialogue you just heard. Tell whether each statement is true (**verdadero**) or false (**falso**). The speaker will confirm the correct answer.

Lección

5

1. Stem-changing verbs (**e:ie**)
2. Some uses of the definite article
3. The present progressive
4. Ordinal numbers

Vocabulario

COGNADOS

el concierto concert	**la oficina** office
la educación education	**las vacaciones**[1] vacation
importante important	

NOMBRES
el almuerzo lunch
la cárcel jail
la cena dinner
el cine movie theater, movies
el desayuno breakfast
la escuela school
la iglesia church
el jabón soap
el mes month
el piso floor, story
la primavera spring
la revista magazine
la semana week
el teatro theater
la toalla towel

VERBOS
cerrar (e:ie) to close
comenzar (e:ie) to begin, to start
comprar to buy
decir[2] to say

desayunar to have breakfast
dormir[3] to sleep
empezar (e:ie) to begin, to start
entender (e:ie) to understand
hacer (yo hago) to do, to make
pedir[2] to ask (for)
perder (e:ie) to lose
preferir (e:ie) to prefer
querer (e:ie) to want
servir[2] to serve
traer (yo traigo) to bring

ADJETIVO
próximo(a) next

OTRAS PALABRAS Y EXPRESIONES
esta noche tonight
primero first
ya lo creo I'll say

---

[1] **Vacaciones** is always used in the plural.
[2] These verbs will be studied in Lección 7.
[3] This verb will be studied in Lección 6.

Resumen de palabras interrogativas	
¿a quién? to whom?	¿A quién llamas?
¿adónde? where to?	¿Adónde vas?
¿cuál(es)? which?	¿Cuál prefieres?
¿cuándo? when?	¿Cuándo vienen ellos?
¿cuánto(a)? how much?	¿Cuánto dinero necesitas?
¿cuántos(as)? how many?	¿Cuántas toallas quieres?
¿de dónde? from where?	¿De dónde es Ud.?
¿de quién(es)? whose?	¿De quién es la revista?
¿dónde? where?	¿Dónde está el cine Rex?
¿por qué? why?	¿Por qué no van al concierto?
¿qué? what?	¿Qué desea comprar, señora?
¿quién(es)? who?	¿Quiénes van a venir a la fiesta?

1 **Stem-changing verbs** (e:ie)
Verbos que cambian en la raíz (e:ie)

In Spanish, some verbs undergo a stem change in the present indicative. For these verbs, when **e** is the last stem vowel and it is stressed, it changes to **ie** as follows.

preferir *(to prefer)*	
prefiero	preferimos
prefieres	
prefiere	prefieren

◆ Notice that the stem vowel is not stressed in the verb form corresponding to **nosotros,** and therefore the **e** does not change to **ie: nosotros preferimos.**

◆ Stem-changing verbs have regular endings like other **-ar, -er,** and **-ir** verbs.

◆ Some other verbs that undergo the same change are:

cerrar	to close	**entender**	to understand
comenzar[1]	to start, to begin	**perder**	to lose
empezar[1]	to start, to begin	**querer**	to want

[1] When **comenzar** and **empezar** are followed by an infinitive, the preposition **a** is used: **Yo comienzo *(empiezo)* a trabajar a las seis.** Notice that these two verbs are synonymous.

—¿**Quieres** ir al cine o al   *"Do you want to go to the*
   teatro esta noche?   *movies or to the theater tonight?"*
—No, **prefiero** ir al   *"No, I prefer to go to the*
   concierto.   *concert."*
—¿A qué hora **empieza**?   *"At what time does it begin?"*
—**Comienza** a las nueve.   *"It starts at nine."*

—¿A qué hora **cierran** las   *"At what time do the stores*
   tiendas?   *close?"*
—A las diez.   *"At ten."*

Práctica

A. Finish the following sentences in your own words, matching the
verbs to the new subjects:

1. Luis comienza a trabajar a las siete y nosotros...
2. Tú prefieres ir al cine y yo...
3. Nosotros cerramos a las nueve y ellos...
4. Yo empiezo a trabajar el lunes y Uds....
5. Rafael quiere aprender francés y nosotros...
6. Yo no entiendo inglés y Uds....

B. Interview a classmate, using the following questions and two of
your own. When you have finished, switch roles.

1. ¿Cuándo comienzan las clases en la universidad?
2. ¿A qué hora empieza la clase de español?
3. Cuando el profesor (la profesora) habla español, ¿tú
   entiendes?
4. ¿A qué hora cierran la biblioteca?
5. ¿Prefieres ir al cine o a un concierto?
6. ¿Quieres ir al teatro el sábado?
7. ¿Quieres ir a un restaurante italiano o prefieres comer comida mexicana?
8. ¿Tú pierdes las llaves a menudo?

C. With a partner, play the roles of two friends who cannot
agree on anything. When one wants to do something, the other
prefers to do something else.

2 Some uses of the definite article

Algunos usos del artículo definido

The definite article is used in the following instances in Spanish.

◆ with expressions of time, the seasons, and the days of the week

—¿Cuándo es su clase de español?	*"When is your Spanish class?"*
—Tengo clase de español **los**[1] lunes, miércoles y viernes, a **las** nueve.	*"I have a Spanish class on Mondays, Wednesdays, and Fridays at nine."*

ATENCIÓN: The definite article is omitted with the seasons and days of the week when used after the verb **ser.**

—¿Es primavera ahora en Argentina?	*"Is it spring in Argentina now?"*
—Sí, es primavera.	*"Yes, it is spring."*
—¿Qué día es hoy?	*"What day is today?"*
—Hoy es domingo.	*"Today is Sunday."*

◆ before nouns used in a general sense

—¿Tomas **café?**	*"Do you drink coffee?"*
—Sí, pero prefiero **el té.**	*"Yes, but I prefer tea."*

◆ with abstract nouns

—**La educación** es muy importante.	*"Education is very important."*
—Ya lo creo.	*"I'll say."*

◆ before **próximo(a)** (*next*) with expressions of time

—¿Tus vacaciones comienzan **la** semana **próxima?**	*"Does your vacation start next week?"*
—Sí, comienzan el lunes.	*"Yes, it starts on Monday."*

---

[1] Notice that the definite article is used here as the equivalent of *on.*

◆ with the nouns **iglesia, escuela,** and **cárcel** when they are preceded by a preposition

—¿Vas a **la iglesia** los viernes?   *"Do you go to church on Fridays?"*

—No, los viernes voy a **la escuela.**   *"No, I go to school on Fridays."*

◆ before the words **desayuno, almuerzo,** and **cena**

—¿**El desayuno** es a las ocho?   *"Is breakfast at eight?"*

—Sí, y **el almuerzo** es a las doce.   *"Yes, and lunch is at twelve."*

Práctica

A. Is the definite article needed or not? Complete the following dialogues, then act them out with a partner.

1. —¿Tú vas a _____ iglesia hoy?
   —No, hoy es _____ sábado, y yo voy a _____ iglesia _____ domingos.
   —¿Vas a _____ escuela _____ lunes?
   —No, _____ lunes no tengo clases.

2. —¿A qué hora es _____ almuerzo?
   —_____ almuerzo es a _____ doce y _____ cena es a _____ ocho.

3. —_____ hombres son más inteligentes que _____ mujeres.
   —¡No! _____ mujeres somos tan inteligentes como _____ hombres.

4. —¿ Adónde vas a ir _____ domingo próximo?
   —Voy a ir a visitar a Julio, que está en _____ cárcel.

5. —¿Qué es muy importante para ti?
   —_____ educación.

B. Interview a classmate, using the following questions. When you have finished, switch roles.

1. ¿Qué días tienes clases en la universidad?
2. ¿A qué hora es tu primera (*first*) clase?
3. ¿A qué hora es la cena en tu casa? (¿y el desayuno? ¿ y el almuerzo?)
4. ¿Van a ir Uds. de vacaciones la semana próxima?
5. ¿Vas a la iglesia los domingos?

6. ¿Qué crees que es más importante, el amor (*love*) o el dinero?
7. ¿Quiénes crees tú que son más inteligentes, los hombres o las mujeres?
8. ¿Te gusta la comida mexicana o prefieres la comida italiana?

3 The present progressive
El presente progresivo

The present progressive describes an action that is in process at the moment we are talking. In Spanish, it is formed with the present tense of **estar** and the Spanish equivalent of the present participle (*-ing* form)[1] of the main verb.

-ing Form Endings		
-ar: **hablar**	-er: **comer**	-ir: **escribir**
habl- **ando**	com- **iendo**	escrib- **iendo**

◆ Some irregular *-ing* forms:

pedir	**pidiendo**	servir	**sirviendo**
decir	**diciendo**	leer	**leyendo**[2]
dormir	**durmiendo**	traer	**trayendo**[2]

—¿Qué **están haciendo** tus hermanos?	*"What are your brothers doing?"*
—**Están estudiando.**	*"They are studying."*
—¿Qué **estás comiendo?**	*"What are you eating?"*
—**Estoy comiendo** pollo.	*"I'm eating chicken."*
—¿Qué **está leyendo** Ud.?	*"What are you reading?"*
—**Estoy leyendo** una revista.	*"I'm reading a magazine."*

ATENCIÓN: Unlike in English the present progressive is never used in Spanish to refer to a future action. Instead, the present indicative is used for actions that will occur in the near future.

Trabajo mañana.   *I'm working tomorrow.*

Verbs such as **ser, estar, ir (yendo),** and **venir (viniendo)** are rarely used in the progressive construction.

---

[1] The equivalent of the *-ing* form of the verb is called **el gerundio** in Spanish.
[2] Notice that the **-i** of **-iendo** becomes **y** between vowels.

Práctica

A. Complete the following dialogues, using the present progressive of the verbs given. Then act them out with a partner.

1. —¿Qué _____ tú? (comer)
   —_____ pollo y papa asada. (comer)
2. —¿Jorge _____? (dormir)
   —No, _____. (leer)
3. —¿Qué _____ Uds.? (servir)
   —_____ las bebidas. (servir)
4. —¿Qué _____ Gerardo ahora? (hacer)
   —_____ en la biblioteca. (trabajar)
5. —¿Qué _____ los chicos? (pedir)
   —_____ el menú. (pedir)
6. —¿A quién _____ Uds.? (esperar)
   —_____ a mi suegra. (esperar)

B. Imagine what these people are doing according to where they are.

Modelo: Yo / en el hotel
   Yo estoy hablando con el gerente.

1. Julia / en su cuarto
2. el mozo / en el restaurante
3. nosotros / en la biblioteca
4. Ud. / en la cafetería
5. mis padres / en la pensión
6. los estudiantes / en la clase de español

4 Ordinal numbers
Los números ordinales

primero(a)	*first*	**sexto(a)**	*sixth*
segundo(a)	*second*	**séptimo(a)**	*seventh*
tercero(a)	*third*	**octavo(a)**	*eighth*
cuarto(a)	*fourth*	**noveno(a)**	*ninth*
quinto(a)	*fifth*	**décimo(a)**	*tenth*

Ordinal numbers agree in gender and number with the nouns they modify.

—¿Qué **oficina** prefiere?　　　*"Which office do you prefer?"*
—Prefiero **la** quinta oficina.　　*"I prefer the fifth (one)."*

◆ The ordinal numbers **primero** and **tercero** drop the final **-o** before masculine singular nouns.

—¿Qué día llegan Uds.?   *"What day are you arriving?"*
—Llegamos el **primer** día   *"We are arriving the first day*
   del mes.   *of the month."*

—¿Dónde está Paco? ¿En el   *"Where is Paco?*
   tercer piso?   *On the third floor?"*
—Sí, está comprando toallas   *"Yes, he's buying*
   y jabón.   *towels and soap."*

◆ Ordinal numbers are seldom used after *the tenth*.

—¿En qué piso viven Uds.?   *"On which floor do you live?"*
—Vivimos en el piso **doce**.   *"We live on the twelfth floor."*

◆ Remember that cardinal numbers are used in Spanish for dates except for *the first*.

—¿Qué día es hoy?   *"What day is it today?"*
—Hoy es el **treinta** de abril.   *"Today is April 30th.*
   Mañana es **el primero**   *Tomorrow is the first (day)*
   de mayo.   *of May."*

Práctica

Complete the following dialogues with the correct ordinal numbers. Then act them out with a partner.

1. —¿La oficina de Alberto está en el _____ piso? *(third)*
  —No, está en el _____ piso. *(second)*
  —Yo quiero una en el _____ piso. *(fifth)*
2. —¿Uds. viajan la _____ semana? *(fourth)*
  —Sí, pero no viajamos el _____ día. *(first)*
3. —¿Septiembre es el _____ mes del año? *(tenth)*
  —No, es el _____. *(ninth)*
4. —¿Ellos viven en el _____ piso o en el _____? *(sixth, seventh)*
  —No, viven en el _____. *(eighth)*

Palabras y más palabras

Circle the word or phrase that best completes each sentence.

1. (El desayuno, La cena) es a las siete de la mañana.
2. Septiembre es el (octavo, noveno) mes del año.
3. La primavera comienza en (marzo, julio).
4. Mi familia y yo vamos a la (iglesia, escuela) los domingos.

5. Vamos a comprar jabón y (semanas, toallas).
6. ¿Qué está (diciendo, trabajando) Marcela?
7. ¿Quieres ir al cine o (al teatro, a la cárcel) esta noche?
8. Ellos (cierran, traen) a los chicos hoy.
9. Pablo está (durmiendo, pidiendo) la cuenta.
10. —María Inés es muy bonita.
    —¡Ya lo (creo, pierdo)!

En el laboratorio

The following material is to be used with the tape or audio CD in the language laboratory.

I. Vocabulario

Repeat each word after the speaker. When repeating words that are cognates, notice the difference in pronunciation between English and Spanish.

COGNADOS:	el concierto la educación importante la oficina las vacaciones
NOMBRES:	el almuerzo la cárcel la cena el cine el desayuno la escuela la iglesia el jabón el mes el piso la primavera la revista la semana el teatro la toalla
VERBOS:	cerrar comenzar comprar decir desayunar dormir empezar entender hacer pedir perder preferir querer servir traer
ADJETIVO:	próximo
OTRAS PALABRAS Y EXPRESIONES:	esta noche primero ya lo creo

II. Práctica

A. Change the verb in each sentence according to the new subject. Repeat the correct answer after the speaker's confirmation. Listen to the model.

Modelo: Nosotros comenzamos temprano. (yo)
      Yo comienzo temprano.

1. (Uds.)	4. (ellos)
2. (tú)	5. (Ud.)
3. (ella)	6. (él)

B. Answer the questions, using the cues provided. Repeat the correct answer after the speaker's confirmation. Listen to the model.

> *Modelo:* —¿Qué día es hoy? (sábado)
> —**Hoy es sábado.**

1. (lunes y miércoles)	4. (iglesia)
2. (educación)	5. (mujeres)
3. (mes próximo)	6. (no, café)

C. Change the verbs in each sentence to the present progressive. Repeat the correct answer after the speaker's confirmation. Listen to the model.

> *Modelo:* —Yo tomo café.
> —**Yo estoy tomando café.**

D. Say the ordinal number that corresponds to each cardinal number. Repeat the correct answer after the speaker's confirmation. Listen to the model.

> *Modelo:* cuatro **cuarto**

III. Para escuchar y entender

1. The speaker will make some statements. Circle **L** (**lógico**) if the statement is logical and **I** (**ilógico**) if it is illogical. The speaker will verify your response.

1. L I	5. L I
2. L I	6. L I
3. L I	7. L I
4. L I	8. L I

2. Listen carefully to the dialogue. It will be read twice.

(Diálogo 1)

Now the speaker will make some statements about the dialogue you just heard. Tell whether each statement is true (**verdadero**) or false (**falso**). The speaker will confirm the correct answer.

3. Listen carefully to the dialogue. It will be read twice.

(Diálogo 2)

Now the speaker will ask you some questions about the dialogue you just heard. Answer each question, omitting the subject. The speaker will confirm the correct answer. Repeat the correct answer.

¿Cuánto sabe usted ahora?

Lección 1   **A.** The present indicative of regular **-ar** verbs

Complete the following exchanges, using the verbs given.

1. —¿Uds. _____ (hablar) inglés?
   —Sí, nosotros _____ (hablar) inglés y francés.
2. —¿Dónde _____ (trabajar) tú?
   —Yo _____ (trabajar) en el restaurante Miramar.
3. —¿Qué _____ (tomar) Uds.?
   —Yo _____ (desear) un refresco y Jorge _____ (desear)
   cerveza.
4. —¿Qué _____ (necesitar) ellos?
   —Ana _____ (necesitar) un mantel y Roberto _____
   (necesitar) servilletas.
5. —¿Ud. _____ (estudiar) inglés?
   —No, yo _____ (estudiar) alemán.

B. Interrogative and negative sentences

Give the Spanish equivalent of the following exchanges.

1. "Do they pay the bill?"
   "No, they don't pay the bill."
2. "At what time do you want to study, Anita?"
   "I don't want to study today."

C. Forms and position of adjectives

Complete the following, using the Spanish equivalent of the
words in parentheses.

1. Nosotros bebemos _____ (*French champagne*).
2. Ana necesita el _____ (*white tablecloth*) y las _____ (*red
   napkins*).
3. Sergio es _____ (*a very handsome young man*).

D. Telling time

Complete the following, using the Spanish equivalent of the
words in parentheses.

—¿Uds. estudian _____? (*in the morning*)
—Sí, estudiamos _____ (*at eight-thirty in the morning*)

—¿Qué hora es?
—_____. (*It's a quarter to seven.*)

E. Cardinal numbers (300–1,000)

Write the following numbers in Spanish.

1. 1.578
2. 11.750
3. 23.380
4. 48.660
5. 420.200

F. Vocabulary

Complete the following sentences, using vocabulary learned in **Lección 1.**

1. ¿A qué _____ estudian Uds.? ¿A las dos?
2. ¿Tú estudias por la mañana, por la tarde o por la _____?
3. Ella es _____; es de Berlín.
4. En Washington hablan _____ y en París hablan _____.
5. Sergio es un muchacho muy _____.
6. ¿_____ chicos hay? ¿Veinte?
7. Yo no necesito mucho. Necesito _____ diez dólares.
8. ¿Uds. toman vino _____ o cerveza?
9. Necesito un mantel y seis _____.
10. Ella necesita un tenedor y una _____.
11. Yo no _____ tomar cerveza.
12. Yo pago la _____.

A. Agreement of articles, nouns, and adjectives

Lección 2

Change the following according to each new noun.

1. la papa asada (pollos)
2. los huevos fritos (papa)
3. el muchacho mexicano (muchachas)
4. el hombre francés (mujeres)
5. el café frío (leche)

B. The present indicative of regular **-er** and **-ir** verbs

Complete the following exchanges, using the verbs given.

1. —¿Qué _____ (beber) Uds.?
   —Nosotros _____ (beber) chocolate caliente.
2. —¿Eva _____ (escribir) en inglés?
   —Sí, y nosotros _____ (escribir) en español.
3. —¿Dónde _____ (vivir) los chicos?
   —Marisa _____ (vivir) en Quito y Rafael _____ (vivir) en Guayaquil.

4. —¿Tú _____ (comer) en la cafetería?
   —No, yo _____ (comer) en un restaurante.
5. —¿A qué hora _____ (abrir) (ellos)?
   —A las once.
6. —¿Qué _____ (leer) Ud.?
   —_____ (leer) el menú.

C. Possession with **de**

Give the Spanish equivalent of the following exchanges.

1. "Is she Sergio's sister?"
   "No, she is Mario's cousin."
2. "Do you need Luisa's address, Miss Fuentes?"
   "No, I need María's phone number."

D. Possessive adjectives

Answer the following questions in the negative.

1. ¿Uds. necesitan sus libros?
2. ¿La profesora de Uds. es de Venezuela?
3. ¿Ud. vive con su madre?
4. ¿Los amigos de Uds. son de Colombia?
5. ¿El profesor necesita su coche hoy?

E. The personal **a**

Give the Spanish equivalent of the following exchanges.

1. "Whom are you calling, Mr. Viñas?"
   "My niece."
2. "Do you take Mrs. Mena's daughter to the university, Miss Soto?"
   "No, I take Mr. Villalba's son."

F. Vocabulary

Circle the word or phrase that does not belong in each group.

1. pollo	pescado	leche
2. botella	mozo	camarero
3. leer	escribir	beber
4. caliente	frito	frío
5. papa	amiga	patata
6. malo	temprano	tarde
7. siempre	de quién	a menudo
8. bueno	frito	asado

A. The irregular verbs **ir, dar,** and **estar**

Lección 3

Write sentences using the subjects and the items given and the present indicative of **ir, dar,** or **estar,** as appropriate. Add any necessary words.

1. Yo / a la universidad / lunes
2. Nosotros / no / número de teléfono
3. Los chicos / la cafetería / ahora
4. ¿Tú / a la fiesta / Nora?
5. Elena / solamente / cinco dólares
6. Yo / cansado / enfermo

B. **Ir a** + infinitive

Answer the following questions, using the cues provided.

1. ¿Qué van a comer Uds.? (pollo frito)
2. ¿A qué hora va a estar Ud. en el hotel? (a las seis)
3. ¿A quién va a esperar su amiga? (a su mamá)
4. ¿Con quién van a viajar ellos? (con Alberto)
5. ¿A quién va a visitar su papá? (al Sr. Mejía)

C. Uses of the verbs **ser** and **estar**

What would you say in the following situations?

1. You want to know where Teresa is from and where she is now. You also want to know whether she is married or single.
2. You don't know what day of the week it is. You are also wondering where Ana's party is taking place.
3. You ask Carlos if he's tired.
4. You are wondering whether Eva is Mario's friend or girlfriend. You also want to know whether she's French or English.

D. Contractions

Complete the following, adding **al, a la, a los, a las, del, de la, de los,** or **de las,** as appropriate.

1. Elsa lleva _____ hijo _____ Sra. Goytisolo _____ universidad.
2. Nosotros llamamos _____ amigos _____ Sr. Villegas y _____ sobrino _____ Sra. Torres.
3. Ellos van _____ hotel con los padres _____ Srta. Barrios.
4. Vamos a llamar _____ sobrinas _____ Dr. Aranda.

E. Vocabulary

Match the questions in column **A** with the answers in column **B**.

A	**B**
1. ¿Es tu abuelo?	a. No, de madera.
2. ¿Cómo es tu novio?	b. A mi novia.
3. ¿La mesa es de metal?	c. Sí, es de Buenos Aires.
4. ¿Elena es tu tía?	d. En el hospital.
5. ¿Es argentina?	e. Sí, es el hijo de mi hermana
6. ¿A quién esperas?	Eva.
7. ¿Paquito es tu sobrino?	f. Sí, es la hija de mi tía Beatriz.
8. ¿Qué bebida deseas?	g. Vino tinto.
9. ¿Dónde están ellos?	h. Sí, es el padre de mi mamá.
10. ¿Carolina es tu prima?	i. A México.
11. ¿Son los padres de tu	j. Sí, son mis suegros.
esposo?	k. Sí, es la hermana de mi papá.
12. ¿Adónde vas?	l. Alto y guapo.

Lección 4 **A.** The irregular verbs **tener** and **venir**

Change the sentence given according to each new subject.

Carlos viene a la universidad con Mirta porque no tiene coche.

1. Yo
2. Nosotras
3. Los chicos
4. Tú

B. Expressions with **tener**

Use expressions with **tener** to say how these people feel, according to each situation.

1. I am in the Sahara desert in the summer. (Yo...)
2. We are in North Dakota in the winter. (Nosotros...)
3. A big dog is chasing Carlos. (Carlos...)
4. Marisa hasn't had anything to eat for 12 hours. (Marisa...)
5. Luis and Beto have a class in two minutes and they are five minutes away from the classroom. (Luis y Beto...)
6. My throat is truly dry. (Yo...)
7. You haven't slept for two days. (Tú...)
8. Liliana is blowing out ten candles on her birthday cake. (Liliana...)

C. Comparative forms

Give the Spanish equivalent of the following exchanges.

1. "Are you as tall as your sister, Anita?"
   "No, she's much taller than I. She's the tallest in the family."
2. "Is your house big, Mr. Varela?"
   "Yes, but it doesn't have as many rooms as your grandparents' house, Rosita."

D. Irregular comparative forms

Say who is oldest and youngest among the girls and which hotels are the best and the worst.

1. Amelia tiene quince años, Laura tiene dieciocho años y Marisol tiene veinte años.
   a.
   b.
2. El hotel Azteca es bueno; el hotel Mirasol no es muy bueno; el hotel Sandoval es muy malo.
   a.
   b.

E. Vocabulary

Circle the word or phrase that best completes each sentence.

1. Tengo que hablar con el (gerente, esposo) del hotel.
2. Olivia (cree, llega) a las dos de la tarde.
3. Tú tienes (más, mal) de cien dólares.
4. No es caro; es (mayor, barato).
5. Estudiamos en (el gimnasio, la biblioteca).
6. Yo (creo, tengo) que ella es una chica muy inteligente.
7. Colorado es más (grande, pequeño) que Rhode Island.
8. ¿Carlos viene con los chicos o viene (mejor, solo)?
9. ¿Tú tienes (el mercado, la llave) del cuarto?
10. Vamos a viajar. Necesitamos las (tiendas, valijas).

A. Stem-changing verbs **(e:ie)**   **Lección 5**

Complete the following exchanges, using the present indicative of the verbs given.

1. —¿Tú _____ (querer) ir a Madrid?
   —No, _____ (preferir) ir a Buenos Aires.
2. —¿A qué hora _____ (empezar) a trabajar Uds.?
   —Nosotros _____ (empezar) a las ocho.

3. —¿Elsa _____ (perder) mucho dinero cuando va a Las Vegas?
   —Sí.
4. —¿Ud. _____ (entender) la lección dos?
   —Sí, pero (yo) no _____ (entender) la lección tres.
5. —¿Cuándo _____ (comenzar) las clases?
   —En agosto.

B. Some uses of the definite article

Complete the following, using the Spanish equivalent of the words in parentheses.

1. Tenemos clases _____. (*on Mondays*)
2. ¿A qué hora es _____? (*dinner*)
3. Ellos van a _____ y yo voy a _____. (*school/church*)
4. Mis vacaciones comienzan _____. (*next Friday*).
5. Eusebio está en _____. (*jail*).
6. Yo creo que _____ es muy importante. (*education*).
7. _____ es una bebida (*drink*) alcohólica. (*Champagne*)

C. The present progressive

Change the following from the present indicative to the present progressive.

1. Yo leo y él duerme.
2. Ella trabaja y ellos estudian.
3. ¿Tú comes pollo?
4. Nosotros esperamos al profesor.
5. ¿Uds. beben vino o cerveza?

D. Ordinal numbers

Complete the following appropriately.

1. Enero es el _____ mes del año.
2. _____ es el sexto mes del año.
3. Septiembre es el _____ mes del año.
4. _____ es el tercer mes del año.
5. Febrero es el _____ mes del año.
6. _____ es el cuarto mes del año.
7. Octubre es el _____ mes del año.
8. _____ es el quinto mes del año.
9. Agosto es el _____ mes del año.
10. Julio es el _____ mes del año.

E. Vocabulary

Circle the word or phrase that does not belong in each group.

1. cine   teatro   iglesia
2. toalla   cárcel   jabón
3. almuerzo   cena   piso
4. cerrar   comenzar   empezar
5. desear   perder   querer
6. semana   desayuno   mes
7. ¡Ya lo creo! primero   próximo

Lección

6

1. Stem-changing verbs
   (**o:ue**)

2. Affirmative and negative
   expressions

3. Pronouns as object of a
   preposition

4. Direct object pronouns

Vocabulario

COGNADOS

alcohólico(a) alcoholic	la excursión excursion, tour
el banco bank	la farmacia pharmacy
el cheque check	

NOMBRES
la cama bed
la carta letter
el colchón mattress
la estampilla, el sello, el timbre (*Méx.*) stamp
la frazada, la manta, la cobija blanket
el guía guide
la librería book store
los lugares de interés places of interest
el mar ocean
la oficina de correos post office
el periódico, el diario newspaper
la playa beach
el pueblo town
el regalo present, gift

VERBOS
almorzar (o:ue) to have lunch

costar (o:ue) to cost
poder (o:ue) to be able
recordar (o:ue) to remember
volar (o:ue) to fly
volver (o:ue) to return, to come (go) back

ADJETIVO
este(a) this

OTRAS PALABRAS Y EXPRESIONES
a casa home
allí there
cerca de near to
¿Cómo se dice... ? How do you say . . . ?
con vista al mar with an ocean view
más tarde, después later
para for
por noche per night
que viene next

1 Stem-changing verbs (o:ue)
Verbos que cambian en la raíz (o:ue)

As you learned in **Lección 5**, certain verbs undergo a change in the stem in the present indicative. When the last stem vowel is a stressed **o**, it changes to **ue**.

volver *(to return)*		
vuelvo	volvemos	
vuelves		
vuelve	vuelven	

♦ Notice that the stem vowel is not stressed in the verb form corresponding to **nosotros;** therefore, the **o** does not change to **ue**.

—¿Cuándo **vuelven** Uds. de la excursión?   *"When are you coming back from the excursion?"*

—**Volvemos** a las siete.   *"We are coming back at seven."*

—¿A qué hora **vuelves** tú?   *"What time are you coming back?"*

—**Vuelvo** a las nueve.   *"I'm coming back at nine."*

Some other common verbs that undergo the same change in the stem are:

almorzar	to have lunch	**poder**	to be able
costar	to cost	**recordar**	to remember
dormir	to sleep	**volar**	to fly

—¿Cuánto **cuesta** una habitación con vista al mar?   *"How much does a room with an ocean view cost?"*

—Cien dólares por noche.   *"One hundred dollars per night."*

—¿**Puede** Ud. comprar el colchón mañana?   *"Can you buy the mattress tomorrow?"*

—Sí. ¡Ah!, no, ahora **recuerdo** que no tengo dinero.   *"Yes. Oh!, no, now I remember that I have no money."*

—¿Cuándo **vuela** Ud.?   *"When are you flying?"*

—**Vuelo** la semana que viene.   *"I'm flying next week."*

—¿Cuándo **pueden** ir
   Uds. a la farmacia?
—**Podemos** ir más tarde.

*"When can you go to the
  pharmacy?"*
"We can go later."

—No **duermo** bien.
—¿Cuántas horas
  duermes?
—**Duermo** solamente
  tres o cuatro horas.

"I don't sleep very well."
"How many hours do you sleep?"

"I sleep only three or four hours."

Práctica

A. Complete the following dialogues with the correct verb forms.
Then act them out with a partner.

1. *almorzar* —¿Dónde _almuerzan_ Uds.? _almorzamos_
   —Nosotros _____ en la cafetería y mis hijos
   _____ en la escuela.

2. *volver* —¿Cuándo _vuelves_ tú de la excursión?
   —Yo _vuelvo_ a las ocho. ¿Y Uds.?
   —Nosotros _volvemos_ mañana a las diez.

3. *costar* —¿Cuánto _cuesta_ un cuarto con vista al mar en
   el hotel Calinda? ¿Ochenta dólares por noche?
  recordar —(Yo) no _recuerdo_.

4. *poder* —¿Uds. _pueden_ ir a la farmacia ahora?
   —No, no _puedo_. ¿Tú _puedes_ ir más tarde?
   —Sí, yo _puedo_ ir más tarde con Daniel.

5. *dormir /* —¿Tú _duermes_ cuando _vuelas_?
  volar —No, porque tengo miedo.

B. Interview a classmate, using the following questions. When you
have finished, switch roles.

1. Cuando viajas, ¿vuelas o vas en ómnibus?
2. ¿Cuánto cuestan tus libros para la universidad?
3. ¿A qué hora vuelves a tu casa?
4. ¿Cuántas horas duermes?
5. ¿Puedes venir a clase la semana que viene?
6. ¿Recuerdas el número de teléfono de tu mejor amigo o
  amiga? (¿Cuál es?)
7. ¿A qué hora almuerzan Uds. en su casa?

C. With a classmate, discuss your daily routine: when and where
you have lunch (about how much it costs), what you can and
cannot do every day, what time you return home, and how many
hours you sleep. Compare notes!

2 Affirmative and negative expressions

Expresiones afirmativas y negativas

Affirmative		*Negative*	
algo	something, anything	**nada**	nothing
alguien	someone, anyone	**nadie**	nobody, no one
alguno(a)		**ninguno(a)**	
algún	any, some	**ningún** } 2	none, not any
algunos(as) } 1			
siempre	always	**nunca**	
alguna vez	ever	**jamás** }	never
algunas veces	sometimes		
también	also, too	**tampoco**	neither
o... o	either . . . or	**ni... ni**	neither . . . nor

◆ A double negative is frequently used in Spanish. In this construction, the adverb **no** is placed immediately before the verb. The second negative word may either precede the verb, follow the verb, or come at the end of the sentence. If the negative word precedes the verb, **no** is not used.

—¿Uds. van al teatro
   algunas veces?
—No, **no** vamos **nunca.**
   (**nunca** vamos.)

"Do you go to the theater
   sometimes?"
"No, we never go."

—¿Compra Ud. **algo** aquí?
—No, aquí **no** compro
   nada nunca. (nunca
   compro **nada** aquí.)

"Do you buy anything here?"
"No, I never buy anything here."

Práctica

A. Answer the following questions in the negative.

1. ¿Necesita Ud. algo?
2. ¿Hay alguien aquí?
3. ¿Estudia Ud. siempre por la noche?
4. ¿Quiere té o café?
5. ¿Hay algunos lugares de interés cerca de aquí?
6. Su amigo no va a la excursión. ¿Va Ud.?
7. ¿Va Ud. a la playa algunas veces?

[1]These follow the same format as **un/uno(s)/una(s)** when they precede a noun. See p. 18.
[2]These are always used in the singular form and follow the same format as **un/uno(a)**
when they precede a noun. See p. 18.

B. With a partner, act out the following dialogues in Spanish.

1. "Are you going to travel by bus?"
"No, I never travel by bus. I always travel by car."
2. "Do you want to go to the movies or to the theater?"
"I do not want to go to the movies or the theater."
"Neither do I."
3. "Is there anybody with the students now?"
"No, there isn't anybody . . . Oh, yes! The guide is with the students."

C. With a classmate, talk about the things that you always do, you sometimes do, and you never do. Compare notes!

3 Pronouns as object of a preposition
Pronombres usados como objetos de preposición

> **Preposition** a word that introduces a noun, pronoun, adverb, or verb and indicates its function in the sentence. They were **with** us. She is **from** Lima.

Prepositional Pronouns

Singular		Plural	
mí	me	**nosotros(as)**	us
ti	you (*familiar*)		
Ud.	you (*formal*)	**Uds.**	you (*formal, plural*)
él	him	**ellos**	them (*masc.*)
ella	her	**ellas**	them (*fem.*)

♦ Notice that only the first and the second persons singular (**mí**, **ti**) have special forms. The other persons use the forms of the subject pronouns.

♦ When used with the preposition **con**, the first and second person singular forms become **conmigo** and **contigo**.

—¿Vas a casa **conmigo**?   *"Are you going home with me?"*
—No, no voy **contigo**.   *"No, I'm not going with you.*
   Voy **con ellos** a la   *I'm going with them to the*
   librería.   *bookstore."*

—¿Es **para nosotros** el   *"Is the present for us?"*
  regalo?
—Sí, es **para Uds.**   *"Yes, it's for you."*
—¿Y la frazada?   *"And the blanket?"*
—Es **para mí.**   *"It's for me."*

—¿Hablan **de ti?**   *"Are they talking about you?"*
—No, no hablan **de mí.**   *"No, they're not talking about me."*

Práctica

A. Complete the following sentences with the correct form of the pronoun.

1. Mi hermana va a la playa con _____. (*us*)
2. El regalo es para _____. (*him*)
3. Ellos siempre hablan de _____, no de _____. (*you, fam./me*)
4. La cama es para _____ y el colchón es para _____, señor. (*her/you*)
5. Ellos vienen con _____; no vienen con _____. (*you, sing., fam./me*)

B. Interview a classmate, using the following questions and two questions of your own. When you have finished, switch roles. Use the appropriate prepositions and pronouns in your responses.

1. ¿Hablas con tus amigos en la clase?
2. ¿Puedes estudiar español conmigo?
3. ¿Trabajas para tus padres?
4. ¿Vives cerca de tus abuelos?
5. ¿Hablas mucho con tus amigos por teléfono?
6. ¿Vas de vacaciones con tu familia?

4 Direct object pronouns
Los pronombres de complemento directo

Direct object   generally a noun or a pronoun that is the receiver of a verb's action and answers the question *"what?"* or *"whom?"*. Take **it.** We know **her.** I call **Mary.**

The forms of the direct object pronouns are as follows.

Subject	Direct Object	
yo	**me** (*me*)	Ella **me** visita.
tú	**te** (*you, familiar*)	Yo **te** espero.
Ud.	{ **lo** (*you, masc., formal*)	Yo **lo** llamo. (a Ud.)[1]
	la (*you, fem., formal*)	Yo **la** llamo. (a Ud.)[1]
él	**lo** (*him, it*)	Él **lo** visita. (a él)[1]
ella	**la** (*her, it*)	Él **la** visita. (a ella)[1]
nosotros nosotras }	**nos** (*us, masc. and fem.*)	Tú **nos** llamas.
Uds.	{ **los** (*you, masc., pl., formal*)	Nosotros **los** llevamos. (a Uds.)[1]
	las (*you, fem., pl., formal*)	Nosotros **las** llevamos. (a Uds.)[1]
ellos	**los** (*them, masc.*)	Él **los** trae. (a ellos)[1]
ellas	**las** (*them, fem.*)	Él **las** trae. (a ellas)[1]

The direct object pronoun replaces the direct object noun and is placed *before* the conjugated verb.

Yo espero **al Sr. Lima.**
Yo   **lo**   espero.

Ella escribe **la carta.**
Ella   **la**   escribe.

Nosotros llevamos **a nuestros amigos.**
Nosotros   **los**   llevamos.

—¿**Me** llamas hoy?   *"Will you call me today?"*
—Sí, **te** llamo después.   *"Yes, I'll call you later."*

—¿Tu lees el periódico?   *"Do you read the paper?"*
—Sí, **lo** leo.   *"Yes, I read it."*

—¿Cuándo traes las   *"When are you bringing the*
   estampillas?   *stamps?"*
—**Las** traigo por la tarde.   *"I'm bringing them in the*
                                       afternoon."

—¿Dónde **las** compras?   *"Where do you buy them?"*
—**Las** compro en la oficina   *"I buy them at the post office."*
   de correos.

---

[1] Used for clarification to avoid confusion between **Ud.** and **él** or **ella,** or between **Uds.** and **ellos** or **ellas.**

◆ In a negative sentence, the **no** must precede the object pronoun.

Yo		leo	**las revistas.**	
Yo			**las**	leo.
Yo	**no**		**las**	leo.

—¿Tú llevas los cheques al banco?	*"Do you take the checks to the bank?"*
—No, yo **no los** llevo.	*"No, I don't take them.*

◆ If a conjugated verb and an infinitive appear together, the direct object pronoun may be placed before the conjugated verb or attached to the infinitive.

Yo **te** voy a llamar. ⎫
Yo   voy a llamar**te**. ⎬ *I'm going to call **you**.*

—¿Vas a traer las mantas?	*"Are you going to bring the blankets?"*
—Sí, **las** voy a traer.	*"Yes, I'm going to bring them.*
—¿Vas a traer**las** hoy?	*"Are you going to bring them today?*
—Sí.	*"Yes."*

◆ In the present progressive, the direct object pronoun can be placed either before the verb **estar** or after the present participle.

Lo está leyendo. ⎫
Está leyéndo**lo**. ⎬ *He's reading **it**.*

Note that when the direct object pronoun is attached to the present participle, a written accent is added to preserve the original stress.[1]

Práctica

A. Tell the person asking you these questions that you are the one who does everything. Follow the model.

Modelo: —¿Quién trae los periódicos?
            —**Yo los traigo.**

1. ¿Quién compra las frazadas?
2. ¿Quién hace la cena?
3. ¿Quién trae las revistas?
4. ¿Quién llama al gerente?
5. ¿Quién compra las estampillas?

---

[1] See Appendix A (p. 306) for rules governing the use of accent marks in Spanish.

6. ¿Quién lleva los cheques al banco?
7. ¿Quién lleva a las chicas al pueblo?
8. ¿Quién escribe las cartas?

B. You are planning a trip to Spain. How are you getting ready for it? What is going to happen there? Answer the following questions, always using direct object pronouns.

1. ¿Habla Ud. bien el español?
2. ¿Sus amigos van a esperarlo (esperarla)?
3. ¿Va a ver *(to see)* a sus profesores allí?
4. ¿Va a visitar los museos?
5. ¿Ud. va a llamarnos?
6. ¿Va a llevarme a España con Ud.?
7. ¿Tiene Ud. sus maletas?
8. ¿Va a llevar el coche?

C. With a partner, act out the following dialogues in Spanish.

1. "Can you call me tomorrow, Anita?"
   "Yes, Paco. I can call you in the afternoon."
2. "Are you going to take us to the bookstore, Miss Navarro?"
   "No, I can't take you today."
3. "Do you have Delia's phone number?"
   "No, I don't have it."

Palabras y más palabras

Match the questions in column **A** with the answers in column **B**.

A	B
1. ¿Quieres cerveza?	a. Cerca de la pensión.
2. ¿Dónde compras los sellos?	b. No, al pueblo.
3. ¿A qué hora van a servir la cena?	c. En la cafetería.
4. ¿Cuánto cuesta este colchón?	d. A casa.
5. ¿Dónde está la farmacia?	e. La semana que viene.
6. ¿Adónde vas?	f. Trescientos dólares.
7. ¿Para quién es la carta?	g. No, no hay ninguno.
8. ¿La vas a llevar a la playa?	h. En la oficina de correos.
9. ¿Hay algunos lugares de interés allí?	i. Una con vista al mar.
10. ¿Dónde almuerzan Uds.?	j. A las nueve.
11. ¿Cuándo llega Rafael?	k. Para ti.
12. ¿Qué habitación quiere?	l. No, no tomo bebidas alcohólicas.

En el laboratorio

The following material is to be used with the tape or audio CD in the language laboratory.

I. Vocabulario

Repeat each word after the speaker. When repeating words that are cognates, notice the difference in pronunciation between English and Spanish.

COGNADOS:	alcohólico el banco el cheque la excursión la farmacia
NOMBRES:	la cama la carta el colchón la estampilla el sello el timbre la frazada la manta la cobija el guía la librería los lugares de interés el mar la oficina de correos el periódico el diario la playa el pueblo el regalo
VERBOS:	almorzar costar poder recordar volar volver
ADJETIVO:	este
OTRAS PALABRAS Y EXPRESIONES:	a casa allí cerca de ¿Cómo se dice... ? con vista al mar más tarde después para por noche que viene

II. Práctica

A. Answer the questions, using the cues provided. Repeat the correct answer after the speaker's confirmation. Listen to the model.

Modelo: —¿Cuándo puede volver Ud.? (mañana)
       —**Puedo volver mañana.**

1. (a las dos y cuarto)
2. (el lunes)
3. (ocho horas)
4. (los sábados)
5. (con Raúl)

B. Change the following negative statements to the affirmative. Repeat the correct answer after the speaker's confirmation. Listen to the model.

Modelo: Ellos nunca van al teatro.
Ellos siempre van al teatro.

C. Answer the questions in the negative. Replace the direct objects with the appropriate direct object pronouns. Repeat the correct answer after the speaker's confirmation. Listen to the model.

Modelo: —¿Ud. llama a Carlos?
—No, no lo llamo.

III. Para escuchar y entender

1. The speaker will make some statements. Circle **L (lógico)** if the statement is logical and **I (ilógico)** if it is illogical. The speaker will confirm your response.

1. L I	5. L I
2. L I	6. L I
3. L I	7. L I
4. L I	8. L I

2. Listen carefully to the narration. It will be read twice.

(Narración)

Now the speaker will make statements about the narration you just heard. Tell whether each statement is true (**verdadero**) or false (**falso**). The speaker will confirm the correct answer.

3. Listen carefully to the dialogue. It will be read twice.

(Diálogo)

Now the speaker will ask you some questions about the dialogue you just heard. Answer each question, omitting the subject. The speaker will confirm the correct answer. Repeat the correct answer.

1. Stem-changing verbs (**e:i**)
2. Irregular first-person forms
3. **Saber** contrasted with **conocer**
4. Indirect object pronouns

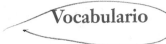
Vocabulario

COGNADOS

la información information	**el pasaporte** passport
la novela novel	**la reservación** reservation

NOMBRES

la agencia de viajes travel agency

el (la) agente de viajes travel agent

la avenida avenue

el avión plane

la carne meat

la embajada embassy

la ensalada salad

España Spain

los folletos turísticos tourist brochures

la oficina de turismo tourist office

el país country

el pasaje, el billete ticket

el postre dessert

la sopa soup

la suerte luck

el viaje trip

el vuelo flight

VERBOS

cancelar to cancel

conducir (yo conduzco), manejar to drive

confirmar to confirm

conocer (yo conozco) to know, to be familiar with

conseguir (e:i) to obtain, to get

nadar to swim

poner (yo pongo) to put, to place

quedar to be located

saber (yo sé) to know how, to know a fact

salir (yo salgo) to go out, to leave

seguir (e:i) to follow, to continue

traducir (yo traduzco) to translate

ver to see

ADJETIVOS

extranjero(a) foreign

helado(a) iced

OTRAS PALABRAS Y EXPRESIONES

¡Buen viaje! Have a nice trip!, Bon voyage!

de memoria by heart

entonces then, in that case

tener suerte to be lucky

1 Stem-changing verbs (e:i)

Verbos que cambian en la raíz (e:i)

Some **-ir** verbs undergo a special stem change in the present indicative. For these verbs, when **e** is the last stem vowel and it is stressed, it changes to **i**.

servir *(to serve)*	
sirvo	servimos
sirves	
sirve	sirven

(handwritten annotations: We, you plural, ellos, ellas)

◆ Notice that the stem vowel is not stressed in the verb form corresponding to **nosotros**; therefore, the **e** does not change to **i**.

—¿Qué **sirven** Uds.?   *"What do you serve?"*
—**Servimos** té helado.   *"We serve iced tea."*

—¿Qué **sirven** en la   *"What do they serve at the*
   cafetería?   *cafeteria?"*
—**Sirven** sopa, ensalada,   *"They serve soup, salad, meat,*
   carne y postre.   *and dessert."*

◆ Some other common verbs that undergo the same **e** to **i** change in the stem are **pedir** (*to ask for, to request, to order*), **seguir** (*to follow, to continue*), and **repetir** (*to repeat*). Verbs like **seguir** (such as **conseguir,** *to obtain*) contain a **u** to preserve the hard **g** sound before an **e** or an **i**. Verbs that follow this pattern drop the **u** before an **a** or an **o: yo sigo, yo consigo.**

—¿Qué **pide** Enrique en   *"What is Enrique requesting at*
   la agencia de viajes?   *the travel agency?"*
—**Pide** información.   *"He is requesting information."*

—¿A quién **siguen** Uds.?   *"Whom are you following?"*
—**Seguimos** al guía.   *"We are following the guide."*

—¿Dónde **consiguen**   *"Where do you get tourist*
   Uds. folletos turísticos?   *brochures?"*
—En la oficina de   *"At the tourist office."*
   turismo.

◆ The verb **decir** (*to say, to tell*) undergoes the same **e** to **i** stem change, but in addition it is irregular in the first person singular: **yo digo.**

—¿Qué **dice** Fernando?   *"What does Fernando say?"*
—**Dice** que podemos   *"He says that we can confirm*
   confirmar la reservación   *the reservation at the hotel*
   en el hotel porque no   *because they are not going to*
   van a cancelar el vuelo.   *cancel the flight.*
—Yo siempre **digo** que él   *"I always say that he is lucky."*
   tiene suerte.

Práctica

A. Complete the following dialogues with the correct verb forms. Then act them out with a partner.

1. —En este restaurante mexicano _sirven_ una sopa muy buena. (servir)
   —Cuando yo vengo aquí, siempre _pido_ tacos. (pedir)
   —Yo siempre _digo_ que los tacos de aquí son los mejores. (decir)

2. —Carlos, ¿dónde _consigues_ tú folletos en español? (conseguir)
   —Yo _____ algunos en Los Ángeles y algunos en la oficina de turismo. (conseguir)
   —¿Tú _____ en la clase de la Dra. Peña? (seguir)
   —Sí, y ella siempre _dice_ que yo soy su mejor estudiante. (decir)

3. —Los chicos _dicen_ que tú sólo _sirves_ carne y ensalada. (decir/servir)
   —No es verdad; algunas veces también _sirves_ sopa y postre. (servir)

B. Tell about yourself by answering the following questions.

1. ¿Dónde consigue Ud. libros de español?
2. ¿Sigue Ud. en la clase de español?
3. En un restaurante mexicano, ¿qué pide Ud.?
4. ¿A qué hora sirven Uds. la cena?
5. ¿Sirve Ud. té helado con la comida?
6. ¿Dice Ud. siempre la verdad?

C. With a classmate discuss your favorite restaurants. Tell what you always say about those restaurants, what type of food they serve, and what you order when you go there. Compare notes!

The three types of stem-changing verbs

Here is a list of stem-changing verbs studied up to now. Every time you learn a new one, add it to the list.

e:ie	o:ue	e:i
cerrar	almorzar ✓	conseguir
comenzar	costar	decir
empezar	dormir	pedir
entender	poder	repetir
perder	recordar	seguir
preferir	volar	servir
querer	volver	

2 Irregular first-person forms

Verbos irregulares en la primera persona

Some common verbs are irregular in the present indicative only in the first person singular. The other persons are regular.

Verb	First-person (yo) form	Regular forms
salir (*to go out, to leave*)	**salgo**	sales, sale, salimos, salen
hacer (*to do, to make*)	**hago**	haces, hace, hacemos, hacen
poner (*to put, to place*)	**pongo**	pones, pone, ponemos, ponen
traer (*to bring*)	**traigo**	traes, trae, traemos, traen
conducir (*to drive*)	**conduzco**	conduces, conduce, conducimos, conducen
traducir (*to translate*)	**traduzco**	traduces, traduce, traducimos, traducen
conocer (*to know*)	**conozco**	conoces, conoce, conocemos, conocen
ver (*to see*)	**veo**	ves, ve, vemos, ven
saber (*to know*)	**sé**	sabes, sabe, sabemos, saben

—¿Tú **sabes** conducir?   *"Do you know how to drive?"*
—Sí, yo **sé** conducir.   *"Yes, I know how to drive. I drive*
    Conduzco el coche   *my brother's car."*
    de mi hermano.

—Mañana **salgo** para España.   *"I'm leaving for Spain tomorrow."*
—¿A qué hora **sale** el avión?   *"What time does the plane leave?"*

—A las siete.	*"At seven."*
—¡Buen viaje!	*"Have a nice trip!"*
—¿Qué **haces** los domingos?	*"What do you do on Sundays?"*
—No **hago** nada.	*"I don't do anything."*
—Entonces, ¿no **ves** a tus amigos?	*"Then, you don't see your friends?"*
—No, no **veo** a nadie.	*"No, I don't see anybody."*

Práctica

Interview a classmate, using the following questions. When you have finished, switch roles.

1. ¿Sales a menudo? ¿Con quién?
2. ¿Ves a tus amigos los sábados? ¿Y los domingos?
3. ¿Haces algo los domingos?
4. ¿Conoces la ciudad de Nueva York? ¿Qué otras ciudades grandes conoces?
5. ¿Conduces bien? ¿Qué coche conduces?
6. ¿Sabes francés? ¿Sabes algún otro idioma?
7. ¿Traduces del español al inglés?
8. ¿Traes tus libros a clase?
9. ¿Dónde pones tus libros?
10. ¿Conoces a alguien de España? ¿A quién?

3 Saber **contrasted with** conocer
Saber **contrastado con** conocer

There are two verbs in Spanish that mean *to know:* **saber** and **conocer.** These verbs are not interchangeable.

♦ **Saber** means to know something by heart, to know how to do something, or to know a fact.

—¿**Sabe** Ud. algunos poemas de memoria?	*"Do you know any poems by heart?"*
—No, no **sé** ninguno.	*"No, I don't know any."*
—¿**Saben** ellos nadar?	*"Do they know how to swim?"*
—Sí, ellos **saben** nadar.	*"Yes, they know how to swim."*
—¿**Sabes** dónde queda la embajada norteamericana?	*"Do you know where the American Embassy is located?"*
—Sí, queda en la avenida Juárez.	*"Yes, it's located on Juárez Avenue."*

◆ **Conocer** means to be familiar or acquainted with a person, a thing, or a place.

—¿**Conoces** al agente de viajes?	*"Do you know the travel agent?"*
—¿Al Sr. Paz? Sí.	*"Mr. Paz? Yes."*
—¿**Conocen** Uds. las novelas de Cervantes?	*"Are you familiar with Cervantes's novels?"*
—Sí, **conocemos** algunas.	*"Yes, we are familiar with some (of them)."*
—¿Qué país extranjero **conoces** tú?	*"What foreign country are you familiar with (do you know)?"*
—**Conozco** Venezuela.	*"I'm familiar with Venezuela."*

Práctica

Tell what these people know or don't know, using **saber** or **conocer.**

1. Ellos / California   *conocer*
2. Ud. / a mi madre   *conoce*
3. Tú / el poema de memoria
4. Él / al agente de viajes
5. Yo no / nadar   *se*
6. ¿Uds. / los poemas de Neruda?
7. Yo no / qué día es hoy
8. Yo no / ningún país extranjero
9. Nosotras no / dónde queda la embajada
10. Ellas / al hijo del profesor

4 Indirect object pronouns
Los pronombres de complemento indirecto

Indirect object   a word or phrase that tells *to whom* or *for whom* something is done. An indirect object pronoun can be used in place of the indirect object. In Spanish, the indirect object pronoun includes the meaning *to* or *for*: Yo **les** mando los libros (*a los estudiantes*). I send the books **to them** (*to the students*).

The forms of the indirect object pronouns are as follows.

Subject	Indirect Object	
yo	**me** (to / for me)	Él **me** da las revistas.
tú	**te** (to / for you, familiar)	Yo **te** doy el periódico.
Ud.	**le** (to / for you, formal, masc. and fem.)	Ella **le** compra un pasaje.
él ⎫ ella ⎭	**le** (to / for him / her)	Yo **le** hablo en inglés.
nosotros ⎫ nosotras ⎭	**nos** (to / for us, masc. and fem.)	Ella **nos** da la lección.
Uds. ⎫ ellos ⎬ ellas ⎭	**les** (to / for you, formal pl., masc. and fem.) **les** (to / for them, masc. and fem.)	Yo **les** digo la dirección. El agente **les** da el dinero.

The forms of the indirect object pronouns are the same as the forms of the direct object pronouns, except in the third person. Indirect object pronouns are usually placed *in front* of a conjugated verb.

—¿Quién **les** compra a Uds. los pasajes?   *"Who buys you the tickets?"*

—Mi padre **nos** compra los pasajes.   *"My father buys us the tickets."*

—¿En qué idioma **le** hablas?   *"In which language do you speak to him (to her)?"*

—**Le** hablo en español.   *"I speak to him (to her) in Spanish."*

◆ When an infinitive follows the conjugated verb, the indirect object pronoun may be placed in front of the conjugated verb or attached to the infinitive.[1]

Te voy a comprar   una maleta.
Voy a comprar**te**   una maleta.

◆ With the present progressive forms, the indirect object pronoun can be placed in front of the conjugated verb or it can be attached to the end of the progressive construction.[1]

Le estoy escribiendo   al agente de viajes.
Estoy escribiéndo**le**[2]   al agente de viajes.

---

[1] This is also true of direct object pronouns.
[2] See Appendix A (p. 306) for rules governing the use of accent marks in Spanish.

ATENCIÓN: The indirect object pronouns **le** and **les** require clarification when the person to whom they refer is not specified. Spanish provides clarification by using the preposition **a** + *noun or personal (subject) pronoun.*

Le doy la información.	*I give the information . . .* (to whom? to him? to her? to you?)
but: **Le** doy la información **a ella** (a Rosa).	*I give the information **to her** (to Rosa).*

◆ This prepositional form is also used to express emphasis.

Me da el pasaporte **a mí.**	*He gives the passport to me* (and to nobody else).

◆ Although the prepositional form provides clarification, it is not a substitute for the indirect object pronoun. The prepositional form may be omitted, but the indirect object pronoun must always be used.

—¿Qué **le** vas a traer (a Roberto)?
—**Le** voy a traer unas novelas.

Práctica

A. Add the missing indirect object pronouns to express for whom the following are being done.

Modelo: Ella va a traer los billetes. (**para él;** *both ways*)
Ella **le** va a traer (va a traer**le**) los billetes.

1. Yo compro el regalo. (**para ti**)
2. Nosotros vamos a traer los postres. (**para Uds.;** *both ways*)
3. Ada compra las bebidas. (**para mí**)
4. Ellos están escribiendo una carta. (**para ella;** *both ways*)
5. Yo voy a traer los pasajes. (**para Ud.;** *both ways*)
6. Fernando compra los sellos. (**para nosotros**)

B. Answer the following questions, using the information in parentheses.

1. ¿Qué vas a comprarle a tu hermano? (un pasaje para España; *both ways*)
2. ¿Qué les da a Uds. el agente? (folletos turísticos)
3. ¿Quién te escribe? (mi novio / mi novia)
4. ¿Qué vas a traerme? (un regalo; *both ways*)
5. ¿Qué les vas a comprar a las chicas? (refrescos; *both ways*)
6. ¿Cuándo nos va a escribir Ud.? (mañana; *both ways*)

C. Answer the following questions.

1. ¿Ud. les pide dinero a sus padres?
2. ¿El profesor le va a dar a Ud. una A en español?
3. ¿Puede Ud. darme el periódico?
4. ¿Uds. pueden traernos unos refrescos?
5. ¿El profesor les trae a Uds. revistas en español?

D. With a partner, act out the following dialogues in Spanish.

1. "Can he bring me the tickets tomorrow, Luis?"
   "Yes, but you have to give him the money tonight."
2. "Do your parents speak to you in Spanish?"
   "No, they speak to us in English."
3. "Does he write to you, Anita?"
   "Yes, he writes to me very often."

Palabras y más palabras

Circle the word or phrase that best completes each sentence.

1. Van a cancelar los (aviones, vuelos).
2. Va a llamar a la agencia de viajes para (confirmar, cancelar) la reservación porque no puede viajar.
3. ¿Vas a España? ¡Buen (viaje, billete)!
4. Viven en la (alberca, avenida) Victoria.
5. La (embajada, ensalada) americana queda en la avenida Morelos.
6. Ellos no saben (traducir, conducir) al español.
7. Te deseamos buena (sopa, suerte).
8. Vamos a servir té (helado, frito).

En el laboratorio

The following material is to be used with the tape or audio CD in the language laboratory.

I. Vocabulario

Repeat each word after the speaker. When repeating words that are cognates, notice the difference in pronunciation between English and Spanish.

COGNADOS:	la información la novela el pasaporte la reservación
NOMBRES:	la agencia de viajes el agente de viajes la avenida el avión la carne la embajada la ensalada España

los folletos turísticos
la oficina de turismo   el país   el pasaje
el billete   el postre   la sopa   la suerte
el viaje   el vuelo

VERBOS: cancelar   conducir   manejar
confirmar   conocer   conseguir   nadar
poner   quedar   saber   salir   seguir
traducir   ver

ADJETIVOS: extranjero   helado

**OTRAS PALABRAS
Y EXPRESIONES:**   ¡Buen viaje!   de memoria   entonces
tener suerte

II. Práctica

A. Change each sentence, using the verb provided. Repeat the correct answer after the speaker's confirmation. Listen to the model.

Modelo: Yo quiero carne. (pedir)
Yo pido carne.

B. Answer the questions, always using the first choice. Omit the subject. Repeat the correct answer after the speaker's confirmation. Listen to the model.

Modelo: —¿Conduces un Ford o un Chevrolet?
—Conduzco un Ford.

C. Answer the questions, using the cues provided. Repeat the correct answer after the speaker's confirmation. Listen to the model.

Modelo: —¿Qué me vas a traer? (los folletos turísticos)
—Te voy a traer los folletos turísticos.

1. (el agente de viajes)   4. (las maletas)
2. (que es tarde)   5. (sopa y ensalada)
3. (inglés)   6. (revistas)

III. Para escuchar y entender

1. The speaker will make some statements. Circle **L (lógico)** if the statement is logical and **I (ilógico)** if it is illogical. The speaker will verify your response.

1. L   I   5. L   I
2. L   I   6. L   I
3. L   I   7. L   I
4. L   I   8. L   I

2. Listen carefully to the narration, in which Ana will tell you about her plans. It will be read twice.

(*Narración*)

Now the speaker will ask you some questions about the narration you just heard. Answer each question, omitting the subject. The speaker will confirm the correct answer. Repeat the correct answer.

3. Listen carefully to the dialogue. It will be read twice.

(*Diálogo*)

Now the speaker will ask you some questions about the dialogue you just heard. Answer each question, omitting the subject. The speaker will confirm the correct answer. Repeat the correct answer.

1. **Pedir** contrasted with **preguntar**

2. Special construction with **gustar, doler,** and **hacer falta**

3. Demonstrative adjectives and pronouns

4. Direct and indirect object pronouns used together

Vocabulario

COGNADOS

la aspirina aspirin	el (la) presidente(a)
el básquetbol basketball	president
la bicicleta bicycle	la raqueta racket
	el tenis tennis

NOMBRES
la bolsa de dormir sleeping bag
el caballo horse
la cabeza head
la entrada ticket (*for an event*)
el (la) entrenador(a) trainer, coach
los esquíes, los esquís skis
la mochila backpack
el (la) niño(a) child, kid
la página deportiva sports page
el partido game, match
los patines skates
la pelota ball
el pie foot
la raqueta de tenis tennis racket
la tienda de campaña tent

VERBOS
doler (o:ue) to hurt, to ache

esquiar to ski
gustar to like, to be pleasing
jugar[1] to play (*e.g. a game*)
mandar, enviar to send
preguntar to ask (*a question*)
prestar to lend
regalar to give (*a present*)

OTRAS PALABRAS Y EXPRESIONES
allá over there
hacer falta to need, to lack
ir a esquiar to go skiing
montar a caballo to ride a horse
montar en bicicleta to ride a bicycle
¿para quién? for whom?
que that, which
si if

---

[1] Present tense: **juego, juegas, juega, jugamos, juegan**

1 Pedir **contrasted with** preguntar
Pedir **contrastado con** preguntar

◆ **Pedir** means *to ask for* or *to request something.*

—¿Qué le **piden** los muchachos al entrenador?	*"What do the boys ask the coach for?"*
—Le **piden** entradas para el partido de básquetbol.	*"They ask him for tickets for the basketball game."*
—¿Vas a **pedir**le dinero a tu tío?	*"Are you going to ask your uncle for money?"*
—Sí, le voy a **pedir** doscientos dólares para comprar una bicicleta.	*"Yes, I am going to ask him for two hundred dollars to buy a bicycle."*

◆ **Preguntar** means *to ask a question.*

—¿Qué vas a **preguntar**le a René?	*"What are you going to ask René?"*
—Voy a **preguntar**le si quiere ir a esquiar.	*"I'm going to ask him if he wants to go skiing."*
—¿Qué le vas a **preguntar** a Ana?	*"What are you going to ask Ana?"*
—Si quiere jugar al tenis, montar a caballo o montar en bicicleta.	*"If she wants to play tennis, to ride a horse, or to ride a bicycle."*

Práctica

Complete the following dialogues, using **pedir** and **preguntar** as appropriate. Then act them out with a partner.

1. —¿Qué le vas a _____ al entrenador?
   —Si vamos a jugar al básquetbol mañana.
2. —¿Cuánto dinero le vas a _____ a tu tía?
   —Cien dólares, para comprar una bicicleta.
3. —¿Qué te está _____ Elsa?
   —Me está _____ adónde voy a ir a esquiar.
4. —¿Qué están haciendo los chicos?
   —Están _____ información sobre (*about*) el partido.
5. —¿Tú siempre les _____ consejo (*advice*) a tus padres?
   —No, nunca les _____ consejo.
6. —¿Qué le quiere _____ a Ester?
   —Le quiero _____ si vamos al cine hoy.

2 Special construction with gustar, doler, **and** hacer falta

Construcción especial con gustar, doler y hacer falta

The verb **gustar** means *to like*. A special construction is required in Spanish to translate the English structure *to like*. This is done by making the English direct object the subject of the Spanish sentence. The English subject then becomes the indirect object of the Spanish sentence.

English:	*I like Spain.*
	subj. d.o.
Spanish:	**Me** gusta España.
	i.o. subj.
Literally:	*Spain appeals to me.*

The two most commonly used forms of **gustar** are: (1) the third person singular **gusta** if the subject is singular or if **gustar** is followed by one or more infinitives; and (2) the third person plural **gustan** if the subject is plural.

Indirect Object Pronouns

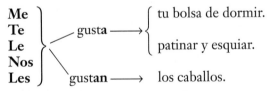

Me
Te
Le
Nos
Les

gusta → tu bolsa de dormir.
patinar y esquiar.
gustan → los caballos.

◆ Note that the verb **gustar** agrees with the subject of the sentence, that is, the person or thing *being liked*.

Me gusta **el café.**   Le gust**an los patines.**

◆ Note that the person who does the liking is the *indirect object*.

Me gusta el café.   **Le** gustan las chicas inteligentes.
I.O.   I.O.

—¿**Les gusta** el café?   *"Do you (pl.) like coffee?"*
—Sí, **nos gusta** mucho   *"Yes, we like coffee very much, but*
   el café, pero **nos gusta**   *we like tea better."*
   más el té.

ATENCIÓN: Note that the words **más** (*better*) and **mucho** immediately follow **gustar**.

♦ The preposition **a** + *noun or pronoun* is used to clarify meaning or to emphasize the indirect object.

> **A Aurora (A ella)** le gusta ese lugar, pero **a mí** no me gusta.
> *Aurora likes that place, but I don't like it.*
>
> **A Roberto** y **a Rosa** les gusta mi tienda de campaña.
> *Roberto and Rosa like my tent.*

♦ The verb **doler** (*to hurt, to ache*) and the expression **hacer falta** (*to need*) use the same construction as **gustar**.

> —¿Qué **les hace falta**, señoras?
> *"What do you need, ladies?"*
>
> —**Nos hacen falta** las entradas.
> *"We need the tickets."*
>
> —¿Por qué estás tomando aspirinas?
> *"Why are you taking aspirin?"*
>
> —Porque **me duele** la cabeza.
> *"Because my head hurts."*
>
> —¿A ti **te duele** la cabeza?
> *"Your head hurts?*
>
> —A mí **me duelen** los pies.
> *My feet hurt."*

ATENCIÓN: In Spanish, the definite article is generally used instead of the possessive adjective with parts of the body.

Práctica

A. Use **gustar** to say what you and the people named like.

> *Modelo:* José / el café
> (A José) **Le gusta** el café.

1. Elsa / tu caballo
2. nosotros / la bolsa de dormir
3. yo / la tienda de campaña
4. ellos / patinar y esquiar
5. tú / jugar al básquetbol
6. Uds. / la comida francesa

B. With a partner, act out the following dialogues in Spanish.

1. "Do you like this novel, Paquito?"
   "Yes, it's very good."
2. "Do you want to go to the store, Mr. Alba?"
   "Yes, I need a tent."
3. "My head hurts!"
   "Why don't you take aspirins, Anita?"

4. "Do you want the red sleeping bag, sir?"
   "No, I like the blue sleeping bag better."
5. "What do we need?"
   "Towels."

C. Interview a classmate, using the following questions. When you have finished, switch roles.

1. ¿Cuándo tomas aspirinas?
2. ¿Te duele la cabeza a menudo? ¿Te duelen los pies?
3. ¿Qué te duele hoy?
4. ¿Qué te hace falta?
5. ¿Les hace falta más dinero a tu familia y a ti?
6. ¿Les gusta a tus amigos y a ti el español?
7. ¿Te gusta esquiar?
8. ¿Qué te gusta más: el básquetbol o el tenis?

D. With a classmate discuss your likes and dislikes as well as those of your family and friends.

3 Demonstrative adjectives and pronouns
Los adjetivos y pronombres demostrativos

Demonstrative   a word that points out a definite person or object: **this, that, these, those**

Demonstrative adjectives

Demonstrative adjectives point out persons or things. They agree in gender and number with the nouns they modify or point out. The forms of the demonstrative adjectives are as follows.

Masculine		Feminine		
Singular	Plural	Singular	Plural	
este	estos	esta	estas	this, these
ese	esos	esa	esas	that, those
aquel	aquellos	aquella	aquellas	that, those *(at a distance)*

—¿Para quién es **esta** raqueta de tenis?

"Whom is this tennis racket for?"

—**Esta** raqueta es para Marta y **esa** pelota es para Rita.

"This racket is for Marta and that ball is for Rita."

—¿Te gusta **este** caballo?

"Do you like this horse?"

—No, me gusta **aquel** caballo blanco que está allá.

"No, I like that white horse over there."

Práctica

Change the demonstrative adjectives so that they agree with the new nouns.

1. Este caballo, _____ raqueta, _____ revistas, _____ programas.
2. Esas ciudades, _____ teatros, _____ biblioteca, _____ museo.
3. Aquella mesa, _____ sillas, _____ hombre, _____ restaurantes.

4. Esta lección, _____ idioma, _____ problemas, _____ universidades.
5. Ese jabón, _____ frazadas, _____ cuartos, _____ toalla.

Demonstrative pronouns

The demonstrative pronouns are the same as the demonstrative adjectives, except that the pronouns have a written accent mark. The forms of the demonstrative pronouns are as follows.

Masculine		Feminine		Neuter	
Singular	Plural	Singular	Plural		
éste	éstos	ésta	éstas	esto	this (one), these
ése	ésos	ésa	ésas	eso	that (one), those
aquél	aquéllos	aquélla	aquéllas	aquello	that (one), those (at a distance)

—¿Qué patines quiere Ud.? ¿**Éstos** o **aquéllos?**

"Which skates do you want? These or those (over there)?"

—Quiero **aquéllos.**

"I want those (over there)."

—¿Qué mochilas van a llevar los niños, **éstas** o **ésas?**

"Which backpacks are the children going to take, these or those?"

—**Éstas.**

"These."

♦ Each demonstrative pronoun has a neuter form. The neuter pronoun has no accent, because there are no corresponding demonstrative adjectives.

♦ The neuter forms are used to refer to situations, ideas, or things that are abstract, general, or unidentified. The neuter pronouns are equivalent to the English *this* or *that* (*matter, business; thing, stuff*).

—¿Qué crees de **eso?**

"What do you think about that (matter, issue)?"

—Creo que es un problema para el presidente del club.

"I think it is a problem for the president of the club."

—¿Qué es **esto?** "*What is this* (thing, stuff)?"
—No sé. "*I don't know.*"

Práctica

Complete the following sentences with the Spanish equivalent of the pronouns in parentheses.

1. El presidente del club quiere este coche y _____ (*that one*).
2. Necesitamos esa pelota y _____ (*that one [over there]*).
3. Compramos esos patines y _____ (*these*).
4. Recibimos este periódico y _____ (*those*).
5. ¿Estudia Ud. esta lección o _____ (*that one*)?
6. ¿Habla Ud. con este señor o con _____ (*that one [over there]*)?
7. ¿Prefieren ellos estas mesas de madera o _____ (*those [over there]*)?
8. ¿Va Ud. a leer este libro o _____ (*those*)?
9. Deseo aquellas mochilas y _____ (*these*).
10. ¿Van Uds. a comprar esa raqueta o _____ (*this one*)?
11. Ellas no saben qué es _____ (*this*).
12. ¿Para quién es _____ (*that*)?

4 Direct and indirect object pronouns used together
Pronombres de complemento directo e indirecto usados juntos

When both an indirect object pronoun and a direct object pronoun are used in the same sentence, the indirect object pronoun always appears first.

D.O.

Ana me da la pluma.   Ana me la da.

I.O.

—¿Cuándo me das el dinero? "*When are you giving me the money?*"
—**Te lo** doy[1] mañana. "*I'll give it to you tomorrow.*"

---

[1] Remember that the present indicative is frequently used in Spanish to express future time.

◆ With an infinitive, the pronouns may be placed either before the main verb or attached to the infinitive.

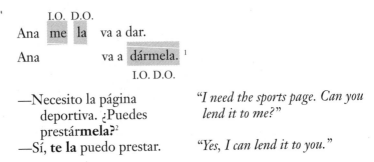

       I.O. D.O.

Ana me la va a dar.

Ana   va a dármela. [1]

                 I.O. D.O.

—Necesito la página deportiva. ¿Puedes prestármela?[2]	*"I need the sports page. Can you lend it to me?"*
—Sí, **te la** puedo prestar.	*"Yes, I can lend it to you."*

◆ With the present progressive, the pronouns can be placed either before the conjugated verb or attached to the present participle.

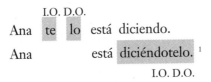

      I.O. D.O.

Ana te lo está diciendo.

Ana   está diciéndotelo. [1]

              I.O. D.O.

◆ If both pronouns begin with **l**, the indirect object pronoun (**le** or **les**) is changed to **se.**

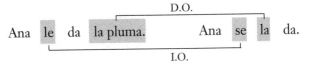

                 D.O.

Ana le da la pluma.   Ana se la da.

                 I.O.

◆ For clarification, it is sometimes necessary to specify the person(s) to whom the indirect object pronoun refers: **a él, a ella, a Ud., a Uds., a ellos, a ellas, a José**, etc.

—¿**Le** vas a regalar los esquíes **a él** o **a ella**?	*"Are you going to give the skis to him or to her?"*
—**Se los** voy a regalar **a ella.**	*"I'm going to give them to her."*
—¿Uds. **les** mandan las cartas **a ellas** o **a ellos**?	*"Do you send the letters to them (fem.) or to them (masc.)?"*
—**Se las** mandamos **a ellos.**	*"We send them to them (masc.)."*

---

[1] See Appendix A (p. 306) for rules governing the use of accent marks in Spanish.

Práctica

A. Mom is always doing things for the family. Explain what she does, using the information provided.

> *Modelo:* **Yo** quiero **una mochila.** (comprar)
> Mamá **me la** compra.

1. **Papá** quiere **café.** (servir)
2. **Nosotros** necesitamos **dinero.** (dar)
3. **Tú** quieres **los periódicos.** (traer)
4. **Yo** quiero **una raqueta.** (prestar)
5. **Mis hijos** necesitan **toallas.** (comprar)
6. **Papá** quiere **la página deportiva.** (traer)
7. **Uds.** necesitan **la bolsa de dormir.** (dar)
8. **Ud.** quiere comer **comida mexicana.** (hacer)

B. You keep changing your mind when someone asks you a question. First you say "yes" and then you say "no." Substitute pronouns for the boldface nouns.

> *Modelo:* —¿Me compra Ud. **la mochila?**
> —**Sí, se la compro.**
> —**No, no se la compro.**

1. ¿Me presta Ud. **sus patines?**
2. ¿Me compra Ud. **la tienda de campaña?**
3. ¿Les paga Ud. **los pasajes** a ellos?
4. ¿Está Ud. pidiéndole **el periódico** a Inés?
5. ¿Nos va a traer Ud. **los esquíes?**
6. ¿Le vas a regalar **la raqueta de tenis** a tu tía?

C. With a partner act out the following dialogues in Spanish.

1. "I need the tent. Can you bring it to me, Paquito?"
   "Yes, I can bring it to you this afternoon, sir."
2. "I need the skates."
   "I can give them to you (*as a gift*), Anita. I don't need them."
3. "Where do you get the tickets, Mario?"
   "My father sends them to me."
4. "Can you lend me the sleeping bag, Mr. Peña?"
   "No, Paquito, I can't lend it to you, because I'm going to need it."

Palabras y más palabras

Complete the following dialogues with words from the lesson vocabulary.

1. —¿Quieres ir a _____ con nosotros?
   —Sí, pero no tengo esquíes.
   —¿Quieres ir a patinar?
   —Sí, pero no tengo _____.
2. —¿Qué te _____ falta para jugar al tenis?
   —Una _____ y una _____.
3. —¿Qué está leyendo el entrenador?
   —La _____ deportiva.
4. —¿Quieres montar a _____?
   —No, prefiero montar en _____.
5. —¿Por qué tomas aspirinas?
   —Porque me _____ la cabeza.
6. —Necesito tu mochila. ¿Me la puedes _____?
   —No te la presto. Te la _____.
7. —¿Quién es ese _____?
   —Es mi hijo Carlitos.
8. —¿Qué le vas a _____ a Sergio?
   —_____ quiere ver el _____ de básquetbol.

En el laboratorio

The following material is to be used with the tape or audio CD in the language laboratory.

I. Vocabulario

Repeat each word after the speaker. When repeating words that are cognates, notice the difference in pronunciation between English and Spanish.

COGNADOS:	la aspirina el básquetbol la bicicleta
	el presidente la raqueta el tenis

NOMBRES:	la bolsa de dormir el caballo
	la cabeza la entrada el entrenador
	los esquíes los esquís la mochila
	el niño la página deportiva el partido

los patines   la pelota   el pie
la raqueta de tenis   la tienda de campaña

VERBOS: doler   esquiar   gustar   jugar   mandar
enviar   preguntar   prestar   regalar

**OTRAS PALABRAS
Y EXPRESIONES:**   allá   hacer falta   ir a esquiar
montar a caballo   montar en bicicleta
¿para quién?   que   si

II. Práctica

A. Answer the questions, using the cues provided. Repeat the correct answer after the speaker's confirmation. Listen to the model.

Modelo: —¿Qué te pide Jorge? (la pelota)
    —**Me pide la pelota.**

1. (mi dirección)
2. (500 dólares)
3. (no, a mi papá)
4. (si pueden ir al cine)
5. (la página deportiva)

B. Repeat each statement or question, replacing **preferir** with **gusta más** or **gustan más** and the appropriate indirect object pronoun. Repeat the correct answer after the speaker's confirmation. Listen to the model.

Modelo: Yo prefiero la bicicleta gris.
    Me gusta más la bicicleta gris.

C. Give the Spanish equivalent of the demonstrative adjective that agrees with each noun mentioned by the speaker. Repeat the correct answer after the speaker's confirmation. Listen to the model.

Modelo: this / raqueta
    esta raqueta

1. this / these
2. that / those
3. that (*over there*) / those (*over there*)

D. Repeat each sentence, changing the direct object to the corresponding direct object pronoun. Make all the necessary changes in the sentence. Repeat the correct answer after the speaker's confirmation. Listen to the model.

Modelo: Le traen **el periódico.**
    Se lo traen.

III. Para escuchar y entender

1. The speaker will make some statements. Circle **L (lógico)** if the statement is logical and **I (ilógico)** if it is illogical. The speaker will verify your response.

1. L I	5. L I
2. L I	6. L I
3. L I	7. L I
4. L I	8. L I

2. Listen carefully to the dialogue. It will be read twice.

(Diálogo 1)

Now the speaker will make some statements about the dialogue you just heard. Tell whether each statement is true (**verdadero**) or false (**falso**). The speaker will confirm the correct answer.

3. Listen carefully to the dialogue. It will be read twice.

(Diálogo 2)

Now the speaker will ask you some questions about the dialogue you just heard. Answer each question, omitting the subject. The speaker will confirm the correct answer. Repeat the correct answer.

1. Possessive pronouns

2. Reflexive constructions

3. Command forms: **Ud.** and **Uds.**

4. Uses of object pronouns with command forms

Vocabulario

COGNADOS

el champú shampoo
generalmente generally
impaciente impatient
el momento moment

el parque park
el perfume perfume
la terraza terrace

NOMBRES
el baño bathroom
el botiquín medicine
cabinet
el cepillo brush
el dormitorio bedroom
el espejo mirror
la máquina de afeitar razor
la medianoche midnight
el pantalón, los pantalones
pants
el peine comb
el pelo hair
la peluquería beauty salon,
beauty parlor
el (la) peluquero(a)
hairdresser
la tarjeta card
la tarjeta de crédito credit
card
la tintorería dry cleaners
la ventana window
el vestido dress

VERBOS
acordarse (o:ue) (de) to
remember
acostarse (o:ue) to go to
bed

atender (e:ie) to wait on,
to attend to
bañar(se) to bathe
(oneself)
cortar(se) to cut (oneself)
doblar to turn
lavar(se) to wash (oneself)
levantarse to get up
llamarse to be named
probarse (o:ue) to try on
sentarse (e:ie) to sit down

ADJETIVOS
corto(a) short
querido(a) dear

**OTRAS PALABRAS Y
EXPRESIONES**
a la derecha to the right
a la izquierda to the left
ahora mismo right now
antes de before
lavarse la cabeza to wash
one's hair
seguir derecho to
continue straight ahead
todavía yet

1 Possessive pronouns

Los pronombres posesivos

Singular		Plural		
Masculine	*Feminine*	*Masculine*	*Feminine*	
el mío	la mía	los míos	las mías	mine
el tuyo	la tuya	los tuyos	las tuyas	yours *(familiar)*
el suyo	la suya	los suyos	las suyas	his hers yours *(formal)*
el nuestro	la nuestra	los nuestros	las nuestras	ours theirs
el suyo	la suya	los suyos	las suyas	yours *(formal)*

The possessive pronouns in Spanish agree in gender and number with the thing possessed. They are generally used with the definite article.

—Aquí están las máquinas de afeitar de ellos. ¿Dónde están **las nuestras?**
"Here are their razors. Where are ours?"

—**Las nuestras** están en el dormitorio.
"Ours are in the bedroom."

—Tus pantalones están aquí. ¿Dónde están **los míos?**
"Your trousers are here. Where are mine?"

—**Los tuyos** están en la tintorería.
"Yours are at the cleaners."

—Mi peine está aquí. ¿Dónde está **el suyo?**
"My comb is here. Where is yours?"

—**El mío** está en el baño.
"Mine is in the bathroom."

◆ After the verb **ser**, the definite article is frequently omitted.

—¿Es **tuyo** este perfume?
"Is this perfume yours?"

—Sí, este perfume es **mío,** pero ése es **tuyo.**
"Yes, this perfume is mine, but that one is yours."

—¿Esta tarjeta de crédito **es suya,** Sr. Muñoz?
"Is this credit card yours, Mr. Muñoz?"

—Sí, **es mía,** gracias.
"Yes, it's mine, thanks."

◆ Since the third person forms of the possessive pronouns (**el suyo, la suya, los suyos, las suyas**) could be ambiguous, they may be replaced for clarification by the following.

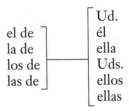

—Estos cepillos y estos peines son de Marta y de Arturo, ¿no?
—Bueno, los cepillos son **de ella,** pero los peines son **de él.**

"These brushes and these combs are Marta's and Arturo's, right?"
"Well, the brushes are hers, but the combs are his."

Práctica

A. Supply the correct possessive pronouns and read the sentences aloud. Follow the models.

> *Modelos:* Yo tengo una tarjeta. Es _____.
> Yo tengo una tarjeta. Es **mía.**
>
> Juan tiene una tarjeta. Es _____. (Es _____.)
> Juan tiene una tarjeta. Es **suya.** (Es **de él.**)

1. Tú tienes un cepillo. Es _____.
2. Juan tiene una entrada. Es _____. (Es _____.)
3. Nosotros tenemos una tarjeta de crédito. Es _____.
4. Ud. tiene unos peines. Son _____. (Son _____.)
5. Yo tengo un coche. Es _____.
6. Uds. tienen dos bicicletas. Son _____. (Son _____.)
7. Yo tengo unos pantalones. Son _____.
8. Lucía tiene tres hijos. Son _____. (Son _____.)

B. Interview a classmate, using the following questions. When you have finished, switch roles.

1. Mi mejor amigo vive en _____. ¿Dónde vive el tuyo?
2. Mis padres son de _____. ¿De dónde son los tuyos?
3. Nuestros abuelos son de _____. ¿De dónde son los de Uds.?
4. Yo tengo mis tarjetas de crédito en el dormitorio. ¿Tú tienes las tuyas?
5. Mis libros de español están aquí. ¿Dónde están los del (de la) profesor(a)? ¿Dónde están los tuyos?
6. Tu pantalón (vestido) es _____. ¿De qué color es el mío?

2 Reflexive constructions
Las construcciones reflexivas

Reflexive pronouns

A **reflexive construction**, such as *I introduce myself*, consists of a reflexive pronoun and a verb. Reflexive pronouns refer to the same person who is the subject of the sentence.

Subjects	Reflexive Pronouns	
yo	**me**	*myself, to / for myself*
tú	**te**	*yourself, to / for yourself* (**tú** form)
nosotros	**nos**	*ourselves, to / for ourselves*
Ud.		*yourself, to / for yourself*
Uds.		*yourselves, to / for yourselves*
él	**se**	*himself, to / for himself*
ella		*herself, to / for herself*
		itself, to / for itself
ellos, ellas		*themselves, to / for themselves*

◆ Note that, with the exception of **se**, reflexive pronouns have the same forms as the direct and indirect object pronouns.

◆ The third person singular and plural **se** is invariable.

◆ Reflexive pronouns are positioned in the sentence in the same manner as object pronouns. They are placed in front of a conjugated verb.

Yo **me** baño a las ocho.   *I bathe at eight.*

They may be attached to an infinitive or to a present participle.

Yo voy a bañar**me** a las ocho.   *I'm going to bathe at eight.*
Yo estoy bañándo**me**.[1]   *I'm bathing.*

◆ In Spanish most verbs can be made reflexive with the aid of a reflexive pronoun to indicate that they act upon the subject.

---

[1] See Appendix A (p. 306) for rules governing the use of accent marks in Spanish.

Julia le prueba el
vestido a su hija.

Julia se prueba
el vestido.

Reflexive verbs

◆ Reflexive verbs are conjugated in the following manner.

lavarse *(to wash oneself, to wash up)*	
Yo **me lavo.**	*I wash (myself).*
Tú **te lavas.**	*You wash (yourself—fam.).*
Ud. **se lava.**	*You wash (yourself—formal).*
Él **se lava.**	*He washes (himself).*
Ella **se lava.**	*She washes (herself).*
Nosotros **nos lavamos.**	*We wash (ourselves).*
Uds. **se lavan.**	*You wash (yourselves).*
Ellos **se lavan.**	*They* (masc.) *wash (themselves).*
Ellas **se lavan.**	*They* (fem.) *wash (themselves).*

◆ Some commonly used reflexive verbs are listed below.

acostarse (o:ue) *to go to bed, to lie down*
afeitarse *to shave*
bañarse *to bathe*
despertarse (e:ie) *to wake up*
levantarse *to get up*
sentarse (e:ie) *to sit down*
vestirse (e:i) *to get dressed*

—¿A qué hora **se levanta**
  Ud., Srta. López?
—Generalmente **me levanto**
  a las ocho, pero no **me**
  acuesto hasta la
  medianoche.

"At what time do you get
  up, Miss Lopez?"
"I generally get up at eight
  o'clock, but I don't go to
  bed until midnight."

◆ Some verbs change their meaning when they are used with reflexive pronouns.

acostar (o:ue)	*to put to bed*	**acostarse**	*to go to bed*
dormir (o:ue)	*to sleep*	**dormirse**	*to fall asleep*
ir	*to go*	**irse**	*to leave, to go away*
levantar	*to lift, to raise*	**levantarse**	*to get up*
llamar	*to call*	**llamarse**	*to be named*
probar (o:ue)	*to try, to taste*	**probarse**	*to try on*
poner	*to put*	**ponerse**	*to put on (e.g.* clothing*)*
quitar	*to take away, to remove*	**quitarse**	*to take off (e.g.* clothing*)*

◆ Notice the use of the reflexive in the following sentences.

—¿Por qué no **te acuestas,**
   querido?   *"Why don't you go to bed, dear?"*

—Primero voy a **acostar** a
   los chicos.   *"First I'm going to put the
    children to bed."*

—Voy a **llamar** al hermano
   de Teresa antes de salir.[1]   *"I'm going to call Teresa's
    brother before going out."*
—¿Cómo **se llama** él?   *"What's his name?"*
—**Se llama** Alberto.   *"His name is Alberto."*

◆ Some verbs are *always* used with reflexive pronouns in Spanish.

acordarse (o:ue) (de)   *to remember*
quejarse (de)   *to complain*

Notice that the use of a reflexive pronoun does not necessarily
imply a reflexive action.

—¿**Se acuerda** Ud. de
   Rosita?   *"Do you remember Rosita?"*
—Sí, **me acuerdo** de ella.   *"Yes, I remember her."*

Práctica

A. Describe what these people do, using the present indicative or
the infinitive of the verbs in parentheses.

   1. Elena _____ (probarse) el vestido.
   2. Ella _____ (acostarse) y Ud. _____ (acostar) a los niños.
   3. Carlos _____ (bañarse) y Luis _____ (vestirse).

---

[1] The infinitive, not the *-ing* form, is used after a preposition in Spanish.

4. Tú siempre _____ (dormirse) en la clase.
5. Nosotros nunca _____ (quejarse) de nada.
6. Yo voy a _____ (probarse) los pantalones.
7. Debes _____ (bañarse) antes de _____ (vestirse).
8. Nosotros vamos a _____ (sentarse) aquí.
9. ¿Por qué no _____ (afeitarse), querido?
10. Pepito, tienes que _____ (lavarse) las manos.

B. Interview a classmate, using the following questions. When you are finished, switch roles.

1. ¿A qué hora te acuestas generalmente?
2. ¿Te duermes en la clase?
3. ¿A qué hora te levantas?
4. ¿Siempre te despiertas temprano?
5. ¿Qué te vas a poner para salir mañana?
6. ¿Te acuerdas del número de teléfono de tus amigos?
7. ¿Siempre pruebas la comida antes de servirla?
8. ¿Uds. se quejan de sus profesores?

C. Describe what you do during a typical day from the time you wake up to the time you go to bed.

Summary of Personal Pronouns

Subject	Direct Object	Indirect Object	Reflexive	Object of Prepositions
yo	me	me	me	mí
tú	te	te	te	ti
Ud. (f.)	la			Ud.
Ud. (m.)	lo	le	se	Ud.
él	lo			él
ella	la			ella
nosotros	nos	nos	nos	nosotros
Uds. (f.)	las			Uds.
Uds. (m.)	los	les	se	Uds.
ellos	los			ellos
ellas	las			ellas

3 Command forms: Ud. and Uds.
El imperativo: Ud. y Uds.

Command form   the form of a verb used to give an order or a direction: **Go! Come back! Turn to the right.**

To form the command for **Ud.** and **Uds.**,[1] drop the **-o** of the first person singular of the present indicative and add the following endings to the stem.

-ar verbs: **-e** (Ud.) and **-en** (Uds.)
-er verbs: **-a** (Ud.) and **-an** (Uds.)
-ir verbs: **-a** (Ud.) and **-an** (Uds.)

ATENCIÓN: Notice that the endings for the **-er** and **-ir** verbs are the same.

			Commands	
Infinitive	*First Person Present Ind.*	*Stem*	**Ud.**	**Uds.**
hablar	Yo hablo	**habl-**	hable	hablen
comer	Yo como	**com-**	coma	coman
abrir	Yo abro	**abr-**	abra	abran
cerrar	Yo cierro	**cierr-**	cierre	cierren
volver	Yo vuelvo	**vuelv-**	vuelva	vuelvan
pedir	Yo pido	**pid-**	pida	pidan
decir	Yo digo	**dig-**	diga	digan
hacer	Yo hago	**hag-**	haga	hagan
traducir	Yo traduzco	**traduzc-**	traduzca	traduzcan

—¿Con quién debo hablar?   *"With whom must I speak?"*
—**Hable** con el peluquero.   *"Speak with the hairdresser."*

—¿Vengo por la mañana o por la tarde?   *"Shall I come in the morning or in the afternoon?"*
—**Venga** por la mañana y **traiga** a su hija.   *"Come in the morning and bring your daughter."*

—¿Cierro la puerta?   *"Shall I close the door?"*
—No, no **cierre** la puerta. **Cierre** la ventana, por favor.   *"No, don't close the door. Close the window, please."*

—Para ir a la peluquería, ¿sigo derecho o doblo a la derecha?   *"To go to the beauty parlor shall I continue straight ahead or shall I turn right?"*
—**Doble** a la izquierda.   *"Turn left."*

[1] The **tú** form will be studied in **Lección 11**.

♦ The command forms of the following verbs are irregular.

	dar	estar	ser	ir
Ud.	dé	esté	sea	vaya
Uds.	den	estén	sean	vayan

—¿Podemos ir solas al parque?	*"Can we go to the park alone?"*
—No, no **vayan** solas. **Vayan** con sus padres.	*"No, don't go alone. Go with your parents."*
—¡Tiene que atenderme ahora mismo!	*"You must wait on me right now!"*
—Un momento, señora. ¡No **sea** impaciente!	*"One moment, madam. Don't be impatient!"*

Práctica

A. Answer the questions in the negative, using the cues provided.

> *Modelos:* —¿Hablo con el peluquero? (dueño)
> —No, **hable** con el dueño.
>
> —¿Tenemos que hablar con el peluquero? (dueño)
> —No, **hablen** con el dueño.

1. ¿Vamos a la peluquería mañana? (hoy)
2. ¿Tenemos que estar allí a las diez? (a las nueve)
3. Para ir a la peluquería, ¿tengo que seguir derecho? (doblar en la calle Lima)
4. ¿Doblo a la derecha? (izquierda)
5. ¿Desayunamos antes de salir? (en la cafetería)
6. ¿Qué perfume compro para Estela? (Chanel número cinco)
7. ¿Qué traemos para la cena? (pollo frito)
8. ¿A qué hora volvemos? (a las tres)
9. ¿Cerramos las ventanas antes de salir? (la puerta)

B. With a partner, prepare a list of ten commands (five affirmative and five negative) that a professor would give to students.

4 Uses of object pronouns with command forms
Uso de los pronombres con el imperativo

Affirmative commands

With all direct *affirmative* commands, the object pronouns are placed *after* the verb and are attached to it, forming a single word.

—¿Dónde pongo el champú?   *"Where shall I put the
                                   shampoo?"*

—**Póngalo**[1] en el botiquín.   *"Put it in the medicine
                                   cabinet."*

—¿Dónde sirvo el café?   *"Where shall I serve (the)
                                   coffee?"*

—**Sírvalo** en la terraza.   *"Serve it on the terrace."*

—¿Qué le doy a la chica?   *"What shall I give the girl?"*
—**Déle** el espejo.   *"Give her the mirror."*

—¿Abrimos la puerta?   *"Shall we open the door?"*
—Sí, **ábranla.**   *"Yes, open it."*

—¿Se lo digo a Ana?   *"Shall I tell (it to) Ana?"*
—Sí, **dígaselo** a Ana.   *"Yes, tell (it to) Ana."*

—¿Dónde me siento?   *"Where shall I sit?"*
—**Siéntese** aquí.   *"Sit here."*

—¿Le corto el pelo?   *"Shall I cut your hair (for
                                   you)?"*
—Sí, **córtemelo**, por favor.   *"Yes, cut it (for me), please."*

Práctica

A. Answer the following questions, using affirmative commands.

> *Modelo:* —El peluquero necesita el champú. ¿Lo traigo ahora?
> —Sí, **tráigalo.**

1. Mi amiga quiere ir a la peluquería. ¿La llevo?
2. Las ventanas están abiertas (*open*). ¿Las cierro?
3. Tienen un disco compacto que me gusta. ¿Lo compro?
4. Los niños están durmiendo. ¿Los despierto?
5. La señora quiere el espejo. ¿Se lo doy?
6. Mi hermana quiere un perfume. ¿Se lo compro?
7. La peluquera necesita los peines. ¿Se los traigo?
8. Mis amigos necesitan mis cintas (*tapes*). ¿Se las presto?

B. Answer the following questions, using the appropriate pronouns
and the cues provided.

> *Modelo:* —¿Cuándo traemos las maletas? (ahora mismo)
> —**Tráiganlas** ahora mismo.

1. ¿Dónde servimos el desayuno? (en la terraza)
2. ¿Compramos pescado para el almuerzo? (sí)

---

[1] See Appendix A (p. 306) for rules governing the use of accent marks in Spanish.

3. ¿Cuándo llamamos a nuestros amigos? (esta tarde)
4. ¿A qué hora nos levantamos? (a las siete)
5. ¿Dónde nos bañamos? (en este baño)
6. ¿Nos ponemos los pantalones blancos? (sí)
7. ¿Nos lavamos las manos antes de comer? (sí)
8. ¿A qué hora nos acostamos hoy? (a la medianoche)

Negative commands

With all *negative* commands, the object pronouns are placed in front of the verb.

—¿Nos levantamos ahora?   *"Shall we get up now?"*
—No, **no se levanten**   *"No, don't get up yet."*
todavía.

—¿Sirvo los refrescos?   *"Shall I serve the sodas?"*
—No, **no los sirva** todavía.   *"No, don't serve them yet."*

—¿Me lavo la cabeza con   *"Shall I wash my hair with*
este champú?   *this shampoo?"*
—No, no **se la lave** con ese   *"No, don't wash it with that*
champú. No es muy   *shampoo. It's not very good."*
bueno.

—¿Le corto el pelo?   *"Shall I cut your hair (for you)?"*
—No, **no me lo corte.** No   *"No, don't cut it (for me). I*
me gusta el pelo corto.   *don't like short hair."*

Práctica

A. Answer the following questions with negative commands. Use the appropriate pronouns.

Modelo: —¿Atiendo **a la señora** ahora?
—No, no **la atienda** todavía.

1. ¿Traemos **el champú**?
2. ¿Llevamos **a Mirta** a la peluquería?
3. ¿**Me** lavo **la cabeza** ahora?
4. ¿Pongo **el perfume** en el botiquín?
5. ¿Le traigo **el espejo** a Ud.?
6. ¿Le doy **el peine** a Roberto?
7. ¿Llevamos **los pantalones** a la tintorería?
8. ¿Esperamos **a Rosa** un momento?
9. ¿**Les** decimos que son muy impacientes?
10. ¿**Nos** acostamos ahora?

B. Say what Mrs. Rodríguez asked her hairdresser to do by trans-
forming the infinitives in the following instructions to command
forms.

Lavarle la cabeza, pero **no usar** el champú que usa siempre.
Cortarle el pelo, pero **no cortárselo** muy corto. **Traerle**
una revista y **darle** una taza (*cup*) de café pero **no ponerle** leche
al café.

C. You and a partner have a group of teenagers coming to stay with
you for a few days. Use **Uds.** commands to prepare a list of ten
to fifteen things they should and shouldn't do.

Palabras y más palabras

Match the questions in column **A** with the answers in column
B.

	A		**B**
1.	¿Cómo vas a pagar? _____	a.	Sí, y me acuesto a la medianoche.
2.	¿Eva está en su dormitorio? _____	b.	Ahora mismo.
		c.	Sí, cuando me baño.
3.	¿Cómo te llamas? _____	d.	Sí, necesito cortarme el pelo.
4.	¿Doblo a la derecha o a la izquierda? _____	e.	Marisol Villalobos.
5.	¿Cuándo salen? _____	f.	No, los voy a llevar a la tintorería.
6.	¿Dónde está el champú? _____	g.	El pantalón negro.
		h.	Sí, está durmiendo.
7.	¿Te levantas temprano? _____	i.	No, no le gusta el pelo corto.
		j.	Con tarjeta de crédito.
8.	¿Vas a la peluquería? _____	k.	En la terraza.
		l.	Siga derecho.
9.	¿Qué vas a hacer antes de comer? _____	m.	Un momento. ¡No sea impaciente!
10.	¿Te lavas la cabeza? _____	n.	Me voy a lavar las manos.
		o.	En el botiquín.
11.	¿Vas a lavar los pantalones? _____		
12.	¿Qué te vas a poner? _____		
13.	¿Dónde sirven el almuerzo? _____		
14.	¡Tengo mucha prisa! ¿Puede venir? _____		
15.	¿Le vas a cortar el pelo a Rita? _____		

En el laboratorio

The following material is to be used with the tape or audio CD in the language laboratory.

I. Vocabulario

Repeat each word after the speaker. When repeating words that are cognates, notice the difference in pronunciation between English and Spanish.

COGNADOS: el champú   generalmente   impaciente
el momento   el parque   el perfume
la terraza

NOMBRES: el baño   el botiquín   el cepillo
el dormitorio   el espejo
la máquina de afeitar   la medianoche
el pantalón   los pantalones   el peine
el pelo   la peluquería   el peluquero
la tarjeta   la tarjeta de crédito
la tintorería   la ventana   el vestido

VERBOS: acordarse   acostarse   atender   bañarse
cortarse   doblar   lavarse   levantarse
llamarse   probarse   sentarse

ADJETIVOS: corto   querido

**OTRAS PALABRAS
Y EXPRESIONES:** a la derecha   a la izquierda
ahora mismo   antes de
lavarse la cabeza   seguir derecho
todavía

II. Práctica

A. Answer the questions, using the cues provided. Repeat the correct answer after the speaker's confirmation. Listen to the model.

Modelo: —Mi maleta es verde. ¿Y la de Eva? (blanca)
—**La suya es blanca.**

1. (grande)   4. (también)
2. (aquí)   5. (en Honduras)
3. (azules)   6. (de Guatemala)

B. Answer the questions, using the cues provided. Repeat the correct answer after the speaker's confirmation. Listen to the model.

Modelo: —¿A qué hora te levantas tú? (a las seis)
—**Me levanto a las seis.**

1. (no, tarde)   4. (aquí)
2. (en el dormitorio)   5. (no, de nada)
3. (no, por la noche)   6. (sí)

C. Change the following statements to commands. Repeat the correct answer after the speaker's confirmation. Listen to the model.

Modelo: **Debe hablar** con el peluquero.
Hable con el peluquero.

III. Para escuchar y entender

1. The speaker will make some statements. Circle **L (lógico)** if the statement is logical and **I (ilógico)** if it is illogical. The speaker will verify your response.

1. L I   6. L I
2. L I   7. L I
3. L I   8. L I
4. L I   9. L I
5. L I   10. L I

2. Listen carefully to the narration, in which Carlos will tell you what he does every day. It will be read twice.

(Narración)

Now the speaker will make some statements about the narration you just heard. Tell whether each statement is true (**verdadero**) or false (**falso**). The speaker will confirm the correct answer.

3. Listen carefully to the dialogue. It will be read twice.

(Diálogo 1)

Now the speaker will make some statements about the dialogue you just heard. Tell whether each statement is true (**verdadero**) or false (**falso**). The speaker will confirm the correct answer.

4. Listen carefully to the dialogue. It will be read twice.

(Diálogo 2)

Now the speaker will ask you some questions about the dialogue you just heard. Answer each question, omitting the subject. The speaker will confirm the correct answer. Repeat the correct answer.

1. The preterit of regular verbs

2. The preterit of **ser, ir,** and **dar**

3. Uses of **por** and **para**

4. Seasons of the year and weather expressions

Vocabulario

COGNADOS

el límite limit	**el tomate** tomato
la milla mile	**la velocidad** velocity, speed
el suéter sweater	

NOMBRES
el abrigo coat
la aspiradora vacuum cleaner
la cocina kitchen
el (la) criado(a) servant
la escoba broom
el impermeable raincoat
el invierno winter
la lata, el bote (*Méx.*) can
la lavadora washing machine
la lluvia rain
la niebla fog
el otoño fall, autumn
el paraguas umbrella
la puerta de atrás back door
la ropa clothes, clothing
la salsa sauce
el supermercado supermarket
los tallarines, los espaguetis spaghetti
el verano summer

VERBOS
ayudar to help
barrer to sweep

cocinar to cook
entrar to enter, to come in
limpiar to clean
llover (o:ue) to rain
nevar (e:ie) to snow
pasar (por) to go by
preparar to prepare

ADJETIVOS
nublado(a) cloudy
pasado(a) past, last

OTRAS PALABRAS Y EXPRESIONES
anoche last night
ayer yesterday
¿Cuál es el límite de velocidad? What's the speed limit?
por hora per hour
los (las) dos both
¿Qué tiempo hace hoy? What's the weather like today?

1 The preterit of regular verbs
El pretérito de los verbos regulares

Spanish has two simple past tenses: the preterit and the imperfect. (The imperfect will be studied in **Lección 12.**) The preterit of regular verbs is formed by dropping the infinitive ending and adding the appropriate preterit ending to the verb stem, as follows. Note that the endings for **-er** and **-ir** verbs are identical.

-ar *Verbs*	-er *Verbs*	-ir *Verbs*
entrar *(to enter)*	**comer** *(to eat)*	**escribir** *(to write)*
stem: **entr-**	**com-**	**escrib-**
entr**é**	com**í**	escrib**í**
entr**aste**	com**iste**	escrib**iste**
entr**ó**	com**ió**	escrib**ió**
entr**amos**	com**imos**	escrib**imos**
entr**aron**	com**ieron**	escrib**ieron**

yo **entré**   *I entered; I did enter*
Ud. **comió**   *you ate; you did eat*
ellos **escribieron**   *they wrote; they did write*

◆ The preterit tense is used to refer to actions or states that the speaker views as completed in the past. Note that Spanish has no equivalent for the English auxiliary verb *did* in questions and negative sentences.

—¿Quién **cocinó** ayer?   *"Who cooked yesterday?"*
—Yo **cociné** y Pablo me **ayudó**.   *"I cooked and Pablo helped me."*

—¿Qué **comieron**?   *"What did you eat?"*
—**Comimos** tallarines.   *"We ate spaghetti."*

—¿Uds. **prepararon** la salsa?   *"Did you prepare the sauce?"*
—No, **abrimos** dos latas de salsa de tomate.   *"No, we opened two cans of tomato sauce."*

—¿A qué hora **volvieron** tus padres anoche?   *"What time did your parents come back last night?"*
—**Volvieron** a las once.   *"They came back at eleven."*

—¿A qué hora **llegaste** de la universidad hoy?   *"What time did you arrive from the university today?"*
—**Llegué** a las ocho y **limpié** mi cuarto.   *"I arrived at eight and cleaned my room."*

ATENCIÓN: **-ar** and **-er** stem-changing verbs do not change stems in the preterit: **Yo *volví* anoche y *cerré* la puerta.** Verbs ending in **-gar** change **g** to **gu** before **e** in the first person singular preterit: **llegué.**[1]

---

[1] For other verbs with orthographic changes, see Appendix B, p. 315.

Práctica

A. Change the following description of Carmen's daily routine to say what happened yesterday, changing all verbs to the preterit.

Yo me <u>levanto</u> a las seis y me <u>baño</u>. <u>Salgo</u> de casa a las siete. Mi hermano y yo <u>desayunamos</u> en la cafetería. <u>Comemos</u> huevos y <u>bebemos</u> café. Mi hermano <u>trabaja</u> en la oficina y yo <u>estudio</u> en la biblioteca. Mis amigos <u>estudian</u> conmigo. Yo <u>vuelvo</u> a casa a las cinco y mi hermano <u>vuelve</u> a las seis. Yo me <u>acuesto</u> a las diez.

B. Complete the following sentences with the preterit of the verbs in parentheses.

1. ¿Dónde _____ (aprender) Ud. a hablar español?
2. ¿Qué _____ (decidir) Uds. anoche? ¿Ir al concierto?
3. Yo no _____ (entender) su carta.
4. ¿Dónde _____ (comprar) tú esa bicicleta?
5. ¿_____ (Abrir) Ud. las puertas?
6. ¿Qué le _____ (preguntar) Ud. a su suegra?
7. ¿A qué hora _____ (pasar) tú por mi casa ayer?
8. Carmen y yo _____ (ayudar) a preparar la cena.
9. ¿Cuántas horas lo _____ (esperar) Uds.?

C. Interview a classmate, using the following questions. When you have finished, switch roles.

1. ¿A qué hora te levantaste hoy?
2. ¿Desayunaste en tu casa?
3. ¿Quién preparó el desayuno?
4. ¿Qué bebiste en el desayuno?
5. ¿Viste a tus amigos ayer?
6. ¿Tus amigos almorzaron contigo?
7. ¿Quién cocinó anoche en tu casa?
8. ¿Le escribiste a alguien ayer?
9. ¿A qué hora volviste a tu casa?
10. ¿A qué hora cenaron Uds.?
11. ¿Comieron tallarines con salsa de tomate?
12. ¿A qué hora te acostaste?

2 The preterit of ser, ir, and dar
El pretérito de los verbos ser, ir y dar

The preterit forms of **ser, ir,** and **dar** are irregular. Note that **ser** and **ir** have the same forms.

ser *(to be)*	ir *(to go)*	dar *(to give)*
fui	fui	di
fuiste	fuiste	diste
fue	fue	dio
fuimos	fuimos	dimos
fueron	fueron	dieron

—¿Uds. **fueron** estudiantes del profesor Vargas el año pasado?

"Were you professor Vargas's students last year?"

—Yo **fui** estudiante suyo pero mi hermano **fue** estudiante de la profesora Rojas.

"I was his student, but my brother was professor Rojas's student."

—¿Tú **fuiste** a la biblioteca anoche?

"Did you go to the library last night?"

—No, Teresa y yo **fuimos** al supermercado.

"No, Teresa and I went to the supermarket."

—¡Ah, **viste** a Teresa! ¿Le **diste** la ropa para su hija?

"Oh, you saw Teresa! Did you give her the clothing for her daughter?"

—Sí, se la **di.**

"Yes, I gave it to her."

Práctica

A. Complete the following dialogues, using the preterit of **ser, ir,** or **dar** as appropriate. Then act them out with a partner.

1. —¿Adónde _____ tú ayer?
   —Por la tarde _____ a una tienda con mi suegro. Él me _____ dinero para comprar ropa.
   —¿_____ Uds. a casa de tía Eva por la noche?
   —Sí, _____ y le _____ el regalo que tú le mandaste.
2. —¿Adónde _____ Uds. anoche?
   —_____ a un concierto. Los padres de Dora nos _____ las entradas.
3. —¿Tú _____ estudiante del profesor Vega el año pasado?
   —No, yo _____ estudiante de la profesora Soto.

B. Answer the following questions.

1. ¿Dieron Ud. y sus amigos una fiesta el viernes pasado?
2. ¿Dio Ud. dinero para la fiesta?
3. ¿Adónde fue Ud. el sábado pasado?

4. ¿Sus amigos fueron con Ud.?
5. ¿Fue Ud. al supermercado la semana pasada?
6. ¿Fue Ud. estudiante en esta universidad el año pasado?

C. Write a short paragraph describing what you did yesterday. Give as many details as possible.

3 Uses of por and para
Usos de por y para

◆ The preposition **por** is used to express the following concepts.

1. Motion (*through, along, by*)

—¿**Por** dónde entró la criada?
"How (through where) did the maid come in?"

—Entró **por** la puerta de atrás.
"She came in through the back door."

—¿A qué hora pasaste **por** mi casa ayer?
"At what time did you go by my house yesterday?"

—Pasé **por** tu casa a las tres.
"I went by your house at three o'clock."

2. Cause or motive of an action (*because of, on account of, on behalf of*)

—¿Por qué no fueron Uds. a la playa ayer?
"Why didn't you go to the beach yesterday?"

—No fuimos **por** la lluvia.
"We didn't go because of the rain."

3. Agency, means, manner, unit of measure (*by, for, per*)

—¿Vas a San Francisco **por** avión?
"Are you going to San Francisco by plane?"

—No, llevo el coche.
"No, I'm taking the car."

—¿Cuál es el límite de velocidad en California?
"What's the speed limit in California?"

—Cincuenta y cinco millas **por** hora.
"Fifty-five miles per hour."

4. In exchange for

—¿Cuánto pagaste **por** el abrigo y **por** el suéter?
"How much did you pay for the coat and sweater?"

—Pagué cien dólares **por** los dos.
"I paid one hundred dollars for both."

5. Period of time during which an action takes place (*during, in, for*)

—¿**Por** cuánto tiempo vas a estar en Puerto Rico?
"*How long are you going to be in Puerto Rico?*"

—Voy a estar allí **por** un mes.
"*I'm going to be there for a month.*"

◆ The preposition **para** is used to express the following concepts.

1. Destination in space (*to*)

—¿A qué hora hay vuelos **para** México?
"*What time are there flights to Mexico?*"

—A las diez y a las doce de la noche.
"*At ten and twelve P.M.*"

2. Goal for a point in the future (*by, for*)

—¿Cuándo necesita Ud. la aspiradora?
"*When do you need the vacuum cleaner?*"

—La necesito **para** mañana.
"*I need it by tomorrow.*"

3. Whom or what something is for

—¿**Para** quién es la lavadora?
"*Whom is the washing machine for?*"

—Es **para** mi suegra.
"*It's for my mother-in-law.*"

4. Purpose (*in order to*)

—¿**Para** qué necesita la criada la escoba?
"*What does the maid need the broom for?*"

—La necesita **para** barrer la cocina.
"*She needs it (in order) to sweep the kitchen.*"

Práctica

A. Complete the following paragraph, using **por** or **para** as appropriate.

Mañana _____ la mañana salimos _____ Chile. Vamos _____ avión y pensamos estar allí _____ tres semanas. Pagamos quinientos dólares _____ el pasaje y vamos a viajar _____ todo el país. En Santiago voy a comprar regalos _____ todos mis amigos. Tengo que estar aquí _____ el veinte de agosto _____ poder comenzar las clases en septiembre.

B. With a partner, act out the following dialogues in Spanish.

1. "How did you enter, Paquito?"
"I came in through the back door."
"Why didn't you take the children to the park?"
"We didn't go because of the rain."

2. "Did you buy the washing machine and the vacuum cleaner for Mom?"
   "Yes, and I paid seven hundred dollars for both!"
3. "I'm going to Costa Rica to visit my mother-in-law. I'm going to be there for a month."
   "Are you going by plane?"
   "No, I'm going by bus."
4. "What is the speed limit here?"
   "I don't know...Fifty-five miles per hour?"
5. "We are leaving for Madrid tomorrow."
   "When are you coming back?"
   "We have to be here by December tenth."
6. "I need the broom to sweep the kitchen and the terrace."
   "I can help you, Anita."

4 Seasons of the year and weather expressions

Las estaciones del año y las expresiones para describir el tiempo

Las estaciones del año

la primavera	*spring*	**el verano**	*summer*
el otoño	*fall*	**el invierno**	*winter*

Expresiones para describir el tiempo

◆ In the following weather expressions, the verb **hacer** (*to make*) followed by a noun is used in Spanish, whereas the verb *to be* followed by an adjective is used in English.

Hace (mucho) **frío.**	*It is (very) cold.*
Hace (mucho) **calor.**	*It is (very) hot.*
Hace (mucho) **viento.**[1]	*It is (very) windy.*
Hace sol.[1]	*It is sunny.*
Hace buen (mal) tiempo.[2]	*The weather is good (bad).*

—¿Cómo es el clima de Phoenix?	*"What is the weather like in Phoenix?"*
—**Hace** mucho **calor** en el **verano**, pero en el **invierno** no **hace** mucho **frío.**	*"It is very hot in the summer, but in winter it's not very cold."*

---

[1] It is also correct to say **hay viento, hay sol.**
[2] **Bueno** and **malo** drop the final **o** before a masculine singular noun.

—¿Cuándo vienes a Chicago? ¿En octubre? — *"When are you coming to Chicago? In October?"*

—Sí, ¿voy a necesitar un abrigo? — *"Yes, am I going to need a coat?"*

—No, en el **otoño** no **hace** mucho **frío. Hace** mucho **viento.** — *"No, it is not very cold in the fall. It is very windy."*

♦ **Hacer** is not used in weather expressions with **llover (o:ue)** (*to rain*) or **nevar (e:ie)** (*to snow*).

Llueve.	*It rains (It's raining).*
Está lloviendo.	*It's raining.*
Nieva.	*It snows (It's snowing).*
Está nevando.	*It's snowing.*

—¿En Oregón **llueve** mucho en la **primavera?** — *"Does it rain a lot in the spring in Oregon?"*

—¡En Oregón **llueve** siempre! — *"In Oregon it always rains!"*

♦ Other words and expressions related to the weather are:

la **lluvia**	*rain*
la **niebla**	*fog*
Está nublado.	*It's cloudy.*

♦ As in English, the Spanish impersonal verbs use third person singular forms only.

—¿Vas a limpiar la terraza? — *"Are you going to clean the terrace?"*

—No, porque **hace** mucho **viento** y **va** a **llover.** — *"No, because it's very windy and it's going to rain."*

Práctica

A. Complete the following sentences, using a word from the list or an appropriate weather expression.

el paraguas   **el suéter**
el impermeable   **el abrigo**

1. ¿Necesitas un paraguas? Sí, porque _____.
2. ¿No necesitas un abrigo? No, porque _____.
3. ¿Quieres un impermeable? No, no está _____.
4. ¿Necesitas un suéter? No, hoy _____.
5. Está nevando. Lleve el _____.
6. Va a llover. Está _____.

B. **¿Qué tiempo hace?** (*How is the weather?*) **¿Qué estación del año es?**

C. With a partner, act out the following dialogues in Spanish.

1. "There are no flights?"
   "No, because there is fog."
2. "Are you going to clean the terrace, Juanita?"
   "No, because it's going to rain."
3. "Does it snow here?"
   "No, it's very cold in the winter, but it never snows."

Palabras y más palabras

Circle the word or phrase that best completes each sentence.

1. Aquí hace mucho frío en el (verano, invierno).
2. Fui al supermercado para comprar una (aspiradora, lata de salsa).
3. Necesito un paraguas y un impermeable porque (está lloviendo, hace calor).
4. La criada necesita la escoba para (cocinar, barrer) la cocina.
5. El límite de velocidad es de 65 millas por (minuto, hora).
6. Nosotras (preparamos, entramos) por la puerta de atrás.
7. Está nublado. Va a (hacer sol, llover).
8. No hay vuelos porque hay (niebla, ropa).
9. Fuimos a México el verano (pasado, que viene).
10. Necesitamos salsa de tomate para los (tallarines, abrigos).

En el laboratorio

The following material is to be used with the tape or audio CD in the language laboratory.

I. Vocabulario

Repeat each word after the speaker. When repeating words that are cognates, notice the difference in pronunciation between English and Spanish.

Cognados:	el límite la milla el suéter el tomate la velocidad
Nombres:	el abrigo la aspiradora la cocina el criado la escoba el impermeable el invierno la lata el bote la lavadora la lluvia la niebla el otoño el paraguas la puerta de atrás la ropa la salsa el supermercado los tallarines los espaguetis el verano
Verbos:	ayudar barrer cocinar entrar limpiar llover nevar pasar preparar
Adjetivos:	nublado pasado

OTRAS PALABRAS Y
EXPRESIONES:
anoche   ayer
¿Cuál es el límite de velocidad?
por hora   los dos
¿Qué tiempo hace hoy?

II. Práctica

A. Answer the questions, using the cues provided. Repeat the correct answer after the speaker's confirmation. Listen to the model.

Modelo: —¿Quién te ayudó ayer? (Roberto)
    —**Me ayudó Roberto.**

1. (ayer)
2. (por la puerta de atrás)
3. (anoche)
4. (tallarines)
5. (a Teresa)
6. (a las nueve)
7. (la puerta)
8. (al supermercado)
9. (a Esteban)
10. (el Dr. Mena)

B. Answer the questions, always using the first choice. Omit the subject. Repeat the correct answer after the speaker's confirmation. Listen to the model.

Modelo: —¿Entraron Uds. por la ventana o por la puerta?
    —**Entramos por la ventana.**

C. Answer the questions, using the cues provided. Repeat the correct answer after the speaker's confirmation. Listen to the model.

Modelo: —¿Dónde hace mucho frío? (Alaska)
    —**Hace mucho frío en Alaska.**

1. (Oregón)
2. (Arizona)
3. (otoño)
4. (Chicago)
5. (sí)

III. Para escuchar y entender

1. The speaker will make some statements. Circle **L (lógico)** if the statement is logical and **I (ilógico)** if it is illogical. The speaker will verify your response.

1. L   I
2. L   I
3. L   I
4. L   I
5. L   I
6. L   I

2. Listen carefully to the dialogue. It will be read twice.

(*Diálogo 1*)

Now the speaker will make some statements about the dialogue you just heard. Tell whether each statement is true (**verdadero**) or false (**falso**). The speaker will confirm the correct answer.

3. Listen carefully to the dialogue. It will be read twice.

(*Diálogo 2*)

Now the speaker will ask you some questions about the dialogue you just heard. Answer each question, omitting the subject. The speaker will confirm the correct answer. Repeat the correct answer.

¿Cuánto sabe usted ahora?

Lección 6   **A.** Stem-changing verbs (o:ue)

Answer the following questions.

1. ¿A qué hora vuelve Ud. a casa?
2. Cuando Uds. van a México, ¿vuelan o van en auto?
3. ¿Recuerdan Uds. los verbos irregulares?
4. ¿Cuántas horas duerme Ud.?
5. ¿Pueden Uds. ir a la playa?

B. Affirmative and negative expressions

Change the following sentences to the affirmative.

1. Ellos no recuerdan nada.
2. No hay nadie en el cuarto.
3. Yo no quiero volar tampoco.
4. No recibimos ningún regalo.
5. Nunca tiene fiestas en su casa.

C. Pronouns as object of a preposition

How would you say the following in Spanish?

1. Can you come with me?
2. Are you going to work with them?
3. The money is for you, Anita.
4. The gift is not for me; it is for her.
5. No, Paco, I can't go with you.

D. Direct object pronouns

Complete the following sentences with the Spanish equivalent of the direct object pronouns in parentheses. Follow the models.

Modelos: Yo llamo (*him*)
   Yo lo llamo.

   Yo quiero llamar (*him*)
   Yo quiero llamarlo.

1. Yo espero (*them*, fem.)
2. Uds. van a comprar (*it*, masc.)
3. Nosotros no queremos visitar (*you*, fam.)
4. Ella lee (*it*, fem.)

5. ¿Ud. llama? (*me*)
6. Él escribe (*them,* masc.)
7. Carlos va a visitar (*us*)
8. Nosotros no esperamos (*you,* formal, sing., masc.)

E. Vocabulary

Complete the following sentences, using words learned in **Lección 6.**

1. Una habitación con _____ al _____ cuesta más.
2. Ellos _____ dos días a la semana en la cafetería.
3. El _____ de esta cama es muy malo.
4. ¿Cuánto _____ el libro de español?
5. Los Ángeles tiene muchos _____ de interés.
6. No quiero ni vino ni cerveza. No tomo bebidas _____.
7. Él _____ siete horas todas las noches.
8. ¿Dónde está la _____ de _____? Necesito comprar estampillas.

A. Stem-changing verbs (**e:i**)   **Lección 7**

Answer the following questions.

1. ¿Qué sirven Uds., sopa o ensalada?
2. ¿Qué pide Ud. para beber cuando va a un restaurante?
3. ¿Dice Ud. su edad?
4. ¿Sigue Ud. en la universidad?
5. ¿Uds. siempre piden postre?

B. Irregular first person forms

Complete the sentences with the present indicative of the verbs in the following list. Use each verb once.

traer   conocer   traducir   hacer   saber
ver   salir   poner   conducir

1. Yo _____ mi coche.
2. Yo siempre _____ con ella.
3. Yo _____ la carne en la mesa.
4. Yo _____ del inglés al español.
5. Yo no _____ al profesor de mi hijo.
6. Yo _____ los folletos turísticos.
7. Yo _____ el postre.
8. Yo no _____ el regalo. ¿Dónde está?
9. Yo no _____ nadar.

C. Saber contrasted with **conocer**

How would you say the following in Spanish?

1. I know your son.
2. He doesn't know French.
3. Do you know how to swim, Miss Vera?
4. Do you know the travel agent?
5. Are the students familiar with Cervantes's novels?

D. Indirect object pronouns

Answer the following questions according to the model.

Modelo: —¿Qué me vas a traer de México?
       (un regalo)
    —Te voy a traer un regalo.

1. ¿Qué te va a dar Carlos? (dinero)
2. ¿Qué le das tú a Luis? (una revista)
3. ¿En qué idioma les habla a Uds. el profesor? (en español)
4. ¿Qué va a decirles Ud. a los niños? (que es tarde)
5. ¿Qué nos pregunta Ud.? (la dirección de la oficina)
6. ¿A quién están escribiéndole Uds.? (a nuestro padre)
7. ¿Cuándo le escribe Ud. a su abuelo? (los lunes)
8. ¿A quién le da Ud. la información? (al agente de viajes)
9. ¿En qué idioma me hablas tú? (en inglés)
10. ¿Qué te compran tus hijos? (nada)

E. Vocabulary

Complete the following sentences, using the words learned in **Lección 7.**

1. Compré el pasaje en la _____ de viajes.
2. Ellos van a _____ en la piscina.
3. Mi hijo sabe de _____ todos los verbos.
4. Necesita confirmar la _____ hoy.
5. ¿Necesitamos los _____ para entrar en México?
6. No podemos viajar hoy porque van a _____ los vuelos.
7. La embajada de Estados Unidos _____ en la _____ Juárez, número 128.

Lección 8   **A. Pedir** contrasted with **preguntar**

Tell what these people are asking or asking for, using **pedir** or **preguntar.**

1. yo / dónde vive
2. Rosa / las entradas
3. nosotros / la hora

    4. los niños / las pelotas
    5. tú / la raqueta
    6. el entrenador / tu edad

B. Special construction with **gustar, doler,** and **hacer falta**

Complete the following sentences with the appropriate forms of **gustar, doler,** and **hacer falta.**

    1. No _____ esas mochilas. Prefiero aquéllas.
    2. ¿Qué _____, Jorge? ¿La tienda de campaña?
    3. A Marta _____ la cabeza. ¿Tienes aspirinas?
    4. A nosotros no _____ dinero. No necesitamos comprar nada.
    5. ¿_____ a Ud. esta bicicleta, o prefiere la otra?
    6. A Rodolfo _____ unos esquíes. ¿Puedes comprárselos?
    7. A mí _____ los pies.
    8. A nosotros no _____ caminar (*to walk*). ¿Podemos ir en coche?

C. Demonstrative adjectives and pronouns

Complete the following sentences with the Spanish equivalent of the words in parentheses.

    1. Necesito _____ (*these*) pelotas y _____ (*those over there*).
    2. ¿Quieres _____ (*this*) caballo o _____ (*that one*)?
    3. Yo prefiero _____ (*these*) patines, no _____ (*those over there*).
    4. Papá, ¿tú quieres comprar _____ (*that*) raqueta o _____ (*this one*)?
    5. Yo no entiendo _____ (*that*, neuter form).

D. Direct and indirect object pronouns used together

How would you say the following in Spanish?

    1. The money? I'll give it to you tomorrow, Mr. Peña.
    2. I know you need my book, Anita, but I can't lend it to you.
    3. I need my backpack. Can you bring it to me, Miss López?
    4. The pens? She is bringing them to us.
    5. When he needs skates, his mother buys them for him.

E. Vocabulary

Complete the following sentences, using words learned in **Lección 8.**

    1. Quiero leer la página _____.
    2. ¿Para _____ son esos patines? ¿Para tu hijo?
    3. Para jugar al tenis, los niños necesitan una _____ y una _____ de tenis.

4. Tengo dos _____ de dormir. Te presto una.
5. Voy a comprar las _____ para el partido del domingo.
6. Me _____ mucho la cabeza.
7. Necesito la tienda de _____ este fin de semana.
8. Me _____ falta diez dólares para comprar el libro.

Lección 9   **A.** Possessive pronouns

Answer the following questions in the negative, according to the model.

Modelo: —¿Estos pantalones son **de Juan?**
   —No, no son **de él.**

1. ¿Son **tuyas** estas tarjetas?
2. ¿Estos cepillos son **de Julia?**
3. ¿El vestido es **suyo**, señora?
4. ¿Es **de Uds.** esta cama?
5. ¿Esta tarjeta de crédito es **de tus padres?**
6. ¿Son **tuyos** estos espejos?
7. ¿Es **de Uds.** esta máquina de afeitar?
8. ¿Es **nuestro** este dormitorio?

B. Reflexive constructions

How would you say the following in Spanish?

1. I get up at seven, I bathe, I get dressed, and I leave at seven-thirty.
2. What time do the children wake up?
3. She doesn't want to sit down.
4. He shaves every day.
5. Do you remember your teachers, Carlitos?
6. They are always complaining.
7. First she puts the children to bed, and then she goes to bed.
8. Do you want to try on these pants, Miss?
9. Where are you going to put the money, ladies?
10. The students always fall asleep in this class.

C. Command form: **Ud.** and **Uds.**

Complete the sentences with the command forms of the verbs in the following list, as appropriate, and read each sentence aloud. Use each verb once.

escribir	venir	dar	hablar	doblar
servir	cerrar	volver	seguir	ser
estar	poner	ir	abrir	traer

1. _____ la puerta, Sr. Benítez.
2. _____ español, señores.
3. _____ a su hija, señora.

4. _____ mañana por la mañana, señoras.
5. No _____ la ventana, señorita. Tengo calor.
6. _____ a la izquierda, señores.
7. _____ derecho, señorita.
8. _____ su nombre y dirección, señores.
9. _____ en la oficina mañana por la tarde, señores.
10. ¡No _____ tan impacientes, señoritas!
11. Sr. Vega, _____ a la casa del director.
12. _____ el martes, señora. El doctor no está hoy.
13. _____ el café en la terraza, señorita.
14. _____ los libros aquí, señores.
15. _____ las cartas mañana, señoras.

D. Uses of object pronouns with command forms

How would you say the following in Spanish?

1. Tell them my address, Mr. Mena.
2. The dress? Don't bring it to me now, Miss Ruiz.
3. Don't tell (it to) my hairdresser, please.
4. Bring the drinks, gentlemen. Bring them to the terrace.
5. Don't get up, Mrs. Miño.
6. The tea? Bring it to her at four o'clock in the afternoon, Mr. Vargas.

E. Vocabulary

Complete the following sentences, using words learned in **Lección 9.**

1. No tengo máquina de _____.
2. Mañana voy a la _____. Necesito _____ la cabeza y cortarme el _____.
3. Lleve los pantalones a la _____, señorita.
4. No tengo dinero; voy a pagar con _____.
5. No está a la derecha; está a la _____.
6. Ponga el botiquín en el baño ahora _____.
7. Voy a _____ a los niños; ya son las nueve de la noche.
8. Para llegar a la universidad, siga Ud. _____.

A. The preterit of regular verbs / preterit of **ser, ir,** and **dar**   **Lección 10**

Rewrite the following sentences according to the new beginnings. Follow the model.

Modelo: Voy al cine. (Ayer...)
   Ayer fui al cine.

1. Ella entra en la cafetería y come tallarines. (Ayer...)
2. María le escribe a su suegra. (Ayer...)
3. Ella me presta su abrigo. (El viernes pasado...)

4. Ellos son los mejores estudiantes. (El año pasado...)
5. Ellos te esperan cerca del supermercado. (El sábado pasado...)
6. Mi hijo va a Cuba. (El verano pasado...)
7. Le doy el impermeable. (Ayer por la mañana...)
8. Nosotros decidimos comprar la aspiradora. (El lunes pasado...)
9. Le pregunto la hora. (Anoche...)
10. Tú no pagas por la ropa. (Anoche...)
11. Somos los primeros. (El jueves pasado...)
12. Me dan muchos problemas. (Ayer...)
13. Mi suegro no bebe café. (Anoche...)
14. Yo no voy a esquiar. (Ayer...)
15. Te damos el suéter. (La semana pasada...)

B. Uses of **por** and **para**

Complete the following sentences, using **por** or **para**.

1. La criada entró _____ la puerta de atrás.
2. Ella pasó _____ mi casa anoche a las nueve.
3. Ellos no vienen _____ la lluvia.
4. No hay viajes _____ Ecuador los sábados.
5. Vamos _____ avión y necesitamos el dinero _____ pagar los pasajes.
6. El límite de velocidad en California es 65 millas _____ hora.
7. ¿_____ quién es el paraguas?
8. Eva pagó doscientos dólares _____ la aspiradora.
9. Necesito la lavadora _____ mañana _____ la mañana.

C. Seasons of the year and weather expressions

How would you say the following in Spanish?

1. It is very windy today.
2. Here it is very cold in the winter.
3. Is it very hot in Cuba in the summer?
4. How is the weather today?
5. Is it sunny or is it cloudy?
6. There are no flights because of the fog.
7. Do you prefer the fall or the spring?

D. Vocabulary

Complete the following sentences, using words learned in **Lección 10.**

1. Necesito el _____ porque hace frío.
2. ¿Cuál es el _____ de velocidad?

3. Ella quiere ponerse el _____ porque va a llover.
4. ¿Dónde compraste la _____ de tomate? ¿En el supermercado?
5. Ponga el vestido en la _____, señorita.
6. Adela siempre _____ unos tallarines muy buenos.
7. ¿Quién barrió la cocina? ¿La _____?
8. ¿Qué _____ hace hoy? ¿Hace frío?

Lección

11

1. Time expressions with **hacer**

2. Irregular preterits

3. The preterit of stem-changing verbs (**e:i** and **o:u**)

4. Command forms **(tú)**

Vocabulario

el accidente accident	**interesante** interesting
el favor favor	**la paciencia** patience

NOMBRES
el arroz rice
la basura trash, garbage
la cafetera coffeepot
el (la) cocinero(a) cook
la cosa thing
el fregadero sink
el (la) invitado(a) guest
la licuadora blender
la liquidación, la venta sale
la marca brand
el piso floor
la reunión, la junta
    meeting
la secadora dryer
la tostadora toaster
los trabajos de la casa
    household chores

VERBOS
apagar to turn off
caminar to walk
despedirse (e:i) to say
    good-bye
divertirse (e:ie) to have
    a good time
elegir (e:i) to choose, to
    select

enseñar to teach
mentir (e:ie) to lie
morir (o:ue) to die

ADJETIVOS
aburrido(a) boring, bored
todo(a) all
todos(as) every

**OTRAS PALABRAS Y
EXPRESIONES**
arroz con pollo chicken
    with rice
casi nunca hardly ever
¿cuánto tiempo? how
    long?
debajo (de) underneath
ir caminando, ir a pie to
    walk, to go on foot
ir de compras to go
    shopping
media hora half an hour
otra vez again
¡Rápido! Quick!
según according to
Ten paciencia. Be
    patient.

1 Time expressions with hacer

Expresiones de tiempo con hacer

Spanish uses the following formula to express how long something has been going on.

> **Hace** + length of time + **que** + verb (in present tense)
> **Hace   quince años   que   vivo en esta ciudad.**
> *I have been living in this city for fifteen years.*

—¿Tienes hambre?	*"Are you hungry?"*
—Sí, **hace** ocho horas **que** no como.	*"Yes, I haven't eaten in eight hours."*
—¿Cuánto tiempo **hace que** Ud. enseña aquí?	*"How long have you been teaching here?"*
—**Hace** tres años **que** enseño aquí.	*"I have been teaching here for three years."*
—¿Cuánto tiempo **hace que** Uds. caminan?	*"How long have you been walking?"*
—**Hace** media hora **que** caminamos.	*"We have been walking for half an hour."*

ATENCIÓN: To ask how long something has been going on, use the expression **¿Cuánto tiempo hace que... ?**

Práctica

A. Use the expression **hace... que** to say how long each action has been taking place.

> *Modelo:* Estamos en enero. / Él empezó a trabajar en octubre.
> **Hace** tres meses **que** él trabaja.

1. Son las tres de la tarde. / Ellos están aquí desde (*since*) las dos y media.
2. Estamos en el año 2000. / Raquel empezó a enseñar en 1997.
3. Hoy es viernes. / Empezamos a trabajar el lunes.
4. Son las cuatro. / Graciela empezó a hablar por teléfono a las cuatro menos cuarto.
5. Son las cinco. / Empezaste a cocinar a las tres.

B. Interview a classmate, using the following questions. When you have finished, switch roles.

1. ¿Cuánto tiempo hace que estudias español?
2. ¿Cuánto tiempo hace que conoces a tu mejor amigo o amiga?
3. ¿Cuánto tiempo hace que no comes?
4. ¿Cuánto tiempo hace que vives en esta ciudad?

5. ¿Cuánto tiempo hace que no ves a tus padres?
6. ¿Cuánto tiempo hace que Uds. no van de vacaciones?
7. ¿Cuánto tiempo hace que no llueve aquí?

2 Irregular preterits
Pretéritos irregulares

The following Spanish verbs are irregular in the preterit.

tener:	tuve, tuviste, tuvo, tuvimos, tuvieron
estar:	estuve, estuviste, estuvo, estuvimos, estuvieron
poder:	pude, pudiste, pudo, pudimos, pudieron
poner:	puse, pusiste, puso, pusimos, pusieron
saber:	supe, supiste, supo, supimos, supieron
hacer:	hice, hiciste, hizo, hicimos, hicieron
venir:	vine, viniste, vino, vinimos, vinieron
querer:	quise, quisiste, quiso, quisimos, quisieron
decir:	dije, dijiste, dijo, dijimos, dijeron[1]
traer:	traje, trajiste, trajo, trajimos, trajeron[1]
conducir:	conduje, condujiste, condujo, condujimos, condujeron[1]
traducir:	traduje, tradujiste, tradujo, tradujimos, tradujeron[1]

—¿Dónde **pusieron** Uds. la lata de la basura?
"Where did you put the garbage can?"

—La **pusimos** debajo del fregadero.
"We put it underneath the sink."

—¿No **vino** la criada?
"Didn't the maid come?"

—Sí, pero **trajo** a su hijo y no **pudo** hacer los trabajos de la casa.
"Yes, but she brought her son and she couldn't do the household chores."

—¿**Vinieron** caminando?
"Did they walk?"

—Sí, **vinieron** a pie.
"Yes, they came on foot"

—¿Qué te **dijeron** de la reunión?
"What did they tell you about the meeting?"

—Me **dijeron** muchas cosas interesantes.
"They told me many interesting things."

ATENCIÓN: Notice that the third person singular form of the verb **hacer** changes the **c** to **z** in order to maintain the soft sound of the **c** in the infinitive.

---

[1] Note that the **-i** is omitted in the third person plural ending of these verbs.

—¿**Hizo** el arroz con pollo
  el cocinero?

—No, no **pudo** hacerlo
  porque **tuvo** que limpiar
  el piso de la cocina.

"Did the cook make the
chicken and rice?"

"No, he wasn't able to do
it because he had to clean
the kitchen floor."

◆ The preterit of **hay** (from the verb **haber**) is **hubo,** which is
used with singular and plural subjects.

Ayer **hubo** una reunión en
  la universidad.

Yesterday there was a meeting
at the university.

Hubo dos accidentes
  la semana pasada.

There were two accidents
last week.

Práctica

A. Complete the following paragraph with the preterit of the verbs
in parentheses.

Isabel le escribe una carta a Teresa.

Toledo, 15 de julio de 19...

Querida Teresa:

Ayer yo _____ (estar) en Madrid, pero no _____
(poder) ir a verte. Salí de Toledo por la mañana y _____ (conducir) por tres horas hasta llegar a Madrid. Allí _____ (tener)
que ir al hospital para ver a Gustavo. Caminé por la ciudad y
_____ (querer) llamarte por teléfono, pero no _____
(poder) encontrar uno. Como siempre, ayer _____ (hacer)
mucho calor. _____ (Venir) de Madrid muy cansada. Esta
mañana hablé por teléfono con Ramón. Él me _____ (decir)
muchas cosas interesantes. ¡Ah...! Me _____ (poner) el
vestido que compré en Madrid y salí con Jorge. El sábado
vuelvo a Madrid para verte.

Tu amiga,

Isabel

B. Complete the following dialogue, using appropriate irregular
verbs in the preterit. Then act it out with a partner.

—¿Dónde _____ Uds. anoche? ¿Adónde fueron?

—_____ en casa de Julio. _____ una cena en su casa.

—¿Tú _____ tu coche o fueron caminando?

—Yo _____ mi coche.

—¿Tus primos fueron a la cena?

—No, ellos no _____ ir porque _____ que trabajar.
—¿Quién _____ la comida?
—La _____ Julio y su esposa.
—¿Qué vestido te _____ para ir a la cena?
—Me _____ el vestido negro.

C. Answer the following questions, using complete sentences.

1. ¿A qué hora vino Ud. a la universidad hoy?
2. ¿Condujo su coche o vino a pie?
3. ¿Trajo sus libros de español?
4. ¿Pudo Ud. venir a clase la semana pasada?
5. ¿Tuvo que trabajar ayer?
6. ¿Dónde estuvo Ud. anoche? ¿Con quién?
7. ¿Qué hizo anoche para la cena?
8. ¿En qué banco puso Ud. su dinero?

D. Interview a classmate, using the questions in **Práctica C** in the **tú** form. When you have finished, switch roles.

3 **The preterit of stem-changing verbs (**e:i **and** o:u**)**

El pretérito de verbos de cambio radical e:i y o:u

e:i verbs

Stem-changing verbs of the **-ir** conjugation, whether they change **e** to **ie** or **e** to **i** in the present indicative, change **e** to **i** in the third person singular and plural of the preterit.

sentir		pedir	
sentí	sentimos	pedí	pedimos
sentiste		pediste	
sintió	sintieron	pidió	pidieron

◆ The following verbs follow the same **e** to **i** pattern.

conseguir   **preferir**
despedirse (*to say good-bye*)   **repetir**

divertirse (*to have a good time*)   **seguir**
elegir (*to choose*)   **servir**
mentir (*to lie*)

—¿Daniel compró la
    licuadora?

"Did Daniel buy the blender?

—No, **prefirió** comprar una
    cafetera.

*"No, he preferred to buy a
    coffeepot."*

—¿Qué marca **eligió**?

"What brand did he choose?"

—Mr. Coffee.

"Mr. Coffee."

—Según Juan, todos **se
    divirtieron** mucho en
    la fiesta.

*"According to Juan, everybody
    had a good time at the
    party."*

—¡Te **mintió**! La fiesta
    estuvo muy aburrida y no
    sirvieron nada para comer.
    Los invitados se **despidieron**
    muy temprano.

*"He lied to you! The party
    was very boring and they
    didn't serve anything to eat.
    The guests said good-bye
    very early."* (i.e., They left
    very early.)

o:u verbs

Stem-changing verbs of the **-ir** conjugation that change **o** to **ue** in
the present indicative change **o** to **u** in the third person singular and
plural of the preterit.

dormir	
dormí	dormimos
dormiste	
durmió	durmieron

◆   Another verb that follows the same **o** to **u** pattern is **morir** (*to die*).

—¿Cuántas horas **durmió**
    Ud. anoche?

*"How many hours did you
    sleep last night?"*

—Yo dormí seis horas, pero
    Ana y Luis sólo **durmieron**
    tres.

*"I slept six hours, but Ana
    and Luis slept only three."*

—¿Cuántas personas **murieron**
    en el accidente?

*"How many people died in
    the accident?"*

—Por suerte, no **murió** nadie.

"Luckily, nobody died."

Práctica

Complete the following dialogues, using the preterit of the verbs in parentheses. Then act them out with a partner.

1. —¿Doblaron?
   —No, _____ (seguir) derecho.
2. —¿Dónde _____ (dormir) Uds. anoche?
   —Yo _____ (dormir) en la casa de Ana, pero Carlos _____ (dormir) en un hotel.
3. —¿_____ (Conseguir) Uds. la licuadora?
   —Sí, por suerte la _____ (conseguir) en El Corte Inglés. También _____ (elegir) dos cafeteras de una marca muy buena.
4. —¿Uds. _____ (despedirse) de los chicos?
   —No, porque no se fueron. No _____ (conseguir) pasaje.
   —¿Entonces ellos fueron a la fiesta?
   —Sí, y _____ (divertirse) mucho.
5. —¿Gerardo te _____ (mentir)?
   —Sí.
6. —¿ _____ (Haber) un accidente aquí ayer?
   —Sí, y _____ (morir) dos personas.

Now create two original exchanges using stem-changing verbs in the preterit.

4 Command forms (tú)
Las formas imperativas (tú)

The affirmative command

The affirmative command for **tú** has exactly the same form as the third person singular of the present indicative.

Verb	Present Indicative Third Person Singular	Familiar Command (tú Form)
hablar	él habla	**habla**
comer	él come	**come**
abrir	él abre	**abre**
cerrar	él cierra	**cierra**
volver	él vuelve	**vuelve**
pedir	él pide	**pide**
traer	él trae	**trae**

—**Cierra** las ventanas y | *"Close the windows and turn*
  apaga las luces antes | *off the lights before going out."*
  de salir.[1] |

—Muy bien. **Espérame** | *"Very well. Wait for me in the*
  en el coche. ¿Vamos a | *car. Are we going to take*
  llevarle la tostadora | *the toaster to Ines?"*
  a Inés? |

—Sí, **tráela**, por favor. | *"Yes, bring it, please."*

ATENCIÓN: Remember that direct, indirect, and reflexive pronouns are always attached to an affirmative command.

◆ Eight Spanish verbs have irregular affirmative familiar command forms.

decir:	**di** *(say, tell)*	salir:	**sal** *(go out, leave)*
hacer:	**haz** *(do, make)*	ser:	**sé** *(be)*
ir:	**ve** *(go)*	tener:	**ten** *(have)*
poner:	**pon** *(put)*	venir:	**ven** *(come)*

—Carlitos, **ven** aquí. | *"Carlitos, come here. Do me*
  Hazme un favor. **Ve** | *a favor. Go and tell your mom*
  y **di**le a tu mamá que | *that I need the broom. Quick!"*
  necesito la escoba. |
  ¡Rápido! |

—¡**Ten** paciencia! | *"Be patient!"*

The negative command

The negative command for **tú** is formed by adding **-s** to the command form for **Ud.**

hable	no hable**s**	*don't talk*
vuelva	no vuelva**s**	*don't return*
venga	no venga**s**	*don't come*
salga	no salga**s**	*don't leave*

—Voy a la tienda porque | *"I'm going to the store because*
  tienen una liquidación. | *they are having a sale."*

—**No** me **digas** que quieres | *"Don't tell me (that) you*
  ir de compras otra vez. | *want to go shopping again."*

—Sí, porque necesito una | *"Yes, because I need a dryer."*
  secadora. |

—Bueno, pero **no vayas** hoy; | *"Okay, but don't go today;*
  ve mañana. | *go tomorrow."*

ATENCIÓN: Remember that all object pronouns are placed *before* a negative command: **No *me lo* traigas hoy.**

[1] The infinitive, not the *-ing* form, is used after a preposition in Spanish.

Práctica

A. You and a partner are doing household chores. Take turns asking each other what to do, answering in the affirmative. Follow the model.

> *Modelo:* —¿Traigo la escoba?
> —Sí, **tráela,** por favor.

1. ¿Pongo el pan (*bread*) en la tostadora?
2. ¿Hago el postre?
3. ¿Lo pongo en la mesa?
4. ¿Limpio el piso?
5. ¿Pongo la lata de la basura debajo del fregadero?
6. ¿Preparo el arroz con pollo?
7. ¿Lavo el mantel?
8. ¿Lo pongo en la secadora después (*afterwards*)?
9. ¿Llamo a Estrella otra vez?
10. ¿Cierro las ventanas?
11. ¿Apago la luz?
12. ¿Me voy?

B. Now answer the questions in **Práctica A** in the negative. Follow the model.

> *Modelo:* —¿Traigo la escoba?
> —No, **no la traigas** ahora.

C. You are leaving a child home alone for a few hours. Using the **tú** form, tell the child what to do and what not to do. Give at least ten commands.

Palabras y más palabras

Say the following in another way, using the vocabulary learned in this lesson.

1. treinta minutos
2. venta
3. reunión
4. ir caminando
5. opuesto (*opposite*) de aprender
6. la uso para hacer café
7. persona que cocina
8. limpiar, barrer, cocinar
9. persona a quien invitamos
10. decir adiós
11. ir a comprar
12. opuesto de vivir

En el laboratorio

The following material is to be used with the tape or audio CD in the language laboratory.

I. Vocabulario

Repeat each word after the speaker. When repeating words that are cognates, notice the difference in pronunciation between English and Spanish.

COGNADOS:	el accidente el favor interesante la paciencia
NOMBRES:	el arroz la basura la cafetera el cocinero la cosa el fregadero el invitado la licuadora la liquidación la venta la marca el piso la reunión la junta la secadora la tostadora los trabajos de la casa
VERBOS:	apagar caminar despedirse divertirse elegir enseñar mentir morir
ADJETIVOS:	aburrido todo todos
OTRAS PALABRAS Y EXPRESIONES:	arroz con pollo casi nunca ¿cuánto tiempo? debajo de ir caminando ir a pie ir de compras media hora otra vez ¡Rápido! según Ten paciencia.

II. Práctica

A. Answer the questions, using the cues provided. Repeat the correct answer after the speaker's confirmation. Listen to the model.

Modelo: —¿Cuánto tiempo hace que vives en La Habana? (tres años)
   —**Hace tres años que vivo en La Habana.**

1. (veinte años)
2. (tres meses)
3. (una hora)
4. (cuatro años)
5. (media hora)
6. (dos semanas)
7. (cinco días)
8. (quince minutos)

B. Answer the questions, using the cues provided. Repeat the correct answer after the speaker's confirmation. Listen to the model.

Modelo: —¿Qué tuviste que hacer ayer? (estudiar español)
—**Tuve que estudiar español.**

1. (una secadora)
2. (anoche)
3. (los estudiantes)
4. (a las siete)
5. (debajo del fregadero)
6. (nada)
7. (el arroz con pollo)
8. (sí, otra vez)

C. The speaker will read some sentences in the present tense. Restate each one, changing the verb to the preterit. Repeat the correct answer after the speaker's confirmation. Listen to the model.

Modelo: Ellos piden café.
Ellos pidieron café.

D. Change the following commands from the negative to the affirmative. Repeat the correct answer after the speaker's confirmation. Listen to the model.

Modelo: **No hables** inglés.
Habla inglés.

III. *Para escuchar y entender*

1. The speaker will make some statements. Circle **L (lógico)** if the statement is logical and **I (ilógico)** if it is illogical. The speaker will verify your response.

1. L I
2. L I
3. L I
4. L I

5. L I
6. L I
7. L I
8. L I

2. Listen carefully to the dialogue. It will be read twice.

(Diálogo)

Now the speaker will make some statements about the dialogue you just heard. Tell whether each statement is true (**verdadero**) or false (**falso**). The speaker will confirm the correct answer.

3. Listen carefully to the narration. It will be read twice.

(Narración)

Now the speaker will ask some questions about the narration you just heard. Answer each question, omitting the subject. The speaker will confirm the correct answer. Repeat the correct answer.

Lección

12

1. **En** and **a** as equivalents of *at*

2. The imperfect tense

3. The past progressive

4. The preterit contrasted with the imperfect

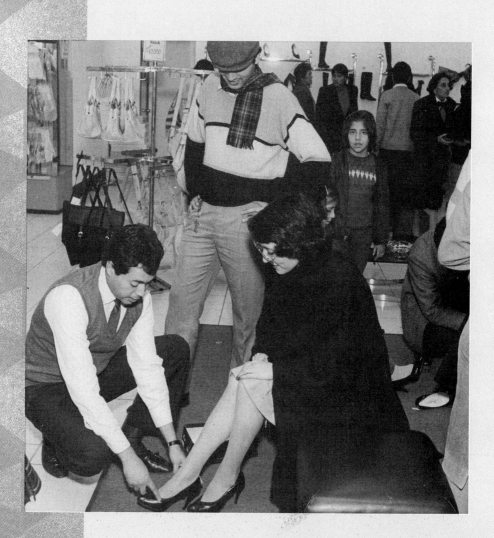

Vocabulario

COGNADOS

el aeropuerto airport	**la computadora** computer
el catálogo catalogue	**el par** pair

NOMBRES
la cartera purse
el centro comercial mall
la joyería jewelry store
la máquina de escribir
  typewriter
el probador fitting room
el sombrero hat
el traje de baño bathing
  suit
la vidriera, el escaparate
  store window
la zapatería shoe store
los zapatos shoes

VERBOS
encontrarse (con) (o:ue)
  to meet (*for an*
  appointment)
mirar to look at
quedarse to stay, to remain
sentir(se) (e:ie) to feel

ADJETIVO
nuevo(a) new

OTRAS PALABRAS Y
EXPRESIONES
anteayer the day before
  yesterday
de vez en cuando once in
  a while
en casa at home
en esa época in those days
escribir a máquina to type
ir de vacaciones to go on
  vacation
juntos(as) together
mirar vidrieras to window
  shop
pues well
todo el día all day long

1 En **and** a **as equivalents of** *at*
En y a **como equivalentes de** *at*

◆ **En** is used in Spanish as the equivalent of *at* to indicate a certain place or location.

—¿Dónde están los chicos? ¿No están **en** casa?   *"Where are the boys? Aren't they at home?"*

—No, están **en** el centro comercial, mirando vidrieras.   *"No, they're at the mall, window shopping."*

◆ **A** is used in Spanish as the equivalent of *at*

1. to refer to a specific moment in time.

—¿Cuándo se encontraron Uds.?   *"When did you meet?"*

—Ayer **a** las once, en la zapatería.   *"Yesterday at eleven, at the shoe store."*

2. to indicate direction towards a point after the verb **llegar**.

—¿**A** qué hora llegaron **al** aeropuerto?   *"What time did they arrive at the airport?"*

—**A** las cinco.   *"At five."*

Práctica

Complete the following dialogues, using **en** or **a**, as appropriate. Then act them out with a partner.

1. —¿_____ qué hora llegaron Uds. _____ California?
   —Llegamos _____ las seis.
   —¿Dónde comieron?
   —_____ un restaurante mexicano que hay _____ el aeropuerto.
2. —¿Dónde está tu esposa ahora? ¿_____ casa?
   —No, está _____ el centro comercial mirando vidrieras.
3. —¿Carlos está _____ la joyería?
   —Sí, él trabaja allí todo el día.
   —¿_____ qué hora te vas a encontrar con él _____ el restaurante?
   —_____ las ocho y media.

2 The imperfect tense
El imperfecto de indicativo

There are two simple past tenses in Spanish: the preterit, which you have studied in **Lecciones 10** and **11,** and the imperfect.

Regular imperfect forms

To form the imperfect tense, add these endings to the verb stem.

The Imperfect Tense		
-ar *Verbs*	-er *and* -ir *Verbs*	
hablar	**comer**	**vivir**
hablaba	comía	vivía
hablabas	comías	vivías
hablaba	comía	vivía
hablábamos	comíamos	vivíamos
hablaban	comían	vivían

◆ Notice that the endings of **-er** and **-ir** verbs are the same. Notice also that there is a written accent mark on the final **í** of **-er** and **-ir** verbs.

◆ Depending on the context, the imperfect tense in Spanish is equivalent to three forms in English.

Yo **vivía** en Chicago.
{
I used to live in Chicago.
I was living in Chicago.
I lived in Chicago.
}

◆ The imperfect is used to refer to habitual or repeated actions in the past, with no reference to when they began or ended.

—¿Tú **llamabas** a tu suegra?   *"Did you used to call your mother-in-law?"*

—Sí, la **llamaba** de vez en cuando.   *"Yes, I used to call her once in a while."*

—¿Dónde **vivía** Ud. en esa época?   *"Where did you live in those days?"*

—Yo **vivía** en Cuba.   *"I lived (was living) in Cuba."*

◆ The imperfect is also used to describe actions or events that the speaker views as in the process of happening in the past.

Yo **empezaba** a probarme la ropa cuando ella vino.	*I was beginning to try on the clothes when she came.*

◆ The imperfect is also used to describe physical, mental, or emotional conditions in the past.

El probador **era** muy grande.	*The fitting room was very big.*
Ella **estaba** enferma.	*She was sick.*

◆ The imperfect tense of **hay** (from the verb **haber**) is **había**.

Irregular imperfect forms

There are only three irregular verbs in the imperfect tense: **ser, ir,** and **ver**.

ser	ir	ver
era	iba	veía
eras	ibas	veías
era	iba	veía
éramos	íbamos	veíamos
eran	iban	veían

—¿Dónde vivían Uds. cuando **eran** niños?	*"Where did you live when you were children?"*
—En Quito, pero **íbamos** a Guayaquil todos los meses a visitar a nuestros abuelos.	*"In Quito, but we went to Guayaquil every month to visit our grandparents."*
—Yo casi nunca **veía** a mis abuelos cuando **era** niña.	*"I hardly ever saw my grandparents when I was a child."*

Práctica

A. Complete the following dialogues, using the imperfect tense of the verbs in parentheses. Then act them out with a partner.

1. —¿Tú _____ (trabajar) cuando _____ (estar) en la universidad?
   —No, pero de vez en cuando _____ (ayudar) a mi mamá con los trabajos de la casa. ¡Y _____ (ser) muy buena cocinera! _____ (Preparar) unos postres muy buenos.

2. —Mamá y yo siempre _____ (ir) al supermercado los
   sábados, y después _____ (limpiar) la casa.
   —Cuando yo _____ (ser) niño, generalmente no _____
   (hacer) nada los sábados.
3. —¿Tú _____ (ver) a tus primos cuando _____ (ser)
   niño?
   —No, casi nunca, pero les _____ (escribir) a menudo.

B. Interview a classmate, using the following questions. When you
have finished, switch roles.

1. ¿Dónde vivías cuando eras niño(a)?
2. ¿A qué escuela ibas?
3. ¿Iban Uds. al cine a veces?
4. ¿Veías a tus abuelos en esa época?
5. ¿Cocinaban tú y tus hermanos cuando eran niños? (¿Qué
   preparaban?)
6. Cuando eras chico(a), ¿qué hacías los domingos?

C. With a classmate, talk about what you used to do when you were
children.

3 The past progressive
El pasado progresivo

The past progressive indicates an action in progress in the past. It is
formed with the imperfect tense of the verb **estar** and the Spanish
equivalent of the present participle (the **gerundio**).

—¿Qué **estabas haciendo**
cuando te llamé?
*"What were you doing when I
called you?"*

—**Estaba escribiendo** a
máquina. Tengo una
máquina de escribir
nueva.
*"I was typing. I have a new
typewriter."*

—Pues ahora necesitas una
computadora...
*"Well, now you need a
computer . . ."*

—¿Qué **estaban haciendo**
las chicas?
"What were the girls doing?"

—**Estaban mirando** un
catálogo. Ana **me
estaba diciendo** que
quería un traje de
baño nuevo.
*"They were looking at a
catalogue. Ana was telling me
that she wanted a new bathing
suit."*

Note that direct and indirect object pronouns, as with other verb tenses, preceed the conjugated verb (**estar**) or are attached to the end of the **gerundio:** estaba diciéndo**me**.

Práctica

A. Tell what the following people were doing when a friend came to visit. Use the cues provided.

> *Modelo:* Elsa / hablar con Jorge
> Elsa **estaba hablando** con Jorge.

1. yo / beber un refresco
2. Uds. / mirar un catálogo
3. tu mamá / limpiar la máquina de escribir
4. Isabel / probarse el traje de baño nuevo
5. los niños / dormir
6. Marta / usar la computadora
7. Carlos y papá / jugar al tenis
8. tu hermana / escribir a máquina

B. With a classmate, talk about what everybody was doing when the professor arrived.

4 The preterit contrasted with the imperfect

El pretérito contrastado con el imperfecto

There are two simple past tenses in Spanish: the imperfect and the preterit. The difference between the two can be visualized this way.

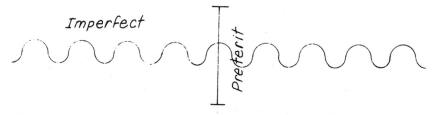

The continuous moving line of the imperfect represents an action or state that was taking place in the past. We don't know when the action started or ended. The vertical line of the preterit represents a completed or finished event in the past.

The following table summarizes the uses of the preterit and the imperfect.

Preterit	Imperfect
1. Records, narrates, and reports an independent past act or event as a completed and undivided whole, regardless of its duration. 2. Sums up a past condition or state viewed as a whole.	1. Describes an action in progress in the past. 2. Indicates a continuous and habitual action: *used to . . .*[1] 3. Describes a physical, mental, or emotional state or condition in the past. 4. Expresses time in the past. 5. Indicates age in the past.

The preterit

—¿Qué **compró** Ud. ayer?   *"What did you buy yesterday?"*

—**Compré** un sombrero y una cartera.   *"I bought a hat and a purse."*

—¿Su esposo **fue** a la tienda también?   *"Did your husband go to the store too?"*

—No, él **estuvo** enfermo todo el día. **Se quedó** en casa.   *"No, he was sick all day long. He stayed home."*

The imperfect

—Anteayer cuando **íbamos** a la zapatería, vimos a María Ortiz mirando vidrieras.   *"The day before yesterday as (when) we were going to the shoe store, we saw María Ortiz window shopping."*

—¿Sí? Ella y yo siempre **íbamos** juntas de vacaciones.   *"Really? She and I always used to go on vacation together."*

—¿Cuántos años **tenías** tú cuando viniste a los Estados Unidos?   *"How old were you when you came to the United States?"*

—**Tenía** quince años.   *"I was fifteen years old."*

---

[1] Note that this use of the imperfect also corresponds to the English *would*, when used to describe a repeated action in the past: **Cuando yo era niña,** *comía* **pollo** *todos los domingos.* *When I was a child, I used to eat chicken every Sunday. (When I was a child, I would eat chicken every Sunday.)*

—¿Por qué te fuiste tan temprano? **Eran** sólo las ocho de la noche.	*"Why did you leave so early?" It was only eight o'clock in the evening."*
—Me fui porque no **me sentía** muy bien.	*"I left because I wasn't feeling very well."*

ATENCIÓN: In the first exchange, **íbamos** describes an action in progress, while in the third exchange, **me sentía** describes a physical state. These verbs in the imperfect act as background for completed actions in the past, which are expressed by the preterit verbs **vimos** and **me fui**.

Práctica

A. Complete the following paragraph with the preterit or the imperfect of the verbs in parentheses, as appropriate.

_____ (Ser) las cuatro de la tarde cuando yo _____ (llegar) a casa ayer. _____ (Preparar) la cena y _____ (escribir) a máquina hasta las ocho. Roberto _____ (venir) a comer conmigo y después (*afterwards*) _____ (mirar) la televisión juntos. Roberto y yo _____ (vivir) en Lima cuando _____ (ser) niños, pero él _____ (irse) a Colombia cuando _____ (tener) quince años. A las diez Roberto _____ (decidir) irse y yo _____ (acostarse) porque no _____ (sentirse) muy bien.

B. With a partner, act out the following dialogues in Spanish.

1. "How old were you when you started to study at the university?"
   "I was seventeen years old."
2. "What time was it when you saw Maribel the day before yesterday?"
   "It was ten o'clock. She was going to the shoe store."
3. "Where did you and your family go on vacation when you were a child?"
   "We used to go to the beach together."
4. "Why did you leave, Anita?"
   "Because I wasn't feeling well."
5. "What did you buy yesterday?"
   "I bought a purse and a hat."

C. Interview a classmate, using the following questions. When you have finished, switch roles.

1. ¿Dónde vivías cuando tenías diez años?
2. ¿Hablabas inglés o español con tus amigos?
3. ¿Adónde ibas de vacaciones?
4. ¿Veías a tus abuelos a menudo?
5. ¿Adónde fuiste anoche?

6. ¿A quién viste?
7. ¿Qué hora era cuando volviste a tu casa ayer?
8. ¿Estuviste enfermo(a) ayer?
9. ¿Cómo te sentías hoy cuando saliste de tu casa?
10. ¿Te dijo tu profesor(a) hoy que hablabas bien el español?

D. With a partner, prepare a list of ten questions you would like to ask your teacher about his or her childhood and youth.

Palabras y más palabras

Match the questions in column **A** with the answers in column **B**.

A	**B**
1. ¿Dónde está el probador? _____	a. En la zapatería.
	b. En mi cartera.
2. ¿Cuándo vino tu cuñado?	c. No, solamente la
3. ¿Qué vas a comprar? _____	mañana.
4. ¿Por qué te quedaste en	d. Un par de zapatos.
tu casa? _____	e. Sí, lo compré ayer.
5. ¿Dónde se van a encontrar	f. Anteayer.
Uds.? _____	g. A la playa.
6. ¿Pasaron todo el día juntos?	h. En Perú.
_____	i. No, solamente de vez
7. ¿Qué estaban haciendo en el	en cuando.
centro commercial? _____	j. A la izquierda.
8. ¿Dónde pusiste el dinero?	k. Mirando vidrieras.
_____	l. No me sentía bien.
9. ¿Tu traje de baño es nuevo?	
_____	
10. ¿Dónde vivías tú en esa	
época? _____	
11. ¿Adónde ibas de vacaciones?	
_____	
12. ¿Veías a tus amigos a menudo?	
_____	

En el laboratorio

The following material is to be used with the tape or audio CD in the language laboratory.

I. Vocabulario

Repeat each word after the speaker. When repeating words that are cognates, notice the difference in pronunciation between English and Spanish.

COGNADOS:	el aeropuerto el catálogo la computadora el par
NOMBRES:	la cartera el centro comercial la joyería la máquina de escribir el probador el sombrero el traje de baño la vidriera el escaparate la zapatería los zapatos
VERBOS:	encontrarse con mirar quedarse sentirse
ADJETIVO:	nuevo
OTRAS PALABRAS Y EXPRESIONES:	anteayer de vez en cuando en casa en esa época escribir a máquina ir de vacaciones juntos mirar vidrieras pues todo el día

II. Práctica

A. Explain what these people used to do by changing the following sentences to the imperfect. Listen to the model.

Modelo: Mis abuelos hablan en español.
     Mis abuelos hablaban en español.

B. Answer the questions, using the cues provided. Repeat the correct answer after the speaker's confirmation. Listen to the model.

Modelo: —¿Qué estabas haciendo tú cuando yo llamé?
        (almorzar)
     —**Estaba almorzando.**

1. (mirar vidrieras)
2. (leer los catálogos)
3. (escribir a máquina)
4. (comprar zapatos)
5. (probarse el traje de baño)

C. Answer the questions, using the cues provided. Notice the use of the preterit or the imperfect. Repeat the correct answer after the speaker's confirmation. Listen to the model.

Modelo: —¿Qué hora era cuando él llegó? (las nueve)
     —**Eran las nueve cuando él llegó.**

1. (en casa)
2. (en México)
3. (esta mañana)
4. (en una fiesta)
5. (sí)

6. (que no podían venir)
7. (sí)
8. (no, pero vine)
9. (no)
10. (a Luisa)

III. Para escuchar y entender

1. The speaker will make some statements. Circle **L (lógico)** if the statement is logical and **I (ilógico)** if it is illogical. The speaker will verify your response.

1. L I
2. L I
3. L I
4. L I

5. L I
6. L I
7. L I
8. L I

2. Listen carefully to the dialogue. It will be read twice.

(*Diálogo 1*)

Now the speaker will make some statements about the dialogue you just heard. Tell whether each statement is true (**verdadero**) or false (**falso**). The speaker will confirm the correct answer.

3. Listen carefully to the dialogue. It will be read twice.

(*Diálogo 2*)

Now the speaker will ask you some questions about the dialogue you just heard. Answer each question, omitting the subject. The speaker will confirm the correct answer. Repeat the correct answer.

1. Changes in meaning with the imperfect and preterit of **conocer, saber,** and **querer**

2. **Hace** meaning *ago*

3. Uses of **se**

4. **¿Qué?** and **¿cuál?** used with **ser**

Vocabulario

COGNADOS

elegante elegant	**el portugués** Portuguese
la persona person	*(language)*
	el tipo type

NOMBRES
el anillo, la sortija ring
el anillo de compromiso
  engagement ring
el ascensor elevator
el camisón nightgown
la chaqueta jacket
el collar necklace
la corbata tie
la escalera stairs
la escalera mecánica
  escalator
la ferretería hardware store
la galería de arte art gallery
la moda fashion
la mueblería furniture store
el (la) nieto(a) grandson,
  granddaughter
el oro gold
la panadería bakery

la talla size
el tiempo time
el traje suit, outfit

VERBOS
  conocer to meet (for the
    first time)
  funcionar to work (*i.e., a
    machine, a motor, etc.*)
  usar to wear, to use

ADJETIVO
  mediano(a) medium

**OTRAS PALABRAS Y
EXPRESIONES**
  **¿Cuánto tiempo hace
  que... ?** ¿How long
  ago . . . ?
  sobre, de about

1 Changes in meaning with the imperfect and preterit of conocer, saber, **and** querer

Cambios de significado del imperfecto y del pretérito de conocer, saber y querer

In Spanish, a few verbs have different meanings when used in the preterit or the imperfect.

Preterit		Imperfect	
conocer		**conocer**	
conocí	*I met*	**conocía**	*I knew, I was acquainted with*
saber		**saber**	
supe	*I found out, I learned*	**sabía**	*I knew* (a fact, how to)
querer		**querer**	
no quise	*I refused*	**no quería**	*I didn't want to*

—Mario, ¿**conocías** a la nieta de Luisa?
      "Mario, did you know Luisa's granddaughter?"

—No, la **conocí** ayer en la mueblería.
      "No, I met her yesterday at the furniture store."

—Rita, ¿**sabías** que la escalera mecánica no funcionaba?
      "Rita, did you know that the escalator wasn't working?"

—No, lo **supe** esta mañana. Tuve que tomar el ascensor.
      "No, I found out this morning. I had to take the elevator."

—¿Por qué no fuiste a la galería de arte?
      "Why didn't you go to the art gallery?"

—Porque mi hermano **no quiso** llevarme. Tuve que quedarme en casa.
      "Because my brother refused to take me. I had to stay home."

Práctica

A. Complete the following dialogue, using the preterit or the imperfect of **saber, conocer,** or **querer,** as appropriate. Then act it out with a partner.

—¿Tú _____ a la nieta de la Sra. Ruiz?

—No, la _____ anteayer.

—¿Tú _____ que ella era la esposa de Roberto?

—No, lo _____ anoche. Me lo dijo Raquel.

—¿Alberto fue a la galería de arte ayer?

—Sí, fue. Él no _____ ir, pero su hermano lo llevó.

—¿Y Rosa? ¿Por qué no fue?

—Rosa no fue porque no _____.

B. With a partner, act out the following dialogues in Spanish.

1. "Why didn't Mario go to the furniture store?"
   "Because he didn't know that they were having a sale."
   "I found out (about it) this morning when I met (ran into)
   Carmen."
2. "Did Laura's grandson go to the concert?"
   "No, he refused to go. He stayed home."
   "I didn't want to go either. But I had to go with my
   husband."
3. "Did you know Mrs. Vega?"
   "No, I met her last night."
4. "I didn't know that the escalator was working."
   "I didn't know it either."

2 Hace meaning *ago*
Hace **como equivalente de** *ago*

In sentences in the preterit and in some cases the imperfect, **hace** +
period of time is equivalent to the English *ago*.[1]

> Llegué **hace dos años.**   *I arrived two years ago.*

When **hace** is placed at the beginning of the sentence, the construction is as follows.

Hace + *period of time* + **que** + *verb (preterit)*
Hace   **dos años**   **que**   **llegué.**

—¿Cuánto tiempo **hace que** Luis te dio el anillo de compromiso?	"How long ago did Luis give you the engagement ring?"
—**Hace dos meses que** me lo dio.	"He gave it to me two months ago."
—¿Cuánto tiempo **hace que** compraste esa corbata y esa chaqueta?	"How long ago did you buy that tie and that jacket?"
—**Hace tres semanas que** las compré.	"I bought them three weeks ago."

---

[1] The imperfect is used with **hacer** to mean *ago* in sentences such as *Hace dos años*, **yo
vivía en Buenos Aires** (*Two years ago, I lived in Buenos Aires*) in which the action or con-
dition described is not viewed as complete or finished.

Práctica

A. Interview a classmate, using the following questions. When you have finished, switch roles.

1. ¿Cuánto tiempo hace que empezaste a estudiar en esta universidad?
2. ¿Cuánto tiempo hace que comiste?
3. ¿Cuánto tiempo hace que tomaste un examen en una de tus clases?
4. ¿Cuánto tiempo hace que conociste a tu mejor amigo o amiga?
5. ¿Cuánto tiempo hace que fuiste a una fiesta?
6. ¿Cuánto tiempo hace que aprendiste a conducir?

B. With a partner, prepare six questions to ask your instructor. Use **hace** to mean *ago* in each question.

3 Uses of se
Usos de se

In Spanish, the pronoun **se** is used before the third person of the verb (either singular or plural, depending on the subject) when the person performing the action is not mentioned or is not known.

La panadería **se abre** a las ocho.	*The bakery opens (is opened) at eight.*
Las oficinas **se cierran** a las cinco.	*The offices close (are closed) at five.*

◆ Notice the use of **se** in the following impersonal constructions, announcements, and general directions.

—Quiero comprar un traje y un camisón. ¿A qué hora **se abren** las tiendas?	*"I want to buy a suit and a night-gown. What time do the stores open?"*
—**Se abren** a las diez.	*"They open at ten."*
—¿A qué hora **se cierra** la ferretería?	*"What time does the hardware store close?"*
—La ferretería **se cierra** a las nueve de la noche.	*"The hardware store closes at 9 P.M."*
—¿En Brasil **se habla** español?	*"Is Spanish spoken in Brazil?"*
—No, **se habla** portugués.	*"No, Portuguese is spoken (there)."*
—¿Te gusta el tipo de ropa que **se usa** ahora?	*"Do you like the type of clothes that is used (worn) today?*
—No, no me gusta. No es muy elegante.	*"No, I don't like it. It isn't very elegant."*

◆ **Se** is also used with the third person singular of the verb as the equivalent of *one, they,* or *people,* when the subject of the verb is not definite.

—¿Cómo **se dice**
  "*necklace*" en español?
—**Se dice** "collar".

"*How does one say* necklace *in Spanish?*"
"*One says* collar."

Práctica

Luis Otero, a student from Chile, is visiting your hometown and needs some information. Answer his questions, using a construction with **se.**

1. ¿A qué hora se abre la librería de la universidad?
2. ¿Se habla español aquí?
3. ¿Cómo se dice "*ferretería*" en inglés?
4. ¿A qué hora se cierra la cafetería?
5. ¿Se abren las oficinas de la universidad los sábados?
6. ¿A qué hora se cierra la oficina de correos?
7. ¿Se abren los bancos los sábados aquí?
8. ¿A qué hora se abre la biblioteca? ¿A qué hora se cierra?

4 ¿Qué? **and** ¿cuál? **used with** ser
¿Qué? y ¿cuál? **usados con el verbo** ser

◆ When asking for a definition, use **¿qué?** to translate as *what.*

—**¿Qué** es el oro?
—Es un metal amarillo.

"*What is gold?*"
"*It is a yellow metal.*"

◆ When asking for a choice, use **¿cuál?** (plural **¿cuáles?**) to translate as *what (which).* **¿Cuál?** implies selection from among many objects or ideas.

—**¿Cuál** es su talla?
—Mediana.

"*What is your size?*"
"*Medium.*"

—**¿Cuáles** son sus ideas
  sobre la moda?
—Yo no sé nada de moda.

"*What are your ideas about fashion?*"
"*I don't know anything about fashion.*"

Práctica

Write the questions that correspond to the following answers, using **qué** or **cuál (cuáles).**

1. —¿_____?
   —348-5490.
2. —¿_____?
   —Calle Victoria, número 1542.
3. —¿_____?
   —Es un metal amarillo.
4. —¿_____?
   —Una enchilada es un tipo de comida mexicana.
5. —¿_____?
   —¿Mis ideas sobre la educación? ¡Creo que es muy importante y necesaria!
6. —¿_____?
   —Rodríguez.
7. —¿_____?
   —Es un lugar donde hay muchas tiendas.
8. —¿_____?
   —Mediana.

Palabras y más palabras

Circle the word or phrase that best completes each sentence.

1. ¿Usaste la escalera mecánica o (el ascensor, la corbata)?
2. Me voy a acostar. ¿Dónde está mi (chaqueta, camisón)?
3. Pedro le dio a Raquel un (anillo, collar) de compromiso.
4. Vamos a la (ferretería, panadería) para comprar un pastel.
5. El ascensor no (trabaja, funciona).
6. Ernesto se va a poner el (traje, camisón) nuevo para ir a la
   galería de arte.
7. Le voy a regalar una (sortija, corbata) de oro.
8. Uso (talla, escalera) mediana.
9. En Brasil se habla (español, portugués).
10. (La talla, El tipo) de ropa que ella usa es muy elegante.
11. Estaban hablando sobre la (escalera, moda) francesa.
12. Compré la cama en la (ferretería, mueblería).

En el laboratorio

The following material is to be used with the tape or audio CD in
the language laboratory.

I. Vocabulario

Repeat each word after the speaker. When repeating words that
are cognates, notice the difference in pronunciation between
English and Spanish.

Cognados:	elegante la persona el portugués el tipo
Nombres:	el anillo la sortija el anillo de compromiso el ascensor el camisón la chaqueta el collar la corbata la escalera la escalera mecánica la ferretería la galería de arte la moda la mueblería el nieto el oro la panadería la talla el tiempo el traje
Verbos:	conocer funcionar usar
Adjetivo:	mediano
Otras palabras y expresiones:	¿Cuánto tiempo hace que... ? sobre de

II. Práctica

A. The speaker will give you information that you will use to say how long ago everything took place. Repeat the correct answer after the speaker's confirmation. Listen to the model.

Modelo: Son las cinco. Nora llegó a las cuatro y media.
Hace media hora que Nora llegó.

B. Answer the questions, using the cues provided. Repeat the correct answer after the speaker's confirmation. Listen to the model.

Modelo: —¿A qué hora se abre el banco? (a las diez)
—**El banco se abre a las diez.**

1. (a las nueve)
2. (portugués)
3. (oro)
4. (no)
5. (a las doce)
6. (un traje de baño)

III. Para escuchar y entender

1. The speaker will make some statements. Circle **L (lógico)** if the statement is logical and **I (ilógico)** if it is illogical. The speaker will verify your response.

1. L   I
2. L   I
3. L   I
4. L   I

5. L   I
6. L   I
7. L   I
8. L   I

2. Listen carefully to the dialogue. It will be read twice.

(*Diálogo 1*)

Now the speaker will make some statements about the dialogue you just heard. Tell whether each statement is true (**verdadero**) or false (**falso**). The speaker will confirm the correct answer.

3. Listen carefully to the dialogue. It will be read twice.

(*Diálogo 2*)

Now the speaker will ask you some questions about the dialogue you just heard. Answer each question, omitting the subject. The speaker will confirm the correct answer. Repeat the correct answer.

1. The past participle

2. The present perfect tense

3. The past perfect
   (pluperfect) tense

Vocabulario

COGNADOS

la gasolina gasoline	el mecánico mechanic
imposible impossible	el tanque tank

NOMBRES
el aceite oil
el acumulador, la batería
  battery
el club automovilístico
  auto club (*e.g., AAA*)
el (la) empleado(a) clerk,
  attendant
el freno brake
la gasolinera, la estación
  de servicio gas station
la goma, la llanta, el
  neumático tire
la goma pinchada flat tire
el limpiaparabrisas
  windshield wiper
el parabrisas windshield
la pieza de repuesto spare
  part
el remolcador, la grúa tow
  truck
el taller repair shop

VERBOS
arreglar to fix
cambiar to change
cubrir to cover
llenar to fill
romper to break

ADJETIVOS
abierto(a) open
cerrado(a) closed
listo(a) ready
vacío(a) empty

**OTRAS PALABRAS Y
EXPRESIONES**
casi almost
en seguida right away
recientemente recently
últimamente lately

1 The past participle
El participio pasado

Past participle   a past form of a verb that may be used in
conjunction with another (auxiliary) verb in certain past
tenses. The past participle may also be used as an adjective:
gone, worked, written

The past participle of regular verbs is formed by adding the following endings to the stem of the verb.

Past Participle Endings		
-ar *Verbs*	-er *Verbs*	-ir *Verbs*
habl- **ado**	ten- **ido**	ven- **ido**

◆ The following verbs have irregular past participles in Spanish.

abrir **abierto**   hacer **hecho**   ver **visto**
cubrir **cubierto**   morir **muerto**   volver **vuelto**
decir **dicho**   poner **puesto**   romper **roto**
escribir **escrito**

◆ In Spanish, most past participles may be used as adjectives. As such, they agree in number and gender with the nouns they modify.

—¿La gasolinera está **abierta**?   *"Is the gas station open?"*
—No, está **cerrada**.   *"No, it's closed. Do you*
  ¿Necesitas gasolina?   *need gas?"*
—No, tengo una goma   *"No, I have a flat tire and*
  pinchada y el parabrisas   *the windshield is broken."*
  está **roto**.

Práctica

A. What are the past participles of the following verbs?

1. dormir	6. cubrir	11. caminar	16. abrir
2. romper	7. recibir	12. pedir	17. ver
3. estar	8. hacer	13. decir	18. volver
4. comer	9. cerrar	14. comprar	19. aprender
5. poner	10. ser	15. morir	20. escribir

B. Using the elements from the two columns and the verb **estar,** create ten descriptive sentences. You may use a verb more than once.

Modelo: ventanas / cerrar
          Las ventanas **están cerradas.**

los hombres	pinchar
Pedro	arreglar
la gasolinera	cerrar
la carta	morir
los frenos	dormir
las puertas	escribir (en español)
el neumático	hacer (de madera)
la mesa	abrir
el parabrisas	romper

2 The present perfect tense
El pretérito perfecto

The present perfect tense is formed by using the present tense of the auxiliary verb **haber** and the past participle of the verb to be conjugated.

This tense is equivalent to the use in English of the auxiliary verb *have* + past participle, as in *I have spoken.*

Present of **haber**[1] *(to have)*	
he	hemos
has	
ha	han

The Present Perfect Tense			
	hablar	**tener**	**venir**
yo	**he** hablado	**he** tenido	**he** venido
tú	**has** hablado	**has** tenido	**has** venido
Ud. ⎫ él ⎬ ella ⎭	**ha** hablado	**ha** tenido	**ha** venido
nosotros	**hemos** hablado	**hemos** tenido	**hemos** venido
Uds. ⎫ ellos ⎬ ellas ⎭	**han** hablado	**han** tenido	**han** venido

—¿Está listo el coche?
"*Is the car ready?*"

—No, porque el mecánico todavía no **ha conseguido** las piezas de repuesto.
"*No, because the mechanic still hasn't obtained the spare parts.*"

—¿Le **ha puesto** un acumulador nuevo?
"*Has he put a new battery in it?*"

—Sí, y también **ha cambiado** los limpiaparabrisas y **ha arreglado** los frenos.
"*Yes, and he has also changed the windshield wipers and has fixed the brakes.*"

—¿**Han llamado** al club automovilístico?
"*Have you called the auto club?*"

—Sí, y el empleado **dice** que el remolcador viene en seguida.
"*Yes, and the clerk says that the tow truck is coming right away.*"

[1] Note that the English verb *to have* has two equivalents in Spanish: **haber** (used only as an auxiliary verb) and **tener.**

—¿**Han comprado** alguna vez esta marca de aceite?   *"Have you ever bought this brand of oil?"*

—No, nunca la **hemos comprado.**   *"No, we have never bought it."*

—¿**Has tenido** que llevar tu coche al taller recientemente?   *"Have you had to take your car to the repair shop recently?"*

—No, últimamente no **he tenido** problemas con el coche.   *"No, lately I have not had problems with my car."*

ATENCIÓN: Note that when the past participle is part of a perfect tense, it is invariable and cannot be separated from the auxiliary verb **haber.**

Práctica

A. Say what the subjects given have or haven't done.

1. yo / comprar / un limpiaparabrisas nuevo
2. el mecánico / arreglar / los frenos
3. tú / no llamar / al club automovilístico
4. ellos / venir / en seguida
5. nosotros / no ver / al empleado
6. Uds. / cambiar / las llantas

B. Interview a classmate, using the following questions. When you have finished, switch roles.

1. ¿Has comprado un coche alguna vez? (¿Cuánto te ha costado?)
2. ¿Cuántas veces (*times*) has cambiado el aceite de tu coche este año?
3. ¿Has tenido una goma pinchada alguna vez?
4. ¿Has cambiado una llanta alguna vez?
5. ¿Has cambiado los frenos de tu coche últimamente?
6. ¿Han tenido tú y tus amigos un accidente alguna vez?
7. ¿Han llamado una grúa alguna vez?
8. ¿Has tenido que comprar un acumulador últimamente?
9. ¿Has llevado tu coche al mecánico recientemente?

3 The past perfect (pluperfect) tense

El pluscuamperfecto

The past perfect tense is formed by using the imperfect tense of the auxiliary verb **haber** and the past participle of the verb to be conjugated.

This tense is equivalent to the use, in English, of the auxiliary verb *had* + past participle, as in *I had spoken*. As in English, the past perfect tense in Spanish describes an action or event completed before some other past action or event.

Imperfect of haber	
había	habíamos
habías	
había	habían

The Past Perfect Tense

	estudiar	beber	ir
yo	**había** estudi**ado**	**había** beb**ido**	**había ido**
tú	**habías** estudi**ado**	**habías** beb**ido**	**habías ido**
Ud. él ella	**había** estudi**ado**	**había** beb**ido**	**había ido**
nosotros	**habíamos** estudi**ado**	**habíamos** beb**ido**	**habíamos ido**
Uds. ellos ellas	**habían** estudi**ado**	**habían** beb**ido**	**habían ido**

—El tanque está casi vacío.	*"The tank is almost empty."*
—Eso es imposible. Carlos me dijo que lo **había llenado.**	*"That's impossible. Carlos told me that he had filled it."*
—Nosotros nunca **habíamos usado** esa marca de aceite.	*"We had never used that brand of oil."*
—¿Por qué la compraron?	*"Why did you buy it?"*
—Porque el mecánico nos **había dicho** que era muy buena.	*"Because the mechanic had told us that it was very good."*

Práctica

A. Complete the following dialogues, using the pluperfect of the verbs in parentheses. Then act them out with a partner.

1. —¿Por qué no le pusiste gasolina al coche?
   —Porque Javier ya _____ (llenar) el tanque.

2. —¿Hablaste con los empleados?
   —No, porque cuando yo llegué, (ellos) ya _____ (irse).
3. —¿Uds. _____ (viajar) a México en coche antes?
   —No, siempre _____ (ir) en avión.
4. —¿Tú _____ (usar) esta marca de gasolina?
   —No, nunca la _____ (usar).
5. —Cuando tú llegaste a casa, ¿tus padres ya _____ (venir)?
   —No, no _____ (llegar) todavía.
6. —¿Ya estaba listo el coche cuando llegaste?
   —No, porque ellos no _____ (traer) las piezas de repuesto.
   —¿Por qué _____ (ir) ellos a la gasolinera?
   —Porque el tanque estaba casi vacío.

B. Say what the subjects given had done to prepare for a car trip across the country.

1. el mecánico / los frenos
2. tú / el tanque
3. yo / la goma pinchada
4. mis padres / una batería nueva
5. mi hermano y yo / el coche

C. Tell a partner five things you had already done today by the time you arrived at Spanish class.

Cuando llegué a la clase de español, ya (*already*) **había tomado** cuatro tazas de café...

Palabras y más palabras

Say the following in a different way, using the vocabulary that you have learned in this lesson.

1. lo que se pone en el tanque de un coche
2. batería
3. gasolinera
4. lo que se usa para limpiar el parabrisas
5. llanta
6. grúa
7. lo que se usa para parar (*to stop*) el coche
8. persona que arregla coches
9. opuesto de posible
10. *Penzoil*, por ejemplo (*for example*)
11. opuesto de abierto
12. la AAA, por ejemplo

En el laboratorio

The following material is to be used with the tape or audio CD in the language laboratory.

I. Vocabulario

Repeat each word after the speaker. When repeating words that are cognates, notice the difference in pronunciation between English and Spanish.

COGNADOS:	la gasolina imposible el mecánico el tanque
NOMBRES:	el aceite el acumulador la batería el club automovilístico el empleado el freno la gasolinera la estación de servicio la goma la llanta el neumático la goma pinchada el limpiaparabrisas el parabrisas la pieza de repuesto el remolcador la grúa el taller
VERBOS:	arreglar cambiar cubrir llenar romper
ADJETIVOS:	abierto cerrado listo vacío
OTRAS PALABRAS Y EXPRESIONES:	casi en seguida recientemente últimamente

II. Práctica

A. Answer the questions in the affirmative, using the past participle of the verb in the question as an adjective in your response. Repeat the correct answer after the speaker's confirmation. Listen to the model.

> *Modelo:* —¿Terminaste la carta?
> —Sí, ya **está terminada.**

B. Change each sentence to the present perfect tense. Repeat the correct answer after the speaker's confirmation. Listen to the model.

> *Modelo:* Yo llamo al club automovilístico.
> **Yo he llamado al club automovilístico.**

C. Restate the model sentence according to the new subjects. Repeat the correct answer after the speaker's confirmation. Listen to the model.

Modelo: Yo no lo había hecho todavía.

1. (Uds.)
2. (nosotras)
3. (tú)

4. (Eva)
5. (ellos)
6. (Ud.)

III. Para escuchar y entender

1. The speaker will make some statements. Circle **L (lógico)** if the statement is logical and **I (ilógico)** if it is illogical. The speaker will verify your response.

1. L I
2. L I
3. L I
4. L I

5. L I
6. L I
7. L I
8. L I

2. Listen carefully to the narration. It will be read twice.

   (Narración)

   Now the speaker will make some statements about the narration you just heard. Tell whether each statement is true (**verdadero**) or false (**falso**). The speaker will confirm the correct answer.

3. Listen carefully to the dialogue. It will be read twice.

   (Diálogo)

   Now the speaker will ask you some questions about the dialogue you just heard. Answer each question, omitting the subject. The speaker will confirm the correct answer. Repeat the correct answer.

1. The future tense

2. The conditional tense

3. Some uses of the prepositions **a, de,** and **en**

Vocabulario

COGNADOS

automático(a) automatic	**el (la) veterinario(a)**
el examen exam	veterinarian

NOMBRES
la agencia de alquiler de
   automóviles car rental
   agency
el barco ship
el (la) cajero(a) cashier
el cajero automático automatic teller machine (ATM)
la cuenta account
la motocicleta, la moto
   motorcycle
el motor engine
el perro dog
la plata silver
el precio price
el reloj clock, watch
el tren train
la vez time (*in a series;*
  as equivalent of occasion)

VERBOS
alquilar to rent
cobrar to charge
depositar to deposit
revisar, chequear to check
terminar to finish

ADJETIVOS
hermoso(a) beautiful
peligroso(a) dangerous

OTRAS PALABRAS Y
EXPRESIONES
cambiar un cheque to
  cash a check
de cambios mecánicos
  with a standard shift
hasta until
sin falta without fail

1 The future tense
El futuro

The English equivalent of the Spanish future is *will* or *shall + verb*.
As you have already learned, Spanish also uses the construction **ir a**
+ *infinitive* or the present tense with a time expression to express future actions or states, very much like the English present tense or
the expression *going to.*

Vamos a ir al cine esta noche.	*We're going (We'll go)*
or: **Iremos** al cine esta noche.	*to the movies tonight.*
Anita **toma** el examen mañana.	*Anita is taking (will*
or: Anita **tomará** el examen mañana.	*take) the exam tomorrow.*

ATENCIÓN: The Spanish future is *not* used to make requests, as is the
  English future. In Spanish, requests are expressed with the verb
  querer.
    ¿Quieres llamar a Tomás?   *Will you call Tomás?*

Regular future forms

Most Spanish verbs are regular in the future. The infinitive serves as the stem of almost all Spanish verbs. The endings are the same for all three conjugations.

The Future Tense			
Infinitive		*Stem*	*Endings*
trabajar	yo	trabajar-	**é**
aprender	tú	aprender-	**ás**
escribir	Ud.	escribir-	**á**
hablar	él	hablar-	**á**
decidir	ella	decidir-	**á**
entender	nosotros	entender-	**emos**
caminar	Uds.	caminar-	**án**
perder	ellos	perder-	**án**
recibir	ellas	recibir-	**án**

ATENCIÓN: Notice that all the endings, except the one for the **nosotros** form, have written accent marks.

—¿Cómo **viajarán** Uds. de Los Ángeles a San Francisco?
"*How will you travel from Los Angeles to San Francisco?*"

—**Alquilaremos** un coche o **viajaremos** en tren.
"*We will rent a car or we will travel by train.*"

—¿Cuánto tiempo **estarán** en San Francisco?
"*How long will you be in San Francisco?*"

—Ana y yo **estaremos** allí por una semana y Jorge **se quedará** un mes. ¿Y adónde **irás** tú?
"*Ana and I will be there for a week and Jorge will stay for a month. And where will you go?*"

—**Iré** a San Diego. Dicen que es una hermosa ciudad.
"*I'll go to San Diego. They say it's a beautiful city.*"

Práctica

The following sentences say what everybody did. Rephrase them using the future tense to say what everyone will do.

1. Nosotros viajamos en tren.
2. Tú alquilaste un coche.
3. Yo fui a México.

4. Juan compró gasolina.
5. El empleado cambió el aceite.
6. Mis padres llamaron a la agencia de alquiler de automóviles.
7. Ud. consiguió las piezas de repuesto.
8. Estela cubrió el coche.
9. El mecánico volvió a la gasolinera.
10. Uds. llenaron el tanque.

Irregular future forms

A few verbs are irregular in the future tense. These verbs use a modified form of the infinitive as a stem. The endings are the same as the ones for regular verbs.

Infinitive	Stem		Future Tense	
decir	dir-	yo	**dir-**	é
hacer	har-	tú	**har-**	ás
saber	sabr-	Ud.	**sabr-**	á
querer	querr-	él	**querr-**	á
poder	podr-	ella	**podr-**	á
poner	pondr-	nosotros	**pondr-**	emos
venir	vendr-	Uds.	**vendr-**	án
tener	tendr-	ellos	**tendr-**	án
salir	saldr-	ellas	**saldr-**	án

♦ The future of **hay** (from the verb **haber**) is **habrá**.

—Mañana **tendré** que ir al banco para depositar un cheque. ¿Tú **podrás** llevarme?

"Tomorrow I'll have to go to the bank to deposit a check. Will you be able to take me?"

—Sí, pero no **vendré** por ti hasta las once porque tengo que trabajar.

"Yes, but I won't come for you until eleven because I have to work."

—¿Qué le **dirán** Uds. a Roberto?

"What will you tell Roberto?"

—Le **diremos** que **saldremos** de la agencia de alquiler de automóviles a las once.

"We will tell him that we'll be leaving the car rental agency at eleven."

—¿Qué **harán** después?

"What will you do afterwards?"

—**Iremos** al banco para cambiar un cheque.

"We will go to the bank to cash a check."

Práctica

A. Complete the following dialogues, using the future tense of the verbs in parentheses. Then act them out with a partner.

1. —¿Qué le _____ (decir) Uds. al empleado?
   —Le _____ (decir) que (nosotros) _____ (tener) que venir mañana.
   —¿Cuándo _____ (estar) listo el coche?
   —Nosotros lo _____ (saber) esta tarde.
2. —¿_____ (Poder) el mecánico traer el coche?
   —Sí, él me ha dicho que _____ (venir) mañana.
   —Muy bien, porque nosotros _____ (salir) para San José por la noche.
3. —¿Cuándo _____ (poder) Uds. depositar el cheque?
   —Lo _____ (hacer) esta tarde después de salir de la agencia de alquiler de automóviles.
4. —¿Qué _____ (hacer) Uds. el domingo?
   —_____ (Ir) a la fiesta que _____ (haber) en el club.
   —¿Qué te _____ (poner) para ir a la fiesta?
   —El traje azul.

B. Interview a classmate, using the following questions. When you have finished, switch roles.

1. ¿A qué hora llegarás a tu casa hoy?
2. ¿Vendrán tú y tus amigos a una fiesta en la universidad esta noche? (¿A cuál?)
3. ¿Habrá mucha gente (*people*)?
4. ¿A qué hora llegarás a tu casa hoy?
5. ¿Podrás venir a clase mañana?
6. ¿Qué más tendrás que hacer mañana?
7. ¿Qué harán tú y tus amigos el domingo?
8. ¿Adónde irás el verano próximo?

C. With a classmate, talk about your plans for the coming month. Use the future tense.

2 The conditional tense
El condicional

The conditional tense in Spanish is equivalent to the conditional in English, expressed by *would* + *verb*.[1] Like the future tense, the

---

[1] The imperfect, not the conditional, is used in Spanish as an equivalent of *used to:* **Cuando era pequeño siempre *iba* a la playa.** *When I was little **I would always go** to the beach.*

conditional uses the infinitive as the stem and has only one set of endings for all three conjugations.

Regular conditional forms

The Conditional Tense			
Infinitive		*Stem*	*Endings*
trabajar	yo	trabajar-	**ía**
aprender	tú	aprender-	**ías**
escribir	Ud.	escribir-	**ía**
ir	él	ir-	**ía**
ser	ella	ser-	**ía**
dar	nosotros	dar-	**íamos**
servir	Uds.	servir-	**ían**
estar	ellos	estar-	**ían**
preferir	ellas	preferir-	**ían**

—¿**Vendería** Ud. su coche por cinco mil dólares?

—No, yo no lo **vendería** por ese precio. **Preferiría** regalárselo a mi hijo.

"Would you sell your car for five thousand dollars?"

"No, I wouldn't sell it at that price. I would prefer to give it (as a gift) to my son."

◆ The conditional is also used to express the future of a past action; that is, the conditional describes an event that in the past was perceived as occurring in the future. In these cases, *would* in English carries the meaning *was going to.*

—¿Qué te dijo el mecánico ayer?

—Me dijo que **revisaría** el motor.

"What did the mechanic tell you yesterday?"

"He told me that he would (was going to) check the motor."

—¿Te dijo cuánto te **cobraría?**

—No, pero me dijo que no **costaría** mucho.

"Did he tell you how much he would charge you?"

"No, but he told me it wouldn't cost very much."

Práctica

Most people don't agree with Eduardo's ideas. Use the cues in parentheses to explain what the people named wouldn't do.

Modelo: Eduardo va a vender su coche. (yo)
Yo no lo vendería.

1. Eduardo va a revisar el motor del coche. (tú)
2. Eduardo va a ponerle una batería nueva al coche. (ellos)
3. Eduardo va a cobrar diez mil dólares por su coche. (Elsa)
4. Eduardo no va a regalarle el coche a su hija. (yo)
5. Eduardo va a comprar un coche nuevo por veinte mil dólares. (nosotros)
6. Eduardo va a trabajar en la agencia de alquiler de automóviles. (Uds.)

Irregular conditional forms

The same verbs that are irregular in the future are also irregular in the conditional. The conditional endings are added to the modified form of the infinitive.

Infinitive	Stem	Conditional Tense		
decir	dir–	yo	**dir–**	ía
hacer	har–	tú	**har–**	ías
saber	sabr–	Ud.	**sabr–**	ía
querer	querr–	él	**querr–**	ía
poder	podr–	ella	**podr–**	ía
poner	pondr–	nosotros	**pondr–**	íamos
venir	vendr–	Uds.	**vendr–**	ían
tener	tendr–	ellos	**tendr–**	ían
salir	saldr–	ellas	**saldr–**	ían

ATENCIÓN: The conditional of **hay** (from the verb **haber**) is **habría**.

—Mi coche no es automático. ¿Tú **podrías** manejarlo?

"*My car is not automatic. Would you be able to drive it?*"

—Sí, pero primero **tendría** que aprender a manejar coches de cambios mecánicos.

"*Yes, but first I would have to learn to drive cars with a standard shift.*"

—Mi hijo quiere comprar una motocicleta.

"*My son wants to buy a motorcycle.*"

—Yo le **diría** que las motocicletas son muy peligrosas.

"*I would tell him that motorcycles are very dangerous.*"

—Voy a abrir una cuenta en el Banco Nacional.

"*I'm going to open an account at the National Bank.*"

—Yo no **pondría** mi dinero en ese banco.

"*I wouldn't put my money in that bank.*"

Práctica

A. Complete the following dialogues, using the conditional of the verbs in parentheses. Then act them out with a partner.

1. —¿A qué hora _____ (salir) Uds.?
   —No _____ (salir) hasta las ocho.
   —Pero, entonces Uds. no _____ (poder) llegar a la agencia a las ocho y media.
   —Bueno, entonces nosotros _____ (tener) que salir antes.
2. —Teresa va a venir en autobús.
   —Yo no _____ (hacer) eso. Yo _____ (venir) en coche.
3. —¿Tú _____ (saber) arreglar el coche?
   —No, yo _____ (tener) que llevarlo al mecánico. Él lo _____ (poder) revisar.
4. —Quiero comprar una moto. ¿Qué crees tú que me _____ (decir) mamá?
   —Probablemente te _____ (decir) que las motocicletas son muy peligrosas.
5. —¿Tú _____ (poder) vender tu coche por diez mil dólares?
   —No, yo no _____ (poder) cobrar tanto. Mi coche es automático, pero no es nuevo.
6. —¿En qué banco _____ (depositar) tú el dinero?
   —Yo lo _____ (poner) en el Banco Nacional. Allí tengo yo mi cuenta.

B. With a partner, take turns telling each other what you would do if you won a million dollars in the lottery. Say at least five things each, and then compare your responses with those of other classmates.

3 Some uses of the prepositions a, de, **and** en
Algunos usos de las preposiciones a, de y en

◆ The preposition **a** (*to, at, in*) is used in the following ways.

1. To introduce the direct object when it is a person,[1] animal, or anything that is given personal characteristics

Esperamos **a** la cajera.	*We're waiting for the cashier.*
Llevé **a** mi perro al veterinario.	*I took my dog to the vet.*

---

[1] When the direct object is not a definite person, the personal **a** is not used: **Busco un buen maestro.**

2. To indicate the time (hour) of day

El coche estará listo **a** las cinco.	*The car will be ready at five.*

3. To express destination or result after verbs of motion when they are followed by an infinitive, a noun, or a pronoun

Siempre venimos **a** alquilar coches aquí.	*We always come to rent cars here.*

4. After the verbs **enseñar, aprender, comenzar,** and **empezar** when they are followed by an infinitive

Él dijo que me **enseñaría a** manejar.	*He said that he would teach me how to drive.*
Voy a **empezar a** arreglar el carro.	*I'm going to start fixing the car.*

5. After the verb **llegar,** when it expresses destination

Llegaremos **a** Lima mañana sin falta.	*We will arrive in Lima tomorrow without fail.*

◆ The preposition **de** (*of, from, about*) is used in the following ways.

1. To refer to a specific time of the day or night

Dijeron que terminarían a las ocho **de** la noche.	*They said that they would finish at eight in the evening.*

2. To distinguish one from a group when using superlatives

Mi sobrina es la más inteligente **de** la familia.	*My niece is the most intelligent in the family.*

3. To indicate possession or relationship

Ésta es la motocicleta **de** mi esposo.	*This is my husband's motorcycle.*
Carlos es el hijo **del** veterinario.	*Carlos is the vet's son.*

4. To indicate the material something is made of

El reloj es **de** plata.	*The watch is made of silver.*

5. To indicate origin

Ellos son **de** La Habana.	*They are from Havana.*

6. As a synonym of **sobre** or **acerca de** (*about*)

Hablaban **de** los precios   *They were speaking about the*
de las casas.   *prices of houses.*

◆ The preposition **en** (*at, in, on, inside, over*) is used in the following ways.

1. To refer to a definite place

Mi coche está **en** la   *My car is at the service station.*
gasolinera.

2. To indicate means of transportation

Muchas veces viajábamos   *We travelled by ship many*
en barco.   *times.*

3. As a synonym of **sobre** (*on*)

Los libros están **en** la   *The books are on the table.*
mesa.

ATENCIÓN: In Mexico and in most Spanish-speaking countries of Latin America, **por** (*by*) is used with certain means of transportation, whereas **en** is used with other means.

Vamos **por** barco. (*or* Vamos **en** barco.)
Vamos **por** avión. (*or* Vamos **en** avión.)
Vamos **por** tren. (*or* Vamos **en** tren.)
but
Vamos **en** autobús.
Vamos **en** automóvil.
Vamos **en** motocicleta.

Práctica

Complete the following dialogues, using **a**, **de**, or **en** as appropriate. Then act them out with a partner.

1. —¿ _____ qué hora llegarán Uds. _____ la agencia
   _____ viajes?
   —Llegaremos _____ las ocho y media _____ la mañana
   sin falta.
2. —¿ _____ quién esperan Uds.?
   —Esperamos _____ la cajera.
   —¿Dónde está ella ahora?
   —Está _____ la oficina _____ la agencia.
3. —¿No trajiste _____ tu perro?
   —No, está enfermo. Lo llevé _____ la veterinaria ayer.

4. —¿Para qué fueron Uds. _____ la agencia?
   —Fuimos _____ alquilar un coche _____ cambios mecánicos.
   —¿Tú sabes manejar ese tipo de coche?
   —No, pero mi hermano me va _____ enseñar _____ manejarlo.

5. —¿Quién es esa chica? ¡Es muy hermosa!
   —Es la hermana _____ Raúl. Es la chica más inteligente _____ la clase.
   —¿ _____ dónde es Raúl?
   —Creo que es _____ Perú.

6. —¿ _____ quién es el reloj que está _____ la mesa?
   —Es _____ Aurelio.
   —¿Es _____ plata?
   —No, es _____ oro blanco.

7. —¿ _____ qué estaban hablando Uds.?
   —Estábamos hablando _____ nuestras vacaciones.
   —¿Adónde fueron?
   —Fuimos _____ San Antonio.
   —¿Fueron _____ autobús?
   —No, fuimos _____ automóvil.

8. —¿Dónde está Teresa?
   —Está _____ el banco. Fue _____ cambiar un cheque.
   —¿Para qué necesitaba el dinero?
   —Para pagarle _____ un mecánico que arregló el motor _____ su coche.

Palabras y más palabras

Complete the following dialogues, using the vocabulary learned in this lesson. Then act them out with a partner.

1. —¿Cuál es el _____ de esa moto?
   —Cuesta doce mil dólares.

2. —Tengo que ir al banco para _____ un cheque.
   —Pues ve hoy sin _____ , porque el banco estará cerrado mañana.

3. —¿A qué hora comienza la clase?
   —Empieza a las dos y _____ a las tres.

4. —¿Cuánto dinero tenemos en nuestra _____ ?
   —Mil dólares, y hoy voy a depositar doscientos.

5. —¿Tu coche es automático?
   —No, es de _____ mecánicos.

6. —¿Le vas a comprar una motocicleta a tu hijo?
   —No, porque son muy _____ .

7. —Quiero alquilar un coche. ¿Quieres ir a la agencia de
   _____ de automóviles conmigo?
   —Si puedes esperar _____ las tres, voy contigo.
8. —¿Cuánto te _____ el mecánico por _____ el motor
   del coche?
   —Cincuenta dólares, pero dice que no puede arreglarlo.

En el laboratorio

The following material is to be used with the tape or audio CD in
the language laboratory.

I. Vocabulario

Repeat each word after the speaker. When repeating words that
are cognates, notice the difference in pronunciation between
English and Spanish.

COGNADOS:	automático el examen el veterinario
NOMBRES:	la agencia de alquiler de automóviles el barco el cajero el cajero automático la cuenta la motocicleta la moto el motor el perro la plata el precio el reloj el tren la vez
VERBOS:	alquilar cobrar depositar revisar chequear terminar
ADJETIVOS:	hermoso peligroso
OTRAS PALABRAS Y EXPRESIONES:	cambiar un cheque de cambios mecánicos hasta sin falta

II. Práctica

A. Rephrase each sentence, using the future tense instead of the expression **ir a** + *infinitive*. Repeat the correct answer after the
speaker's confirmation. Listen to the model.

  Modelo: Vamos a salir muy tarde.
      Saldremos muy tarde.

B. Answer the questions, always using the second choice. Repeat
the correct answer after the speaker's confirmation. Listen to the
model.

  Modelo: —¿Comprarías un coche o una casa?
      —**Compraría una casa.**

C. Answer the questions in complete sentences, using the cues provided. Repeat the correct answer after the speaker's confirmation. Listen to the model.

Modelo: —¿Cómo van ellos? (coche)
      —**Van en coche.**

1. (la cajera)
2. (las ocho)
3. (autobús)
4. (la mesa)

5. (las vacaciones)
6. (la agencia)
7. (Carlos)
8. (sí)

III. Para escuchar y entender

1. The speaker will make some statements. Circle **L (lógico)** if the statement is logical and **I (ilógico)** if it is illogical. The speaker will verify your response.

1. L   I
2. L   I
3. L   I
4. L   I
5. L   I

6. L   I
7. L   I
8. L   I
9. L   I
10. L   I

2. Listen carefully to the dialogue. It will be read twice.

   (*Diálogo 1*)

   Now the speaker will make some statements about the dialogue you just heard. Tell whether each statement is true (**verdadero**) or false (**falso**). The speaker will confirm the correct answer.

3. Listen carefully to the dialogue. It will be read twice.

   (*Diálogo 2*)

   Now the speaker will ask you some questions about the dialogue you just heard. Answer each question, omitting the subject. The speaker will confirm the correct answer. Repeat the correct answer.

¿Cuánto sabe usted ahora?

Lección 11   **A.** Time expressions with **hacer**

How would you say the following in Spanish?

1. "How long have you (*pl.*) been working in San Juan?"
   "We have been working in San Juan for five years."
2. "How long have they been waiting?"
   "They have been waiting for three hours."
3. "How long has she been studying Spanish?"
   "She has been studying Spanish for two years."

B. Irregular preterits

Rewrite the sentences, beginning with the expressions provided. Follow the model.

Modelo: Tenemos que salir. (Ayer)
       Ayer tuvimos que salir.

1. María no está en la clase. (Ayer)
2. No pueden venir. (Anoche)
3. Pongo el dinero en el banco. (El mes pasado)
4. No haces nada. (El domingo pasado)
5. Ella viene con Juan. (Ayer)
6. No queremos venir a clase. (El lunes pasado)
7. Yo no digo nada. (Anoche)
8. Traemos la tostadora. (Ayer)
9. Yo conduzco mi coche. (Anoche)
10. Ellos traducen las lecciones. (Ayer)

C. The preterit of stem-changing verbs (**e:i** and **o:u**)

Rewrite the sentences, beginning with the expressions provided. Follow the model.

Modelo: Él no pide dinero. (Ayer)
       Ayer él no **pidió** dinero.

1. Ella elige la secadora. (Ayer)
2. Marta no duerme bien. (Anoche)
3. No le pido nada. (Ayer)
4. Ella te miente. (La semana pasada)
5. Ellos sirven los refrescos. (El sábado pasado)

6. No lo repito. (Ayer)
7. Ella sigue estudiando. (Anoche)
8. Tú no consigues nada. (El lunes pasado)

D. The affirmative familiar command (**tú** form)

Change the commands from the **Ud.** (*formal*) form to the **tú** (*informal*) form. Follow the model.

Modelo: Salga con los niños.
            Sal con los niños.

1. Venga acá, por favor.
2. Hable con la profesora.
3. Dígame su dirección.
4. Lávese las manos.
5. Póngase el abrigo.
6. Tráiganos el arroz con pollo.
7. Compre los libros.
8. Hágame un favor.
9. Apague la luz.
10. Vaya de compras hoy.
11. Salga temprano.
12. Aféitese aquí.
13. Tenga paciencia.
14. Sea buena.
15. Coma con nosotros.

E. The negative familiar command (**tú** form)

How would you say the following in Spanish?

1. Don't tell (it to) him.
2. Don't go out now.
3. Don't get up.
4. Don't bring the dessert now.
5. Don't drink coffee.
6. Don't talk to them.
7. Don't go to the store.
8. That dress? Don't put it on!
9. Don't do that.

F. Vocabulary

Complete the following sentences, using words learned in **Lección 11.**

1. Ayer fui de _____ porque necesitaba un vestido.
2. Ana, _____ la luz, por favor.

3. Los domingos nosotros siempre comíamos _____ con pollo.
4. No me gusta hacer los _____ de la casa.
5. Ayer hubo una gran _____ en Sears. Todo estaba muy barato.
6. En _____ hora estamos en tu casa.
7. Vamos a tomar un taxi porque ella no quiere _____.
8. Nosotros casi _____ comemos carne.
9. Me voy a _____ del invitado porque se va.
10. ¿Vas a salir otra _____?

Lección 12   **A. En** and **a** as equivalents of *at*

Write sentences using the words provided with **en** or **a**, as appropriate. Follow the model.

Modelo: Yo / estar / universidad
        Yo estoy en la universidad.

1. Nosotros / llegar / aeropuerto / seis y media
2. Mi cuñada / estar / casa
3. Ellos / estar / joyería
4. La fiesta / ser / las doce
5. ¿Raúl / estar / clase?

B. The imperfect tense

Answer the following questions using the model as a guide.

Modelo: —¿Qué querían ellos? (arroz con pollo)
        —Querían arroz con pollo.

1. ¿Dónde vivían Uds. cuando eran chicos? (en Alaska)
2. ¿Qué idioma hablabas tú cuando eras chico(a)? (alemán)
3. ¿A quién veías siempre cuando eras chico(a)? (a mi abuela)
4. ¿En qué banco ponían Uds. el dinero? (en el Banco Nacional)
5. ¿A qué hora se acostaban ellos? (a las nueve)
6. ¿Adónde iba Rosa? (a la universidad)
7. ¿Qué compraba Ud.? (arroz)
8. ¿Qué enseñaba Elsa? (español)

C. The past progressive

Complete the sentences with the past progressive of **hacer, hablar, estudiar, comer, leer, trabajar, escribir,** or **comprar** as appropriate. Use each verb once.

1. Nosotros _____ arroz con pollo cuando llegó Elsa.
2. ¿Qué _____ tú cuando yo llamé?

3. Elena _____ a máquina cuando llegó el Dr. Vargas.
4. Yo _____ por teléfono (*on the phone*) con mi cuñado.
5. ¿Uds. _____ el reloj (*watch*) en la joyería?
6. Ud. _____ el periódico cuando yo vine.
7. Los niños _____ la lección.
8. Roberto _____ en la zapatería cuando yo lo vi.

D. The preterit contrasted with the imperfect

How would you say the following in Spanish?

1. We went to bed at eleven last night.
2. She was typing when I saw her.
3. We used to go to Lima every summer.
4. It was ten-thirty when I called my sister-in-law.
5. She said she wanted to read.

E. Vocabulary

Complete the following sentences, using words learned in **Lección 12.**

1. Mi hija compró ayer un _____ de baño nuevo.
2. Ellos vieron el sombrero en el _____ de JC Penney.
3. No podemos irnos. Tenemos que _____ aquí _____ el día.
4. Necesito la _____ de escribir.
5. Voy a _____ con Rosa a las cinco.
6. El mes pasado fuimos de _____ a México.
7. No quiero ir sola. ¿Por qué no vamos _____ tú y yo?
8. Tengo que estar en el _____ a las ocho porque el avión sale a las ocho y media.
9. Voy a probarme los _____ nuevos.
10. Nos gusta ir al centro _____ a mirar _____.

A. Changes in meaning with imperfect and preterit of **conocer,**   **Lección 13**
saber, and **querer**

Complete the sentences with the preterit or the imperfect of the verbs **conocer, saber,** and **querer,** as appropriate.

1. Yo no _____ a los abuelos de María. Los _____ ayer.
2. Nosotros no _____ que ella era casada. Lo _____ anoche.
3. Mamá no fue a la fiesta porque no _____ ir.
4. Yo no _____ ir a la fiesta, pero cuando _____ que Carlos iba a ir, decidí ir también.

B. Hace meaning *ago*

Write two sentences for each set of items. Follow the model.

Modelo: Un año / yo / conocer / él
Hace un año que yo lo conocí.
Yo lo conocí hace un año.

1. tres meses / nosotros / llegar / a California
2. dos horas / el chico / tomar / café
3. dos días / ellos / terminar / la lección
4. veinte años / ella / venir / a esta ciudad
5. dos días / tú / ver / a tu nieta

C. Uses of **se**

Answer the following questions

1. ¿Qué idiomas se hablan en los Estados Unidos?
2. ¿Cómo se dice *mattress* en español?
3. ¿A qué hora se cierra la oficina de correos?
4. ¿Cómo se escribe su nombre?
5. ¿A qué hora se abren las bibliotecas?

D. ¿**Qué**? and ¿**cuál**? used with **ser**

How would you say the following in Spanish?

1. What is a raincoat?
2. What is your address?
3. What is a library?
4. What is your telephone number?
5. What are his ideas about this?

E. Vocabulary

Complete the following sentences, using words learned in **Lección 13.**

1. Compré la mesa en la _____.
2. En Brasil se habla _____.
3. No voy a subir por la escalera; voy a usar el _____.
4. Carlos me llevó a la _____ de arte.
5. El anillo es de _____.
6. La escalera _____ no funciona.
7. Me voy a poner la _____ porque tengo frío.
8. Elena es mi _____. Es la hija de mi hijo.
9. Otro nombre para anillo es _____.
10. Teresa usa _____ mediana.

A. The past participle

Complete the following chart.

Infinitive	Past Participle
1. trabajar	1. trabajado
2. recibir	2. _____
3. _____	3. vuelto
4. usar	4. _____
5. escribir	5. _____
6. _____	6. ido
7. aprender	7. _____
8. _____	8. abierto
9. cubrir	9. _____
10. comer	10. _____
11. _____	11. visto
12. hacer	12. _____
13. ser	13. _____
14. _____	14. dicho
15. cerrar	15. _____
16. _____	16. muerto
17. _____	17. roto
18. dormir	18. _____
19. estar	19. _____
20. _____	20. puesto

B. Past participles used as adjectives

How would you say the following in Spanish?

1. The book is written in English.
2. The window is broken.
3. The door is open.
4. Are the banks closed?
5. The table is covered.

C. The present perfect tense

Complete the sentences with the present perfect of **hablar, hacer, abrir, venir, decir, estudiar, escribir, tener, poner, romper,** or **comer**, as appropriate. Use each verb once.

1. Yo _____ muchas veces a este lugar.
2. ¿_____ Uds. la lección?
3. Nosotros todavía no _____ con el mecánico.
4. Ella me _____ que tengo que venir el sábado y el domingo.

5. ¿No _____ (tú) las cartas todavía?
6. Hoy nosotros no _____ nada porque no _____ tiempo.
7. ¿Quién _____ las puertas?
8. ¿Dónde _____ Ud. las sillas?
9. Elena y Carlos no _____ todavía.
10. Ellos _____ el parabrisas.

D. The past perfect (pluperfect) tense

How would you say the following in Spanish?

1. I had already brought the battery.
2. They had not called the clerk.
3. They had broken the windows.
4. He had already seen the professor.
5. Had you covered the tables, Miss Peña?

E. Vocabulary

Complete the following sentences, using words learned in **Lección 14.**

1. Voy a la estación de _____ porque necesito comprar _____.
2. Otro nombre para batería es _____.
3. Tengo que llenar el tanque porque está casi _____.
4. Tengo que cambiar la _____ porque está _____.
5. Voy a llamar al club _____ porque necesito una grúa.
6. ¿Qué marca de _____ usa Ud.? ¿Penzoil?
7. La gasolinera no está abierta; está _____.
8. El coche no está listo todavía porque necesita varias piezas de _____.

Lección 15   A. The future tense

Complete the following sentences, using the future tense of the verb in parentheses.

1. ¿Cuándo _____ (ir) Uds. a la agencia de alquiler de automóviles?
2. El cajero _____ (venir) mañana a las ocho.
3. Ellos _____ (pagar) la cuenta el viernes.
4. ¿Tú _____ (llevar) al perro al veterinario?
5. El examen _____ (ser) mañana.
6. ¿Dónde _____ (poner) tú la moto?
7. Ellos _____ (manejar) mi coche.
8. El mecánico _____ (revisar) los frenos.
9. ¿Qué _____ (hacer) Uds. el domingo por la tarde?
10. Yo _____ (alquilar) un coche el próximo sábado.

B. The conditional tense

Complete the sentences with the conditional tense of **servir, poner, haber, trabajar, seguir, vender, levantarse, preferir,** or **ir.** Use each verb once.

1. Él dijo que nosotros _____ a Europa el verano próximo.
2. ¿Ellos _____ su casa a ese precio? Yo creo que sí.
3. ¿Dijo Ud. que no _____ clases esta tarde?
4. Yo no _____ el café en la terraza.
5. Tú no _____ en una gasolinera.
6. ¿_____ Ud. su dinero en ese banco?
7. ¿Qué _____ Uds.: ir a México o ir a Guatemala?
8. ¿_____ Uds. estudiando español?
9. ¿_____ tú a las tres de la mañana?

C. Some uses of the prepositions **a, de,** and **en**

How would you say the following in Spanish?

1. We won't arrive at the university at six.
2. Did you take your dog to the vet, María?
3. Later we will travel by plane.
4. She's at the car rental agency.
5. What are they talking about?

D. Vocabulary

Complete the following sentences, using words learned in **Lección 15.**

1. Necesito alquilar un coche. Voy a la _____ de alquiler de automóviles.
2. Mi mamá dice que las motocicletas son muy _____.
3. Yo no sé manejar coches de cambios _____; sólo sé manejar coches _____.
4. Voy al banco para _____ cien dólares en mi cuenta.
5. Los aretes de Rosalía no son de oro; son de _____.
6. El mecánico va a _____ el motor del auto.
7. Mañana sin _____ voy a llevar a mi perro al veterinario.
8. El _____ de español fue ayer.

1. The present subjunctive
2. The subjunctive with verbs of volition
3. The absolute superlative

Vocabulario

NOMBRES
el asiento seat
el boleto[1] ticket
el descuento discount
la estación de trenes train station
el fin de semana weekend
el itinerario, el horario schedule
el rápido, el expreso express train

VERBOS
  aconsejar to advise
  buscar to look for, to pick up, to get
  esperar to hope
  mandar to order
  negar (e:ie) to deny
  recomendar (e:ie) to recommend

reservar to reserve
rogar (o:ue) to beg
sugerir (e:ie) to suggest

ADJETIVOS
  bello(a) beautiful
  bueno(a) kind
  difícil difficult
  fácil easy
  largo(a) long
  lento(a) slow
  mareado(a) dizzy
  ocupado(a) busy
  rápido(a) fast

OTRAS PALABRAS Y EXPRESIONES
  cuanto antes as soon as possible
  por ciento percent
  sumamente extremely

1 The present subjunctive
El presente de subjuntivo

Uses of the subjunctive

While the indicative mood is used to express events that are factual and definite, the subjunctive mood is used to refer to events or conditions that the speaker views as uncertain, unreal, or hypothetical. Since the subjunctive mood reflects feelings or attitudes towards events or conditions, certain expressions of volition, doubt, surprise, fear, and so forth are followed by the subjunctive.

Except for its use in main clauses to express commands, the Spanish subjunctive is most often used in subordinate or dependent clauses.

The subjunctive is also used in English, although not as often as in Spanish. For example:

I suggest that he arrive tomorrow.

[1] Used when traveling by train or by bus.

The expression that requires the use of the subjunctive is in the main clause, *I suggest*. The subjunctive appears in the subordinate clause, *that he arrive tomorrow*. The subjunctive mood is used because the action of arriving is not yet realized; it is only what is *suggested* that he do.

There are four major concepts that require the use of the subjunctive in Spanish.

1. *Volition:* demands, wishes, advice, persuasion, and other impositions of will

Ella **quiere** que yo **compre** los boletos.	*She wants me to buy the tickets.*
Te **aconsejo** que **vayas** en el rápido.	*I advise you to go on the express train.*
Deseo que **vengas** con nosotros.	*I want you to come with us.*

2. *Emotion:* pity, joy, fear, surprise, hope, regret, etc.

Espero que Uds. **puedan** venir.	*I hope that you can come.*
Siento mucho que Luisa **esté** mareada.	*I'm very sorry that Luisa is dizzy.*

3. *Doubt, disbelief,* and *denial:* uncertainty, negated facts

Dudo que nos **den** un diez por ciento de descuento.	*I doubt that they'll give us a ten percent discount.*
No es verdad que el horario **cambie** la próxima semana.	*It isn't true that the schedule is changing next week.*
Ella **niega** que Juan **sea** su novio.	*She denies that Juan is her boyfriend.*

4. *Unreality:* expectations, indefiniteness, nonexistence

Busco a **alguien** que **pueda** hacerlo.	*I'm looking for someone who can do it.*
¿Hay **alguien** en la clase que **hable** alemán?	*Is there anyone in the class who speaks German?*
No hay **nadie** aquí que **sepa** su dirección.	*There is nobody here who knows his address.*

Formation of the present subjunctive

The present subjunctive is formed by dropping the **-o** from the stem of the first person singular of the present indicative and adding the following endings.

The Present Subjunctive of Regular Verbs		
-ar *Verbs*	**-er** *Verbs*	**-ir** *Verbs*
trabajar	**comer**	**vivir**
trabaj**e**	com**a**	viv**a**
trabaj**es**	com**as**	viv**as**
trabaj**e**	com**a**	viv**a**
trabaj**emos**	com**amos**	viv**amos**
trabaj**en**	com**an**	viv**an**

ATENCIÓN: Notice that the endings for **-er** and **-ir** verbs are the same.

The following table shows you how to form the first person singular of the present subjunctive from the infinitive of the verb.

Verb	First Person Singular (Indicative)	Stem	First Person Singular (Present Subjunctive)
habl**ar**	hablo	**habl-**	hable
aprend**er**	aprendo	**aprend-**	aprenda
escrib**ir**	escribo	**escrib-**	escriba
de**cir**	digo	**dig-**	diga
ha**cer**	hago	**hag-**	haga
tra**er**	traigo	**traig-**	traiga
ve**nir**	vengo	**veng-**	venga
cono**cer**	conozco	**conozc-**	conozca

Práctica

Give the present subjunctive of the following verbs.

1. **yo:**   comer, venir, hablar, hacer, salir, ponerse
2. **tú:**   decir, ver, traer, trabajar, escribir, conocer
3. **él:**   vivir, aprender, salir, estudiar, levantarse, hacer
4. **nosotros:** escribir, caminar, poner, desear, tener, afeitarse
5. **ellos:**   salir, hacer, llevar, conocer, ver, bañarse

Subjunctive forms of stem-changing verbs

Stem-changing **-ar** and **-er** verbs maintain the basic pattern of the present indicative. Their stems undergo the same changes in the present subjunctive.

recomendar *(to recommend)*		recordar *(to remember)*	
recomiende	recomendemos	recuerde	recordemos
recomiendes		recuerdes	
recomiende	recomienden	recuerde	recuerden
entender *(to understand)*		**mover** *(to move)*	
entienda	entendamos	mueva	movamos
entiendas		muevas	
entienda	entiendan	mueva	muevan

Stem-changing **-ir** verbs change the unstressed **e** to **i** and the unstressed **o** to **u** in the first person plural:

mentir *(to lie)*		dormir *(to sleep)*	
mienta	mintamos	duerma	durmamos
mientas		duermas	
mienta	mientan	duerma	duerman

Subjunctive forms of irregular verbs

dar	estar	saber	ser	ir
dé	esté	sepa	sea	vaya
des	estés	sepas	seas	vayas
dé	esté	sepa	sea	vaya
demos	estemos	sepamos	seamos	vayamos
den	estén	sepan	sean	vayan

◆ The subjunctive of **hay** (impersonal form of **haber**) is **haya**.

Práctica

Give the present subjunctive of the following verbs.

1. **yo:**   dormir, mover, cerrar, sentir, ser
2. **tú:**   mentir, volver, ir, dar, recordar
3. **ella:**   estar, saber, perder, dormir, ser
4. **nosotros:** pensar, recordar, dar, morir, cerrar
5. **ellos:**   ver, preferir, dar, ir, saber

2 The subjunctive with verbs of volition
El subjuntivo usado con verbos de deseo

All impositions of will, as well as indirect or implied commands, require the subjunctive in subordinate clauses. The subject in the main clause must be different from the subject in the subordinate clause.

◆ Some verbs of volition:

aconsejar	*to advise*	querer	
desear		recomendar	*to recommend*
mandar	*to order*	rogar	*to beg*
necesitar		sugerir	*to suggest*
pedir			

◆ Note the sentence structure for the use of the subjunctive in Spanish.

Yo quiero	que	*Ud.* estudie.
main clause		subordinate clause
I want		*you* to study.

—Quiero ir a Sevilla este fin de semana.
"*I want to go to Seville this weekend.*"

—Entonces **te aconsejo** que **compres** los boletos cuanto antes.
"*Then I advise you to buy the tickets as soon as possible.*"

—Sí, voy a **pedirle** a Ernesto que me **lleve** a la estación de trenes para comprarlos.
"*Yes, I'm going to ask Ernesto to take me to the train station to buy them.*"

—**Te sugiero** que **viajes** por la noche.
"*I suggest you travel at night.*"

—¿Por qué?
"*Why?*"

—Porque el tren de por la noche es más rápido.
"*Because the night train is faster.*"

—¿Qué quieren hacer Uds. hoy?
"*What do you want to do today?*"

—Queremos ir al aeropuerto para reservar los asientos para el vuelo del sábado.
"*We want to go to the airport to reserve the seats for the Saturday flight.*"

—Yo no puedo ir con Uds. porque mi hermano **quiere** que **vaya a** la estación a buscarle un itinerario.	*"I can't go with you because my brother wants me to go to the station to get him a schedule."*

ATENCIÓN: If there is no change of subject, the infinitive is used.

—¿Adónde quiere **ir** Ud.?
—Quiero **ir** a Sevilla.

Práctica

A. Change the following sentences according to the new beginnings.

Modelo: Yo quiero buscar los libros. Yo quiero que tú...
Yo quiero que tú **busques**[1] los libros.

1. Nosotros queremos comprar los boletos.
   Nosotros queremos que Uds...
2. Yo necesito reservar un asiento.
   Yo necesito que tú...
3. Ella desea ir a la estación de trenes.
   Ella desea que nosotros...
4. ¿Ud. quiere tomar el rápido?
   ¿Ud. quiere que ellos...?
5. Mis padres desean conseguir un itinerario.
   Mis padres desean que yo...
6. Oscar necesita estar allí a las diez.
   Oscar necesita que Ud...
7. Carlos quiere ir a buscar a su hermana.
   Carlos quiere que Marta...

B. Use your imagination to complete the following sentences, using the infinitive or the subjunctive, as appropriate.

1. Yo le sugiero a mi amigo(a) que...
2. Ellos necesitan que tú...
3. Nosotros queremos...
4. Mis padres me ruegan que...
5. Yo necesito...
6. El (La) profesor(a) nos manda que...
7. Yo les recomiendo que...
8. Mi hermano(a) desea...
9. Yo te pido que...
10. Mi madre siempre me aconseja que...

[1] Verbs ending in **-car** change **c** to **qu** in the present subjunctive. For other verbs with orthographic changes, see Appendix B, p. 315.

C. With a partner, act out the following dialogues in Spanish.

1. "My friend needs the tickets."
   "I suggest that you give them to him as soon as possible, Anita."
2. "I need to be in Seville this afternoon."
   "I advise you to take the express train, miss."
3. "I'm dizzy."
   "Then I recommend that you lie down, Miss Vega."
4. "I want to go to the airport to reserve a seat."
   "Why don't you ask your friend to do it, Paquito?"
5. "I recommend that you travel during the weekend, sir."
   "Why?"
   "Because you can get a ten percent discount."

3 The absolute superlative
El superlativo absoluto

In Spanish, there are two ways of expressing a high degree of a given quality without comparing one person or thing to another.

◆ By modifying the adjective with an adverb **(muy, sumamente).**

—¿Cómo estuvo el vuelo?	*"How was the flight?"*
—Estuvo **muy** aburrido y fue **sumamente** largo.	*"It was very boring and extremely long."*

◆ By adding the suffix **-ísimo (-a, -os, -as)** to the adjective. This form is known as the absolute superlative. If the word ends in a vowel, the vowel is dropped before adding the suffix. Notice that the **í** of the suffix always has a written accent.

alt**o**	alt-	**í**simo	alt**í**simo
ocupad**a**	ocupad-	**í**sima	ocupad**í**sima
lent**os**	lent-	**í**simos	lent**í**simos
buen**as**	buen-	**í**simas	buen**í**simas
difícil	dificil-	**í**simo	dificil**í**simo
ric**a**	riqu-[1]	**í**sima	riqu**í**sima
larg**os**	largu-[1]	**í**simos	largu**í**simos

—¿Fuiste a Madrid el verano pasado?	*"Did you go to Madrid last summer?"*
—Sí, es una ciudad **bellísima,** pero no es fácil conducir allí. ¡Es **dificilísimo!**	*"Yes, it is a very beautiful city, but it is not easy to drive there. It is extremely difficult!"*

[1] This is an orthographic change.

—¿Pueden ir al aero-
puerto con nosotros?

—No, estamos
ocupadísimas.

*"Can you go to the airport
with us?"*

"No, we are extremely busy."

Práctica

Change the underlined words in the following sentences to the absolute superlative.

1. Mi novia es <u>muy bella.</u>
2. Mi novio es <u>sumamente alto.</u>
3. Ellos están <u>muy ocupados.</u>
4. Es <u>muy fácil</u> llegar a la estación de trenes.
5. Ellas son <u>muy buenas.</u>
6. La cajera está <u>sumamente ocupada.</u>
7. Ellos son <u>muy lentos.</u>
8. Las clases son <u>sumamente difíciles</u> allí.
9. Ella está <u>sumamente aburrida.</u>
10. El tren es <u>muy rápido.</u>

Palabras y más palabras

Match the questions in column **A** with the answers in column **B.**

A

1. ¿Vas a viajar en tren? _____
2. ¿Qué descuento te dieron?
3. ¿Cuándo vas a reservar el asiento? _____
4. ¿Qué me recomiendas? _____
5. ¿Cómo estuvo el examen? _____
6. ¿Por qué no viajan en ese tren? _____
7. ¿Se siente mal? _____
8. ¿Adónde van de vacaciones? _____
9. ¿A qué hora sale el rápido? _____
10. ¿Quieres que llame a Rosa? _____
11. Tú comes mucho, ¿no? _____
12. ¿Cómo es Elsa? _____

B

a. Que vayas hoy mismo.
b. ¡Es muy lento!
c. Esperamos ir a Bogotá.
d. Sí, te ruego que lo hagas en seguida.
e. No sé. No tengo el itinerario.
f. Cuanto antes.
g. Sumamente difícil.
h. Sí, no lo niego.
i. Sí, y espero conseguir boleto en el expreso.
j. Muy buena.
k. Sí, está mareada.
l. El diez por ciento.

En el laboratorio

The following material is to be used with the tape or audio CD in the language laboratory.

I. Vocabulario

Repeat each word after the speaker.

NOMBRES:	el asiento el boleto el descuento la estación de trenes el fin de semana el itinerario el horario el rápido el expreso
VERBOS:	aconsejar buscar esperar mandar negar recomendar reservar rogar sugerir
ADJETIVOS:	bello bueno difícil fácil largo lento mareado ocupado rápido
OTRAS PALABRAS Y EXPRESIONES:	cuanto antes por ciento sumamente

II. Práctica

A. Say what Carmen wants everybody to do, using the present subjunctive and the cues provided. Repeat the correct answer after the speaker's confirmation. Listen to the model.

Modelo: ¿Qué quiere Carmen que yo haga? (reservar el asiento)
Quiere que Ud. reserve el asiento.

1. (comprar los boletos)
2. (ir a la estación de trenes)
3. (buscar el horario)
4. (darle un descuento)
5. (estar aquí a las dos)
6. (pedir un itinerario)
7. (viajar en el rápido)
8. (venir cuanto antes)
9. (cerrar la puerta)
10. (volver mañana)

B. Rephrase each sentence, changing **muy** + *adjective* to the absolute superlative. Repeat the correct answer after the speaker's confirmation. Listen to the model.

Modelo: Mi novio es muy alto.
Mi novio es altísimo.

III. Para escuchar y entender

1. The speaker will make some statements. Circle **L (lógico)** if the statement is logical and **I (ilógico)** if it is illogical. The speaker will verify your response.

1. L I			5. L I	
2. L I			6. L I	
3. L I			7. L I	
4. L I			8. L I	

2. Listen carefully to the narration. It will be read twice.

(*Narración*)

Now the speaker will make some statements about the narration you just heard. Tell whether each statement is true (**verdadero**) or false (**falso**). The speaker will confirm the correct answer.

3. Listen carefully to the dialogue. It will be read twice.

(*Diálogo 1*)

Now the speaker will make some statements about the dialogue you just heard. Tell whether each statement is true (**verdadero**) or false (**falso**). The speaker will confirm the correct answer.

4. Listen carefully to the dialogue. It will be read twice.

(*Diálogo 2*)

Now the speaker will ask you some questions about the dialogue you just heard. Answer each question, omitting the subject. The speaker will confirm the correct answer. Repeat the correct answer.

1. The subjunctive to express emotion

2. The subjunctive with some impersonal expressions

3. Formation of adverbs

Vocabulario

COGNADOS

la **calculadora** calculator
el **contrato** contract
  especial special
  general general
la **literatura** literature

necesario(a) necessary
posible possible
probable probable
reciente recent

NOMBRES
el (la) **abogado(a)** lawyer
la **beca** scholarship
la **conferencia** lecture
el (la) **consejero(a)** adviser
el **examen final** final exam
el **examen parcial**
  midterm exam
la **física** physics
la **matrícula** tuition
la **nota** grade
la **química** chemistry
el **requisito** requirement

VERBOS
  alegrarse (de) to be glad
  firmar to sign
  matricularse to register
  sentir (e:ie) to regret,
    to be sorry
  temer to fear

ADJETIVOS
  claro(a) clear
  cuidadoso(a) careful

OTRAS PALABRAS Y
EXPRESIONES
  conviene it is advisable
  es difícil it's unlikely
  es (una) lástima it is a
    pity
  es mejor it is better
  es seguro it is certain
  ojalá if only . . . , I hope
  pronto soon
  puede ser it may be
  sacar una nota to get a
    grade

1 The subjunctive to express emotion

El subjuntivo para expresar emoción

In Spanish, the subjunctive is always used in a subordinate clause when the verb in the main clause expresses any kind of emotion, such as fear, joy, pity, hope, pleasure, surprise, anger, regret, and sorrow.

◆ Some verbs of emotion:

alegrarse (de)   *to be glad*

esperar   *to hope*

sentir (e:ie)   *to regret, to be sorry*

temer   *to fear*

—¿Vas a hablar con tu
  consejero hoy?
—Sí, y **espero** que me **diga**
  qué requisitos generales
  debo tomar.

"*Are you going to talk with
your adviser today?*"
"*Yes, and I hope he'll tell me
what general requirements I
have to take.*"

—¿Vas a tomar la clase de
  literatura española?
—Sí, ya me matriculé.
—**Me alegro** de que
  podamos tomarla juntos.

"*Are you going to take the
Spanish literature class?*"
"*Yes, I registered already.*"
"*I'm glad that we can take
it together.*"

—Mañana tengo dos
  exámenes parciales, uno
  en química y otro en
  física. **Temo** que mis
  notas no **sean** buenas.
—Entonces tienes que
  estudiar. **Siento** que no
  puedas ir con nosotros
  a la conferencia.

"*Tomorrow I have two midterm
exams, one in chemistry and
the other in physics. I'm afraid
that my grades won't be good.*"

"*Then you have to study. I'm
sorry that you can't go with
us to the lecture.*"

ATENCIÓN: The subject of the subordinate clause must be different
from that of the main clause for the subjunctive to be used. If
there is no change of subject, the infinitive is used instead.

—¿Vas a terminar el trabajo
  para las cinco?
—Temo no **poder** terminarlo
  tan pronto.

"*Are you going to finish the
work by five?*"
"*I'm afraid I won't be able
to finish it so soon.*"

—Tengo el examen final
  mañana.
—Espero que **saques** una
  buena nota.

"*I have the final exam
tomorrow.*"
"*I hope that you get a good
grade.*"

Práctica

A. Complete the dialogues, using the infinitive or the present subjunctive as appropriate. Then act them out with a partner.

1. —Temo no _____ (poder) ir a la conferencia con Uds.
   —Espero que tú _____ (poder) ir la semana que viene.

2. —Esperamos _____ (sacar) una buena nota en el examen final.
   —Temo que Uds. no _____ (poder) estudiar mucho.
3. —No puedo matricularme en la clase de literatura.
   —Siento que tú no _____ (tomar) la clase conmigo.
   —Yo también siento no _____ (poder) tomarla.
4. —Jorge se alegra de no _____ (tener) que tomar la clase de física.
   —Espero que tampoco (él) _____ (tener) que tomar la de química.
5. —Me alegro de _____ (ver) que has sacado una buena nota en literatura.
   —¡Espero _____ (poder) sacar una buena nota en química!

B. Use your imagination to complete the following sentences with either the subjunctive or the infinitive, as appropriate.

1. Yo espero que mi profesor(a)…
2. Nosotros nos alegramos de…
3. Yo temo…
4. Siento que Uds…
5. Ellos sienten no…
6. Yo me alegro de que mis padres…
7. Nosotros tememos que…
8. Mis amigos se alegran de que…

2 The subjunctive with some impersonal expressions

El subjuntivo con algunas expresiones impersonales

In Spanish, some impersonal expressions that convey emotion, uncertainty, unreality, or an indirect or implied command are followed by a verb in the subjunctive. This occurs only when the verb of the subordinate clause has an expressed subject. The most common impersonal expressions include the following.

conviene	*it is advisable*	**es mejor**	*it is better*
es difícil	*it is unlikely*	**es necesario**	*it is necessary*
es importante	*it is important*	**ojalá**	*if only . . . !* or *I hope . . .*
es (im)posible	*it is (im)possible*	**puede ser**	*it may be*
es (una) lástima	*it is a pity*		

—¿Crees que va a llover
   mañana?
—**Ojalá** que no **llueva**
   porque **es posible** que
   Enrique me **lleve** al
   partido de tenis.

*"Do you think it's going to
rain tomorrow?"*
*"I hope it won't rain, because
it's possible that Enrique will
take me to the tennis
match."*

—¿Viene hoy el abogado?
—**Es difícil** que **venga** hoy.

"Is the lawyer coming today?"
*"It is unlikely that he'll come
today."*

—¿Cuándo quiere Ud. que
   yo escriba las cartas?
—**Es importante** que las
   escriba hoy.

*"When do you want me to
write the letters?"*
*"It is important that you
write them today."*

—¿Cuándo quiere Ud. que
   los estudiantes tomen el
   examen?
—**Es mejor** que lo **tomen**
   en seguida.

*"When do you want the
students to take the exam?"*

*"It is better that they take
it right away."*

—**Es lástima** que Ud. no
   pueda conseguir una beca.
—Sí, porque yo no tengo
   dinero para pagar la
   matrícula.

*"It is a pity that you can't get
a scholarship."*
*"Yes, because I don't have
money to pay the tuition."*

—¿Cuándo tengo que
   matricularme?
—**Es necesario** que **se
   matricule** hoy.

"When do I have to register?"

*"It is necessary that you
register today."*

ATENCIÓN: When the impersonal expression implies certainty, the
   indicative is used.

—¿Vienen ellos hoy?
—Sí, **es seguro** que **vienen**
   hoy.

"Are they coming today?"
*"Yes, it is certain that they'll
come today."*

When a sentence is completely impersonal (that is, when no
subject is stated), the expressions on page 256 are followed by the
infinitive.

—¿Cuándo vamos a firmar
   el contrato?
—**Conviene firmarlo** esta
   semana.

*"When are we going to sign
the contract?"*
*"It is advisable to sign it
this week."*

Práctica

A. Complete the following sentences using the infinitive, the indicative, or the subjunctive.

1. Conviene que Uds. _____ (tomar) los requisitos ahora.
2. Es imposible _____ (matricularse) a esta hora.
3. Es mejor que ellos no _____ (ir) a la conferencia.
4. Ojalá que el consejero _____ (venir) pronto.
5. Es seguro que la profesora nos _____ (dar) un examen parcial hoy.
6. Es difícil que él _____ (conseguir) una beca.
7. Es seguro que la abogada _____ (tener) el contrato.
8. Es importante _____ (ir) a la conferencia de hoy.

B. With a partner, act out the following dialogues in Spanish.

1. "I don't know what classes to take . . ."
   "It's advisable to take the general requirements first."
2. "Will the lawyer be here today?"
   "It's unlikely that he'll come today."
3. "It's a pity that Marta can't pay the tuition."
   "I hope that she gets a scholarship."
4. "Do you think it's necessary to see the adviser?"
   "Yes, it's very important to speak with her."
5. "It may be that they'll sign the contract tomorrow."
   "I hope their lawyer can be there."

3 Formation of adverbs
Formación de adverbios

> **Adverb** a word that modifies a verb, an adjective, or another adverb. It answers the questions "How?", "When?", "Where?": She walked **slowly**. She'll be here **tomorrow**. She is **here**.

Most Spanish adverbs are formed by adding **-mente** (the equivalent of *-ly* in English) to the adjective.

especial *special*	especial**mente** *specially, especially*
reciente *recent*	reciente**mente** *recently*
probable *probable*	probable**mente** *probably*
general *general*	general**mente** *generally*

◆ If the adjective ends in **-o**, the ending changes to **-a** before adding **-mente.**

lent**o** *slow*   lent**amente** *slowly*
rápid**o** *rapid*   rápid**amente** *rapidly*
clar**o** *clear*   clar**amente** *clearly*

◆ If two or more adverbs are used together, both change the **-o** to **-a,** but only the last adverb takes the **-mente** ending.

lent**a** y cuidados**amente**   *slowly and carefully*

◆ If the adjective has a written accent mark, the corresponding adverb retains it.

fácil   fácilmente

—Traje esta calculadora   *"I brought this calculator*
  especialmente para Ud.   *especially for you."*
—Gracias.   *"Thanks."*

—El niño escribe la carta   *"The child is writing the letter*
  lenta y **cuidadosamente.**   *slowly and carefully."*
—¡Pero la escribe muy   *"But he is writing it very*
  bien!   *well!"*

Práctica

A. Complete the following sentences, using appropriate adverbs.

1. Ella habló _____ y _____, pero no le entendí.
2. _____ ellos van a tomar el examen hoy.
3. _____ estudio por la noche.
4. Compré una calculadora _____.
5. Ellos caminan _____.
6. Trajo los libros de literatura _____ para mí.
7. Ellos escriben _____.

B. How would you say the following sentences in Spanish?

1. She reads slowly.
2. Do it carefully, Miss Peña.
3. The chair is especially for you, sir.
4. She is going to do it rapidly, but carefully.
5. When did you see it, ma'am? Recently?
6. The lesson? We can translate it easily.

Palabras y más palabras

Circle the word or phrase that best completes each sentence.

1. No tengo que pagar la matrícula porque me dieron una (beca/nota).
2. Voy a firmar (el contrato/la química).
3. La (química/abogada) es un requisito.
4. Ojalá que ellos puedan venir (claro/pronto).
5. Para sacar una buena nota, es (necesario/lástima) estudiar mucho.
6. Para saber qué clases debo tomar, voy a hablar con mi (abogado/consejero).
7. (Siento/Conviene) que Uds. estén enfermos.
8. El examen (parcial/cuidadoso) es mañana.
9. Estudiamos las ideas de Isaac Newton en la clase de (literatura/física).
10. Fui a una (calculadora/conferencia) que hubo en la universidad.

En el laboratorio

The following material is to be used with the tape or audio CD in the language laboratory.

I. Vocabulario

Repeat each word after the speaker. When repeating words that are cognates, notice the difference in pronunciation between English and Spanish.

COGNADOS:	la calculadora el contrato especial general la literatura necesario posible probable reciente
NOMBRES:	el abogado la beca la conferencia el consejero el examen final el examen parcial la física la matrícula la nota la química el requisito
VERBOS:	alegrarse de firmar matricularse sentir temer
ADJETIVOS:	claro cuidadoso
OTRAS PALABRAS Y EXPRESIONES:	conviene es difícil es una lástima es mejor es seguro ojalá pronto puede ser sacar una nota

II. Práctica

A. Restate each of the following sentences, inserting the cue at the beginning and making any necessary changes. Repeat the correct answer after the speaker's confirmation. Listen to the model.

Modelo: El cliente firma el contrato. (Espero)
Espero que el cliente firme el contrato.

1. (Temo)
2. (Espero)
3. (Siento)
4. (Temo)
5. (Me alegro de)
6. (Espero)
7. (Espero)
8. (Me alegro de)

B. Restate each of the following sentences, inserting the cue at the beginning and making any necessary changes. Repeat the correct answer after the speaker's confirmation. Listen to the model.

Modelo: Él conduce muy rápido. (Es difícil)
Es difícil que él conduzca muy rápido.

1. (No conviene)   5. (Puede ser)
2. (Es necesario)   6. (Ojalá)
3. (Es imposible)   7. (Es una lástima)
4. (Es mejor)   8. (Es importante)

C. Give the adverb that corresponds to each adjective. Repeat the correct answer after the speaker's confirmation. Listen to the model.

Modelo: especial
especialmente

III. Para escuchar y entender

1. The speaker will make some statements. Circle **L (lógico)** if the statement is logical and **I (ilógico)** if it is illogical. The speaker will verify your response.

1. L I   5. L I
2. L I   6. L I
3. L I   7. L I
4. L I   8. L I

2. Listen carefully to the dialogue. It will be read twice.

   (Diálogo 1)

   Now the speaker will make some statements about the dialogue you just heard. Tell whether each statement is true **(verdadero)** or false **(falso)**. The speaker will confirm the correct answer.

3. Listen carefully to the dialogue. It will be read twice.

   (Diálogo 2)

   Now the speaker will make some statements about the dialogue you just heard. Tell whether each statement is true **(verdadero)** or false **(falso)**. The speaker will confirm the correct answer.

4. Listen carefully to the dialogue. It will be read twice.

   (Diálogo 3)

   Now the speaker will ask you some questions about the dialogue you just heard. Answer each question, omitting the subject. The speaker will confirm the correct answer. Repeat the correct answer.

1. The subjunctive to express doubt, disbelief, and denial

2. The subjunctive to express indefiniteness and nonexistence

3. Diminutive suffixes

Vocabulario

COGNADOS

la ambulancia ambulance	**la emergencia** emergency
el (la) dentista dentist	**el (la) paramédico(a)** paramedic

NOMBRES
el árbol tree
el consultorio doctor's office
el dolor pain
la inyección shot, injection
la muleta crutch
la Navidad Christmas
el (la) paciente patient
la pierna leg
la radiografía X-ray
la sala ward room
la sala de emergencia emergency room
la sala de rayos X X-ray room
el tiempo time
el tobillo ankle

VERBOS
cuidar to take care
dudar to doubt
enyesar to put a cast on
fracturarse, romperse to break (a bone)
pasar to happen
torcerse (o:ue) to twist

ADJETIVO
seguro(a) sure

OTRAS PALABRAS Y EXPRESIONES
en este momento at this moment
poner una inyección to give a shot
todos los días every day

1　The subjunctive to express doubt, disbelief, and denial
El subjuntivo para expresar duda, incredulidad y negación

In Spanish, the subjunctive mood is always used in a subordinate clause when the main clause expresses doubt, uncertainty, or disbelief.

◆ Doubt or uncertainty

—Necesito hablar con el médico.
—**Dudo** que él **esté** en su consultorio hoy, y **no estoy seguro** de que **pueda** verla mañana.

"I need to speak with the doctor."
"I doubt that he is in his office today, and I'm not sure that he can see you tomorrow."

—¿Puedes llevar a Teresa a la
sala de emergencia? **Dudo**
que **sea** necesario llamar
una ambulancia.

*"Can you take Teresa to the
emergency room? I doubt that
it's necessary to call an
ambulance."*

—Sí, la llevo en seguida.

"Yes, I'll take her right away."

ATENCIÓN: In the affirmative, the verb **dudar** *(to doubt)* takes the
subjunctive in the subordinate clause even when there is no
change of subject.

—¿Puedes ir conmigo al
médico?

*"Can you go to the doctor
with me?"*

—**(Yo) dudo** que **(yo) pueda**
ir contigo hoy.

*"I doubt that I can go with
you today."*

When the speaker expresses no doubt and is certain of the real-
ity, the indicative is used.

—¿Qué pasó?

"What happened?"

—**Hubo** un accidente.

"There was an accident."

—¿Llamaron a los
paramédicos?

"Did they call the paramedics?"

—Sí, y **no dudo** que
vienen en seguida.

*"Yes, and I don't doubt that
they will come right away."*

—¿**Está** Ud. **seguro** de que
él **tiene** que usar muletas?

*"Are you sure that he has to
use crutches?"*

—Sí, porque se torció el[1]
tobillo.

*"Yes, because he twisted his
ankle."*

◆ Disbelief

The verb **creer** *(to believe, to think)* is followed by the subjunctive
when used in negative sentences in which it expresses disbelief.

—Carlos dice que lo van a
llevar a la sala de rayos X.

*"Carlos says that they are going
to take him to the X-ray
room."*

—¿Para qué? **No creo** que él
necesite una radiografía.

*"What for? I don't think he
needs an X-ray."*

Creer is followed by the indicative in affirmative sentences in
which it expresses belief.

—¿Enrique se fracturó la[1]
pierna?

"Did Enrique break his leg?"

—Sí, y **creo** que **tienen** que
enyesársela.

*"Yes, and I think they have to
put it in a cast."*

---

[1] Note that the definite article, rather than the possessive adjective, is used in Spanish
with parts of the body.

◆ Denial

When the main clause denies what is said in the subordinate clause, the subjunctive is used.

—Dicen que esa dentista
   tiene unos mil pacientes.
—**Es verdad** que **tiene**
   muchos pacientes, pero
   no es verdad que **tenga**
   mil.

"They say that dentist has
about a thousand patients."
"It's true that she has many
patients, but it's not true
that she has a thousand."

ATENCIÓN: When the clause confirms rather than denies what is said in the subordinate clause, the indicative is used. *Es verdad* **que** *tiene* **muchos pacientes.**

Práctica

A. Complete the following dialogues, using the present indicative or the present subjunctive of the verbs in parentheses. Then act them out with a partner.

1. —¿Tus padres pueden llevarme al hospital?
   —Estoy seguro de que _____ (poder) llevarte, pero dudo que _____ (ir) ahora.
2. —Me torcí el tobillo. ¿Tú crees que voy a necesitar usar muletas?
   —Creo que _____ (tener) que usarlas, pero no creo que las _____ (necesitar) por mucho tiempo.
3. —¿Adónde llevaron a Marta?
   —Creo que _____ (estar) en la sala de emergencia.
4. —Roberto se rompió una pierna.
   —Sí, y estoy seguro de que el médico _____ (tener) que enyesársela.
5. —Yo creo que Antonio _____ (ser) paramédico y _____ (manejar) una ambulancia.
   —Es verdad que _____ (manejar) una ambulancia, pero no es verdad que _____ (ser) paramédico.

B. Use your imagination to complete the following sentences with either the subjunctive or the indicative, as appropriate.

1. Yo estoy seguro de que mis padres...
2. Dudo que la casa del profesor...
3. Es verdad que yo...
4. No estoy seguro de que mi amigo...
5. No es verdad que mi familia...
6. No creo que mi nota en esta clase...
7. No dudo que mis amigos...
8. Creo que el profesor...

2 The subjunctive to express indefiniteness and nonexistence
El subjuntivo para expresar lo indefinido y lo no existente

The subjunctive is always used when a subordinate clause refers to someone or something that is indefinite, unspecified, or nonexistent.

—Ellos **buscan una** enfermera[1] que **pueda** cuidar al paciente en su casa.	*"They are looking for a nurse who can take care of the patient in his home."*
—No conozco a **ninguna** enfermera[2] que **quiera** hacer eso.	*"I don't know any nurse who wants to do that."*
—¿**Hay alguien** aquí que **pueda** ponerme una inyección ahora mismo? Tengo mucho dolor.	*"Is there anyone here who can give me a shot right now? I have a lot of pain."*
—No, porque todos están ocupados en este momento, y no tienen tiempo.	*"No, because everybody is busy at this moment, and they don't have time."*

ATENCIÓN: If the subordinate clause refers to existent, definite, or specific persons or things, the indicative is used.

Conozco a una enfermera que **puede** cuidar al paciente en su casa.

Hay alguien aquí que **puede** ponerme una inyección ahora mismo.

Práctica

A. Complete the following dialogues, using the present subjunctive or the present indicative of the verbs in parentheses. Then act them out with a partner.

1. —¿Hay alguna enfermera que no _____ (estar) ocupada en este momento?
   —Sí, hay una en el consultorio del Dr. Vargas que no _____ (estar) ocupada ahora.

---

[1] The personal **a** is not used when the noun does not refer to a specific person.
[2] The personal **a** is used before indefinite expressions such as **alguien, algún, nadie, ningún,** etc.

2. —Necesito a alguien que _____ (poder) cuidar a los niños.
    —Yo conozco a una señora que _____ (cuidar) niños en su casa.
3. —Daniel se fracturó el tobillo y tiene mucho dolor. Necesitamos llevarlo al hospital. ¿Hay alguien aquí que _____ (tener) coche?
    —Sí, aquí hay varias personas que _____ (tener) coche.
4. —¿Hay alguien que _____ (saber) dónde están las radiografías del Sr. Rojas?
    —Sí, están en la sala de rayos X.
5. —Yo necesito ponerme una inyección todos los días. ¿Conoces a alguien que _____ (poder) enseñarme a hacerlo?
    —No, no conozco a nadie que _____ (poder) enseñarte.
6. —¿Qué buscan ellos?
    —Buscan un médico que no _____ (tener) muchos pacientes.
7. —¿Conoces a algún dentista que _____ (ser) bueno y que _____ (trabajar) los sábados?
    —Sí, el Dr. Rodríguez _____ (ser) muy bueno y _____ (trabajar) los sábados.

B. Use your imagination to complete the following sentences with either the subjunctive or the indicative, as appropriate.

1. Yo quiero una casa que...
2. No hay ningún restaurante que...
3. En mi familia no hay nadie que...
4. Yo vivo en una casa que...
5. Conozco a una chica (un chico) que...
6. En mi clase de español hay muchos estudiantes que...
7. En la ciudad donde yo vivo hay muchos restaurantes que...
8. Yo no conozco a nadie que...

3 Diminutive suffixes
Los sufijos diminutivos

To express the idea of small size, and also to denote affection, special suffixes are used in Spanish. The most common suffixes are **-ito(a)** and **-cito(a)**. There are no set rules for forming the diminutive, but usually if the word ends in **-a** or **-o**, the vowel is dropped and **-ito(a)** is added.

niño	niñ	+ ito =	**niñito**	*(little boy)*
niña	niñ	+ ita =	**niñita**	*(little girl)*
abuelo	abuel	+ ito =	**abuelito**	*(grandpa)*
Ana	An	+ ita =	**Anita**	*(Annie)*

◆ If the word ends in a consonant other than **-n** or **-r**, the suffix **-ito(a)** is added.

| árbol + **ito** = | **arbolito** | *(little tree)* |
| Luis + **ito** = | **Luisito** | *(Louie)* |

◆ If the word ends in **-e, -n,** or **-r**, the suffix **-cito(a)** is added.

coche + **cito** =	**cochecito**	*(little car)*
mujer + **cita** =	**mujercita**	*(little woman)*
Carmen + **cita** =	**Carmencita**	*(Carmen)*

—Hola, **abuelito.** ¿Me trajiste el **arbolito** de Navidad?
—Sí, **Tomasito.**

"Hello, grandpa. Did you bring me the little Christmas tree?"
"Yes, Tommy."

—Me gusta tu **cochecito.**
—Gracias, **Carmencita.**

"I like your little car."
"Thanks, Carmen."

Práctica

Give the diminutive form of each of the following words.

1. primo
2. escuela
3. árbol
4. Raúl
5. coche
6. hermana
7. dolor
8. Adán
9. Adela
10. mamá

Palabras y más palabras

Match the questions in column **A** with the answers in column **B**.

A

1. ¿Tuvo un accidente? _____
2. ¿Dónde está el Dr. Mena? _____
3. ¿Se fracturó la pierna? _____
4. ¿Tienes tiempo para ir a la farmacia? _____
5. ¿Hubo un accidente? _____
6. ¿Le van a hacer una radiografía? _____
7. ¿Qué le pasó a Daniel? _____
8. ¿Qué hizo la enfermera? _____

B

a. Sí, se la van a enyesar.
b. Sí, lo llevamos a la sala de rayos X.
c. Sí, y vinieron los paramédicos.
d. Todos los días.
e. Me puso una inyección.
f. En su consultorio.
g. Un arbolito de Navidad.
h. Con un paciente.
i. Sí, lo llevaron en una ambulancia.

9. ¿Cuándo cuidas tú a los niños?   j. Porque tengo mucho
_____   dolor.

10. ¿Con quién está el dentista?   k. Se torció el tobillo.
_____   l. No, en este momento

11. ¿Por qué tomas aspirinas?   estoy ocupada.
_____

12. ¿Qué compraste? _____

En el laboratorio

The following material is to be used with the tape or audio CD in the language laboratory.

I. Vocabulario

Repeat each word after the speaker. When repeating words that are cognates, notice the difference in pronunciation between English and Spanish.

COGNADOS: la ambulancia   el dentista
la emergencia   el paramédico

NOMBRES: el árbol   el consultorio   el dolor
la inyección   la muleta   la Navidad
el paciente   la pierna   la radiografía
la sala   la sala de emergencia
la sala de rayos X   el tiempo
el tobillo

VERBOS: cuidar   dudar   enyesar   fracturarse
romperse   pasar   torcerse

ADJETIVO: seguro

**OTRAS PALABRAS
Y EXPRESIONES:**   en este momento   poner una inyección
todos los días

II. Práctica

A. Restate each of the following sentences, inserting the cue at the beginning and making any necessary changes. Repeat the correct answer after the speaker's confirmation. Listen to the model.

Modelo: No dudo que el médico viene hoy. (Dudo)
Dudo que el médico venga hoy.

1. (No estoy seguro)   6. (Hay alguien)
2. (No creo)   7. (Creen)
3. (Es verdad)   8. (Estamos seguros)

4. (Tememos)   9. (No hay nadie)
5. (Necesito)   10. (No es verdad)

B. The speaker will say some nouns. Change each one to the diminutive form.

III. Para escuchar y entender

1. The speaker will make some statements. Circle **L (lógico)** if the statement is logical and **I (ilógico)** if it is illogical. The speaker will verify your response.

   1. L   I   5. L   I
   2. L   I   6. L   I
   3. L   I   7. L   I
   4. L   I   8. L   I

2. Listen carefully to the narration. It will be read twice.

   (Narración 1)

   Now the speaker will make some statements about the narration you just heard. Tell whether each statement is true **(verdadero)** or false **(falso).** The speaker will confirm the correct answer.

3. Listen carefully to the dialogue. It will be read twice.

   (Diálogo)

   Now the speaker will make some statements about the dialogue you just heard. Tell whether each statement is true **(verdadero)** or false **(falso).** The speaker will confirm the correct answer.

4. Listen carefully to the narration. It will be read twice.

   (Narración 2)

   Now the speaker will ask you some questions about the narration you just heard. Answer each question, omitting the subject. The speaker will confirm the correct answer. Repeat the correct answer.

1. The subjunctive after certain conjunctions

2. The present perfect subjunctive

3. Uses of the present perfect subjunctive

Vocabulario

COGNADOS

horrible horrible
el resultado result
el termómetro
  thermometer

el testamento testament,
  will

NOMBRES
el análisis test
la autopista freeway
el (la) ayudante assistant
el (la) cirujano(a) surgeon
la fiebre fever
el jarabe syrup
el (la) oculista eye doctor
la operación, la cirugía
  surgery
el (la) pasajero(a) passenger
la pastilla pill
el peso weight

VERBOS
  bajar to go down, to
  decrease

chocar to collide
sobrevivir to survive

**OTRAS PALABRAS Y
EXPRESIONES**
  a menos que unless
  antes de que before
  en caso de que in case
  **en cuanto, tan pronto
   como** as soon as
  hacer ejercicio to exercise
  hasta que until
  para que in order that
  ponerse a dieta to go on
   a diet
  sin que without

1 The subjunctive after certain conjunctions

El subjuntivo después de ciertas conjunciones

The subjunctive is used after conjunctions of time when the main clause refers to the future or is a command.

◆ Some conjunctions of time.

tan pronto como	*as soon as*
en cuanto	*as soon as*
hasta que	*until*
cuando	*when*

—Eva, ¿cuándo va a llamarte el médico?

"Eva, when is the doctor going to call you?"

—Me llamará **tan pronto como sepa** el resultado de los análisis.

"He will call me as soon as he finds out the results of the tests."

—Carlos, ¿a qué hora van a empezar la operación?

"Carlos, at what time are they going to begin the surgery?"

—La van a empezar **en cuanto llegue** el ayudante de la cirujana.

"They're going to begin it as soon as the surgeon's assistant arrives."

—Tomás, ¿cuándo vamos a salir para el hospital?

"Tomás, when are we going to leave for the hospital?"

—No podemos salir **hasta que** el carro **esté** arreglado.

"We can't leave until the car is fixed."

—**Cuando llegue** Marta, dígale que **compre** el jarabe y un termómetro.

"When Marta arrives, tell her to buy the syrup and a thermometer."

—Muy bien. Se lo diré **cuando venga.**

"Very well. I'll tell her when she comes."

ATENCIÓN: If the action already happened or if there is no indication of a future action, the indicative is used after the conjunction of time.

—¿A qué hora van a empezar la operación?

"At what time are they going to begin the surgery?"

—Siempre empiezan **en cuanto llegan** los cirujanos.

"They always begin as soon as the surgeons arrive."

—¿Qué haces con el niño cuando tú tienes que trabajar?

"What do you do with the child when you have to work?"

—**Cuando** yo **trabajo,** mi mamá viene a cuidarlo.

"When I work, my mother comes to take care of him."

◆ There are certain conjunctions that, by their very meaning, imply uncertainty or conditional fulfillment; they are therefore always followed by the subjunctive. Here are some of them.

a menos que	*unless*	**en caso de que**	*in case*
antes de que	*before*	**para que**	*in order that*
con tal que	*provided that*	**sin que**	*without*

—¿Va Ud. a firmar el testamento hoy?

"Are you going to sign the will today?"

—No puedo firmarlo **sin que** mi abogado lo **lea.**

"I can't sign it without my lawyer reading it."

—¿Vas a tomar las pastillas   *"Are you going to take the*
   esta noche?   *pills tonight?"*
—Sí, voy a tomarlas **a menos**   *"Yes, I'm going to take them*
   que me **baje** la fiebre.   *unless the fever goes down."*

Práctica

A. Complete the following dialogues, using the present indicative
or the present subjunctive of the verbs in parentheses. Then act
them out with a partner.

1. —¿Cuándo vas a volver a la oficina?
   —En cuanto me _____ (bajar) la fiebre y me _____
   (sentir) mejor.
2. —¿Cuándo te va a llamar Jorge?
   —No me va a llamar hasta que el doctor le _____ (dar) el
   resultado de los análisis.
3. —¿Qué vas a hacer?
   —Voy a llamar a Tito para que me _____ (traer) el jarabe
   cuando _____ (venir) esta tarde.
4. —Todos los días, yo llamo a mamá tan pronto como
   _____ (llegar) a casa.
   —Cuando (tú) la _____ (llamar) hoy, dile que me mande
   las pastillas.
5. —¿Vas a comprar el termómetro?
   —No puedo comprarlo a menos que tú me _____ (llevar)
   a la farmacia.
6. —¿Te vas a ir de vacaciones?
   —No puedo irme antes de que el cirujano _____ (decidir)
   si necesito la operación o no.
   —Yo puedo quedarme contigo en caso de que (tú) me
   _____ (necesitar).
7. —¿Por qué tomas estas pastillas?
   —Porque son muy buenas. Siempre me siento mejor en
   cuanto las _____ (tomar).
8. —Tengo que salir de casa sin que los niños me _____
   (ver).
   —Sí, porque cuando tú _____ (irse), ellos siempre lloran
   (*cry*).

B. Use your imagination to complete the following sentences with
the present indicative or the present subjunctive, as appropriate.

1. No te bajará la fiebre a menos que...
2. El cirujano va a comenzar la operación en cuanto...
3. Ella siempre me llama tan pronto como...
4. Todas las noches lo espero hasta que...
5. Voy a limpiar la casa en caso de que...

6. Carlos siempre llama a su abogado cuando…
7. No puedo ir al hospital antes de que…
8. No puedo comprarte el jarabe sin que tú…

2 The present perfect subjunctive
El pretérito perfecto de subjuntivo

The present perfect subjunctive is formed with the present subjunctive of the auxiliary verb **haber** and the past participle of the main verb.

The Present Perfect Subjunctive		
	Present Subjunctive *of* **haber** **+**	*Past Participle* *of the Main Verb*
yo	**haya**	**hablado**
tú	**hayas**	**comido**
Ud. él ella	**haya**	**vivido**
nosotros	**hayamos**	**hecho**
Uds. ellos ellas	**hayan**	**puesto**

Práctica

Conjugate the following verbs in the present perfect subjunctive for each subject given.

1. **yo:**   hacer, venir, comer, levantarse
2. **tú:**   trabajar, poner, decir, acostarse
3. **ella:**   escribir, cerrar, abrir, sentarse
4. **nosotros:**   romper, hablar, llegar, vestirse
5. **ellos:**   morir, vender, alquilar, bañarse

3 Uses of the present perfect subjunctive
Usos del pretérito perfecto de subjuntivo

The present perfect subjunctive is used in the same way as the present perfect tense in English, but only in sentences that require the subjunctive in the subordinate clause. It describes events that have ended prior to the time indicated in the main clause.

—¿Ya han pagado Uds. la
cuenta del oculista?

*"Have you already paid the
eye doctor's bill?"*

—No recuerdo... no, **no
creo** que la **hayamos
pagado** todavía.

*"I don't remember . . . No, I
don't think we've paid it yet."*

—Hubo un accidente en la
autopista. Chocaron dos
autobuses, y **temo** que
hayan muerto todos los
pasajeros.

*"There was an accident on the
freeway. Two buses collided
and I fear that all the
passengers (have) died."*

—¡Qué horrible![1] **Ojalá** que
algunos **hayan
sobrevivido.**

*"How horrible! I hope that
some (of them) (have)
survived."*

—Inés se ha puesto a dieta.

"Inés has gone on a diet."

—Sí, pero **no creo** que **haya
perdido** mucho peso
porque nunca hace
ejercicio.

*"Yes, but I don't think she has
lost a lot of weight because
she never exercises."*

Práctica

A. Complete the following dialogues, using the present perfect
subjunctive. Then act them out with a partner.

1. —¿Crees que el cirujano ha terminado ya la operación?
   —No, no creo que la _____ (terminar).
2. —Dicen que Mario se ha puesto a dieta.
   —Dudo que se _____ (poner) a dieta, porque él no necesita perder peso. Además, él siempre hace ejercicio.
3. —Ha habido *(There has been)* un accidente en la autopista.
   Chocaron un ómnibus y un coche.
   —Ojalá que no _____ (morir) nadie.
   —Temo que los pasajeros del coche no _____
   (sobrevivir).
   —¡Qué horrible!
4. —Gloria ha ido a la oculista.
   —Me alegro de que _____ (decidir) ir, porque no ve muy
   bien.
5. —¿Hay alguien aquí que _____ (estar) en México este verano?
   —No, aquí no hay nadie que _____ (ir) a México.
6. —¿El Sr. Vega ya ha hecho el testamento?
   —No, no creo que lo _____ (hacer) todavía.

---

[1] The Spanish equivalent of *how* + adjective is **qué** + adjective.

B. Use your imagination to complete the following sentences, using the present perfect subjunctive.

1. Yo me alegro de que mis padres…
2. Ojalá que tú…
3. Yo no creo que mi médico…
4. Mi familia espera que yo…
5. El (La) profesor(a) espera que nosotros…
6. Yo siento que Uds…
7. En mi familia no hay nadie que…
8. Yo dudo que mi hermano(a)…

Palabras y más palabras

Complete the following exchanges, using the vocabulary learned in this lesson. Then act them out with a partner.

1. —¿Cuándo sabrás el _____ de los análisis?
   —En _____ me llame el médico.
2. —¿Hubo un accidente?
   —Sí, fue horrible. No _____ nadie.
3. —¿Qué hiciste para perder _____?
   —Hice ejercicio y me puse a _____.
4. —¿Para qué le das aspirina?
   —Para que le baje la _____.
5. —¿Qué pasó?
   — _____ un coche y un ómnibus en la _____.
6. —No veo bien.
   —Pues ve al _____.
7. —¿A quién espera el cirujano?
   —Espera a su _____ para poder empezar la _____.
8. —¿Qué va a comprar en la farmacia?
   —Un jarabe, un _____ y unas _____.

En el laboratorio

The following material is to be used with the tape or audio CD in the language laboratory.

I. Vocabulario

Repeat each word after the speaker. When repeating words that are cognates, notice the difference in pronunciation between English and Spanish.

COGNADOS: horrible el resultado el termómetro
el testamento

NOMBRES:	el análisis la autopista el ayudante
	el cirujano la fiebre el jarabe
	el oculista la operación la cirugía
	el pasajero la pastilla el peso
VERBOS:	bajar chocar sobrevivir
OTRAS PALABRAS Y EXPRESIONES:	a menos que antes de que
	en caso de que en cuanto
	tan pronto como hacer ejercicio
	hasta que para que ponerse a dieta
	sin que

II. Práctica

A. Restate each of the following sentences, inserting the cue at the beginning and making any necessary changes. Repeat the correct answer after the speaker's confirmation. Listen to the model.

Modelo: Siempre me llama tan pronto como llega. (Me va a llamar)
Me va a llamar tan pronto como llegue.

1. (Los voy a llamar)
2. (Voy a comprar)
3. (Ella va a venir)
4. (No voy a poder hacer nada)
5. (Van a traer)
6. (Vamos a estar aquí)

B. Restate each of the following sentences, inserting the cue at the beginning and using the present perfect subjunctive. Make any other necessary changes. Repeat the correct answer after the speaker's confirmation. Listen to the model.

Modelo: El doctor ha llegado. (Espero)
Espero que el doctor haya llegado.

1. (Espero)
2. (Siento)
3. (No creo)
4. (No es verdad)
5. (Dudo)
6. (No es verdad)
7. (No es cierto)
8. (Me alegro de)

III. Para escuchar y entender

1. The speaker will make some statements. Circle **L (lógico)** if the statement is logical and **I (ilógico)** if it is illogical. The speaker will verify your response.

1. L   I
2. L   I
3. L   I
4. L   I
5. L   I
6. L   I
7. L   I
8. L   I

2. Listen carefully to the dialogue. It will be read twice.

(Diálogo 1)

Now the speaker will make some statements about the dialogue you just heard. Tell whether each statement is true **(verdadero)** or false **(falso).** The speaker will confirm the correct answer.

3. Listen carefully to the dialogue. It will be read twice.

(Diálogo 2)

Now the speaker will make some statements about the dialogue you just heard. Tell whether each statement is true **(verdadero)** or false **(falso).** The speaker will confirm the correct answer.

4. Listen carefully to the dialogue. It will be read twice.

(Diálogo 3)

Now the speaker will ask you some questions about the dialogue you just heard. Answer each question, omitting the subject. The speaker will confirm the correct answer. Repeat the correct answer.

Lección

20

1. The imperfect subjunctive
2. Uses of the imperfect subjunctive
3. *If* clauses

Vocabulario

COGNADOS

americano(a) American	**el crédito** credit
el consulado consulate	**la fotocopia** photocopy

NOMBRES
la billetera wallet
el correo post office
la cortina curtain
la diligencia errand
la entrevista interview
el informe report
el (la) jefe(a) boss, chief
el paquete package
el préstamo loan
el talonario de cheques
  checkbook

VERBOS
  asistir (a) to attend

devolver (o:ue) to return
  (something), to give back
preocuparse to worry
recoger to pick up

**OTRAS PALABRAS Y
EXPRESIONES**
como since
echar al correo to mail
hacer diligencias to do
  errands
pedir prestado(a) to
  borrow
un montón de a lot of

1 The imperfect subjunctive
El imperfecto de subjuntivo

			The Imperfect Subjunctive	
Verb	*Preterit, Third Person Plural*	*Stem*	*Imperfect Subjunctive*	
hablar	hablaron	**habla-**	que yo habla-	**ra**
comer	comieron	**comie-**	que tú comie-	**ras**
vivir	vivieron	**vivie-**	que Ud. vivie-	**ra**
traer	trajeron	**traje-**	que él traje-	**ra**
ir	fueron	**fue-**	que ella fue-	**ra**
saber	supieron	**supie-**	que nosotros supié-	**ramos**
decir	dijeron	**dije-**	que Uds. dije-	**ran**
poner	pusieron	**pusie-**	que ellos pusie-	**ran**
estar	estuvieron	**estuvie-**	que ellas estuvie-	**ran**

The imperfect subjunctive is the past tense of the subjunctive. It is formed in the same way for all verbs, regular and irregular. The **-ron** ending of the third person plural of the preterit is dropped and the following endings are added to the stem: **-ra, -ras, -ra, -ramos, -ran.**[1]

◆ Notice the written accent mark in the first person plural form.

Práctica

Give the imperfect subjunctive of the following verbs.

1. **yo:**   bajar, aprender, abrir, cerrar, estar, acostarse
2. **tú:**   salir, sentir, temer, recordar, venir, ponerse
3. **Ud.:**   llevar, romper, morir, revisar, volar, alegrarse
4. **nosotros:**   esperar, traer, pedir, volver, servir, vestirse
5. **ellos:**   tener, ser, dar, estar, poder, irse

2 Uses of the imperfect subjunctive
Usos del imperfecto de subjuntivo

◆ The imperfect subjunctive is always used in a subordinate clause when the verb of the main clause is in the past and requires the subjunctive mood.

—¿Qué te sugirió él?	*"What did he suggest to you?"*
—Me **sugirió** que **pidiera** un préstamo en el banco.	*"He suggested that I ask for a loan at the bank."*
—¿Lo pediste?	*"Did you ask for it?"*
—No, porque como no tengo crédito **temí** que no me lo **dieran.**	*"No, because since I don't have credit I was afraid that they wouldn't give it to me."*
—Mamá me **pidió** que **comprara** estampillas y que **echara** estas cartas al correo.	*"Mom asked me to buy stamps and to mail these letters."*
—A mí me **dijo** que **fuera** a la tintorería para recoger las cortinas.	*"She told me to go to the cleaners to pick up the curtains."*
—Y a papá le **pidió** que **hiciera** otras diligencias.	*"And she asked Dad to do other errands."*

[1] See Appendix B: Verbs, for the **-se** endings of the imperfect subjunctive, which are less frequently used.

—El jefe me **dio** el informe para que **hiciera** fotocopias y las **llevara** al consulado americano.	*"The boss gave me the report so that I could make photocopies and take them to the American consulate."*
—¿Ya lo hiciste?	*"Did you do it already?"*
—No, porque también me **dijo** que **escribiera** a máquina un montón de cartas.	*"No, because he also told me to type a lot of letters."*

◆ The imperfect subjunctive is also used when the verb of the main clause is in the present, but the subordinate clause refers to the past.

—Es una lástima que no **pudieras** asistir a la reunión ayer.	*"It's a pity that you weren't able to attend the meeting yesterday."*
—No pude ir porque tuve que ir a una entrevista.	*"I couldn't go because I had to go to an interview."*

◆ The imperfect subjunctive form of **querer (quisiera)** is used as a polite form of request.

—**Quisiera** pedirle un favor.	*"I would like to ask you a favor."*

Práctica

A. Complete the following dialogues using the imperfect subjunctive. Then act them out with a partner.

1. —Anita, te dije que _____ (hacer) fotocopias de este informe.
   —No pude porque papá me pidió que _____ (ir) a la oficina de correos.

2. —Mamá quería que yo _____ (recoger) las cortinas en la tintorería.
   —A mí me pidió que _____ (hacer) un montón de diligencias.

3. —Es una lástima que Julio no _____ (poder) ir a la entrevista ayer.
   —No pudo ir porque su jefe le pidió que _____ (asistir) a una junta.

4. —Siento que ellos no te _____ (dar) el préstamo.
   —Era difícil que me lo _____ (dar) porque no tengo buen crédito.

5. —Alicia nos pidió que _____ (comprar) estampillas y que _____ (echar) unas cartas al correo.
   —¡Pero mamá quería que (nosotros) _____ (ir) con ella al consulado americano!

B. Use your imagination to complete the following sentences, using the imperfect subjunctive.

1. Siento que ayer tú no…
2. Yo les pedí a mis amigos que…
3. Mis padres querían que yo…
4. El profesor nos dijo que…
5. Yo quería que mi hermano(a)…
6. Yo me alegré de que Uds…

3 *If* clauses
Oraciones condicionales

In Spanish, the imperfect subjunctive is used in a clause introduced by **si** *(if)* when it refers to statements considered contrary to fact, hypothetical, or unlikely to happen. The resultant clause usually has a verb in the conditional.

Si yo fuera Ud…	*If I were you…*
—**Si** yo **tuviera** dinero, iría de vacaciones con Uds.	*"If I had money, I would go on vacation with you."*
—¿No se lo puedes pedir prestado a tu padre?	*"Can't you borrow it from your father?"*
—No, porque **si** mi padre me lo **prestara,** tendría que devolvérselo antes de septiembre, y yo necesito el dinero para pagar la matrícula.	*"No, because if my father were to lend it to me,[1] I would have to give it back to him before September, and I need the money to pay for registration."*
—**Si tuviéramos** tiempo, podríamos llevar estos paquetes al correo ahora.	*"If we had time, we could take these packages to the post office now."*
—No te preocupes. Podemos llevarlos mañana.	*"Don't worry. We can take them tomorrow."*
—No puedo comprar la computadora porque no tengo mi talonario de cheques.	*"I can't buy the computer because I don't have my checkbook."*
—**Si** yo **fuera** tú, usaría una tarjeta de crédito.	*"If I were you, I would use a credit card."*
—Tienes razón. Si tengo mi *MasterCard* en la billetera voy a usarla.	*"You're right. If I have my MasterCard in my wallet I am going to use it."*

---

[1] Many colloquial English speakers use the simple past tense to express a contrary-to-fact or hypothetical situation, e.g., "… *if my father lent it to me*."

ATENCIÓN: When an *if* clause is not contrary to fact or hypothetical, or when there is a possibility that the situation it describes will happen, the indicative is used.

Vamos a comprar los billetes **si** nos **dan** el dinero.	*We are going to buy the tickets if they give us the money.*

◆ The present subjunctive is **never** used with an *if* clause.

Práctica

A. Complete the following dialogues, using the imperfect subjunctive. Then act them out with a partner.

1. —Si yo _____ (tener) dinero, le compraría una computadora a Pepe.
   —Si yo _____ (ser) tú, no le compraría nada.
2. —Si Estrella me _____ (devolver) el dinero que le presté, yo podría pagar mis cuentas.
   —Estoy segura de que si ella _____ (poder), te lo devolvería.
3. —Ernesto se preocupa mucho por sus hijos.
   —Yo también me preocuparía si mis hijos _____ (ser) como los de él.
4. —Si Carolina _____ (venir) hoy, podríamos ir al consulado juntas.
   —Si nosotras no _____ (trabajar) hoy, iríamos contigo.
5. —Si tú _____ (tener) un examen y un amigo te _____ (pedir) que _____ (hacer) un montón de diligencias, ¿qué harías?
   —Le diría que no.

B. Use your imagination to complete the following sentences, using either the imperfect subjunctive or the present indicative, as appropriate.

1. Yo llevaría el paquete al correo si...
2. Ella te compraría una billetera si...
3. Nosotros pagaríamos con un cheque si...
4. Haré las fotocopias hoy si...
5. Ellos van a asistir a la reunión si...
6. ¿Qué harías tú si... ?
7. Mi papá pediría un préstamo si...
8. Te voy a devolver el dinero si...

Palabras y más palabras

Circle the word or phrase that best completes each sentence.

1. No tengo dinero. Se lo voy a pedir (prestado / preocupado) a mi tío.
2. Ella (devuelve / asiste) a la universidad.
3. Tengo que ir a la tintorería para (comprar / recoger) mis pantalones.
4. Voy a (echar / bajar) estas cartas al correo.
5. Estoy muy ocupada. Tengo que (hacer / chocar) muchas diligencias.
6. Voy al banco para pedir un (paquete / préstamo) porque necesito dinero.
7. No tengo mi (talonario / informe) de cheques.
8. Compré (billeteras / cortinas) para las ventanas de mi cuarto.
9. Fui al (consulado / correo) americano para recoger mi pasaporte.
10. Ella (se sienta / se preocupa) mucho por sus hijos.

En el laboratorio

The following material is to be used with the tape or audio CD in the language laboratory.

I. Vocabulario

Repeat each word after the speaker. When repeating words that are cognates, notice the difference in pronunciation between English and Spanish.

COGNADOS:	americano el consulado el crédito la fotocopia
NOMBRES:	la billetera el correo la cortina la diligencia la entrevista el informe el jefe el paquete el préstamo el talonario de cheques
VERBOS:	asistir devolver preocuparse recoger
OTRAS PALABRAS Y EXPRESIONES:	como echar al correo hacer diligencias pedir prestado un montón de

II. Práctica

A. Restate each of the following sentences, inserting the cue at the beginning and making any necessary changes. Repeat the correct answer after the speaker's confirmation. Listen to the model.

Modelo: Ella quiere que yo vaya con él. (Ella quería)
Ella quería que yo fuera con él.

1. (Fue una lástima)
2. (No creí)
3. (Esperaba)
4. (Dudábamos)
5. (No había nadie)
6. (Necesitaba)
7. (No quería)
8. (No creían)

B. Restate each of the following sentences, inserting the cue at the beginning and making any necessary changes. Repeat the correct answer after the speaker's confirmation. Listen to the model.

Modelo: Iré si tengo tiempo. (Iría)
Iría si tuviera tiempo.

1. (Le hablaría)
2. (Compraríamos)
3. (Lo harían)
4. (Se lo diría)
5. (Vendríamos)
6. (Me alegraría)
7. (Lo compraría)
8. (Lo haríamos)

III. Para escuchar y entender

1. The speaker will make some statements. Circle **L (lógico)** if the statement is logical and **I (ilógico)** if it is illogical. The speaker will verify your response.

1. L I
2. L I
3. L I
4. L I

5. L I
6. L I
7. L I
8. L I

2. Listen carefully to the narration. It will be read twice.

(Narración)

Now the speaker will make some statements about the narration you just heard. Tell whether each statement is true (**verdadero**) or false (**falso**). The speaker will confirm the correct answer.

3. Listen carefully to the dialogue. It will be read twice.

   (Diálogo 1)

   Now the speaker will make some statements about the dialogue you just heard. Tell whether each statement is true (**verdadero**) or false (**falso**). The speaker will confirm the correct answer.

4. Listen carefully to the dialogue. It will be read twice.

   (Diálogo 2)

   Now the speaker will ask you some questions about the dialogue you just heard. Answer each question, omitting the subject. The speaker will confirm the correct answer. Repeat the correct answer.

¿Cuánto sabe usted ahora?

Lección 16 **A.** The present subjunctive

Complete the following sentences, using the Spanish equivalent of the verbs in parentheses in the present subjunctive. Follow the model.

> *Modelo:* …que yo _____ *(speak)*
> …que yo **hable**

1. …que nosotros _____ *(close)*
2. …que ellos _____ *(go)*
3. …que tú _____ *(open)*
4. …que Pablo _____ *(recommend)*
5. …que Ud. _____ *(leave)*
6. …que yo _____ *(return)*
7. …que Uds. _____ *(want)*
8. …que ella _____ *(understand)*
9. …que nosotros _____ *(have)*
10. …que las chicas _____ *(put)*
11. …que tú _____ *(bring)*
12. …que los estudiantes _____ *(give)*
13. …que yo _____ *(be:* **estar***)*
14. …que Teresa _____ *(be:* **ser***)*
15. …que Uds. _____ *(know:* **saber***)*

B. The subjunctive with verbs of volition

How would you say the following in Spanish?

1. "Do you want to go to the hospital with me, Anita?"
   "I can't. Alberto wants me to go to the train station with him."
2. "What do you want to do this weekend, Pedro?"
   "I don't know…What do you suggest that I do?"
   "I suggest that you study."
3. "Do you need me to bring you the train schedule, Miss Rojas?"
   "Yes, and I beg you to come this afternoon, Mr. Varela."
   "What time do you want me to be at your house?"
   "At two."
4. "I am going to ask him to buy the tickets."
   "I prefer to buy them this afternoon."

C. The absolute superlative

Change the following to the absolute superlative.

1. sumamente difícil
2. muy lenta
3. sumamente buenas
4. muy alto
5. muy largo
6. sumamente rápido
7. muy inteligentes
8. sumamente fáciles

D. Vocabulario

Complete the following sentences, using words learned in **Lección 16.**

1. ¡Son las cinco! Tienes que salir cuanto _____.
2. Me dieron un _____ del diez por _____.
3. Quiero reservar un _____ para el vuelo a Mérida.
4. Todos los trenes son muy lentos, menos *(except for)* el _____.
5. Vamos a estar en la _____ de trenes a las diez.
6. Alberto dice que ella es muy bonita. ¡Yo no lo _____!

A. The subjunctive to express emotion   **Lección 17**

How would you say the following in Spanish?

1. "I hope to get the scholarship."
   "I'm afraid you can't get it because your grades are not very good."
2. "I'm glad to be here with you, Anita."
   "I hope that you can go to the party with me tonight, Carlos."
3. "I'm afraid we cannot register in the physics class."
   "I'm sorry you don't have the money, girls . . . "
4. "We hope to take a literature class."
   "We're glad that you want to take literature."

B. The subjunctive with some impersonal expressions

Complete the following sentences, using the present subjunctive or the infinitive, as appropriate.

1. Conviene _____ (matricularse) en agosto.
2. Es difícil que mi abogado _____ (poder) verme mañana.
3. Es importante _____ (sacar) buenas notas.
4. Es posible que ellos me _____ (dar) una beca.
5. Es lástima que esa clase _____ (ser) un requisito.
6. Yo creo que es mejor no _____ (firmar) el contrato.
7. Es necesario _____ (tomar) una clase de química.
8. Ojalá que el profesor _____ (tener) tiempo de preparar la conferencia.

C. Formation of adverbs

Complete the following sentences, using the Spanish equivalent of the words in parentheses.

1. Ella vino _____ para verte. *(especially)*
2. Tomé una clase de literatura _____ . *(recently)*
3. Yo hablé _____ y _____, y los estudiantes me entendieron. *(slowly* and *clearly)*
4. Nosotros _____ nos levantamos a las seis. *(generally)*
5. Ellos todo lo hacen muy _____. *(easily)*

D. Vocabulary

Complete the following sentences, using words learned in **Lección 17.**

1. Necesito la _____ para mi clase de matemáticas.
2. El examen _____ es en octubre y el examen _____ es en diciembre.
3. Me _____ de que saques buenas _____ en la clase.
4. No puedo tomar clases. No tengo dinero para pagar la _____.
5. Puede _____ que la profesora vuelva mañana.
6. Ud. no necesita traer dinero porque no es _____ comprar nada.
7. Estudiamos las ideas de Isaac Newton en nuestra clase de _____.
8. Mi _____ quiere que tome una clase de física.

Lección 18   **A.** The subjunctive to express doubt, disbelief, and denial

How would you say the following in Spanish?

1. "Dr. Soto says she can take care of my patients."
   "I'm sure she can."
2. "I don't think the doctor is in his office."
   "Then I have to call his house."
3. "I doubt that Mr. Soto can take his wife to the emergency room."
   "Can her daughter take her?"
   "I don't think she's home."
4. "I'm sure that she needs crutches!"
   "It's true that her leg hurts, but it isn't true that she needs crutches . . . "

B. The subjunctive to express indefiniteness and nonexistence

Rephrase these sentences according to the new beginnings.

1. Tengo un paciente que es de México.
   No tengo ningún paciente…

2. Hay alguien que puede llevarlo a la sala de rayos X.
   No hay nadie…
3. Hay una enfermera que habla español.
   No hay ninguna enfermera…
4. Hay dos personas aquí que saben poner inyecciones.
   Busco a alguien…
5. Necesito a alguien que cuide a mis hijos.
   Hay una señora…

C. Diminutive suffixes

Give the diminutive form of the following words.

1. Carmen
2. árbol
3. niños
4. café
5. camión

6. favor
7. piernas
8. brazo
9. hermana
10. noche

D. Vocabulario

Complete the following sentences, using words learned in **Lección 18.**

1. Lo llevaron al hospital en una _____ .
2. Se rompió la pierna. Va a necesitar _____ para caminar.
3. Lo llevaron a la _____ de emergencia.
4. El doctor está en su _____ .
5. Lo llevaron a la sala de rayos X para hacerle una _____ .
6. Le van a _____ una inyección.
7. Yo me rompí el brazo; me lo van a _____ .
8. En este _____ llegan los paramédicos.

A. The subjunctive after certain conjunctions   **Lección 19**

Complete the following sentences, using the Spanish equivalent of the words in parentheses.

1. No va a hacer testamento hasta que _____ . (*her lawyer comes*)
2. Yo siempre espero hasta que mi ayudante _____ el resultado. (*brings me*)
3. Yo podré ir a trabajar en cuanto me _____ . (*the fever goes down*)
4. Cuando él _____ el resultado de los análisis, se va a alegrar. (*knows*)
5. No sobrevivirán a menos que _____ al hospital inmediatamente. (*they take them*)
6. En cuanto el cirujano _____ al hospital, siempre habla con sus ayudantes. (*arrives*)

7. No te sentirás mejor a menos que _____ estas pastillas.
   (*you take*)
8. Voy a comprar aspirinas en caso de que Adela _____ . (*has a fever*)

B. The present perfect subjunctive

Give the present perfect subjunctive of the verbs given.

1. ...que yo _____ (llegar)
2. ...que Uds. _____ (volver)
3. ...que Teresa _____ (ir)
4. ...que tú _____ (decir)
5. ...que nosotros _____ (hacer)
6. ...que Ud. _____ (preferir)
7. ...que Carlos _____ (abrir)
8. ...que los niños _____ (poner)

C. Uses of the present perfect subjunctive

Rephrase the following sentences according to the new beginnings.

1. Nosotros hemos hecho el trabajo.
   Ellos no creen que nosotros...
2. Yo he estado enfermo.
   Ella duda que yo...
3. Han muerto muchos.
   No es verdad que...
4. Ha ido a México.
   No hay nadie que...
5. Tú le has escrito una carta.
   Ella no cree que tú...
6. Ellos han hablado con la enfermera.
   Espero que...
7. Uds. no han visto a sus pacientes.
   Siento que Uds...
8. Ana y yo hemos ido a su consultorio.
   No es cierto...

D. Vocabulario

Complete the following sentences, using words learned in **Lección 19.**

1. Los _____ ya están en el tren.
2. Necesito el _____ para ver si tiene fiebre.
3. Hubo un accidente en la _____.
4. Te traje un _____ para la tos (*cough*).
5. Tengo que salir _____ de que lleguen los chicos.
6. Para bajar de peso me voy a poner a _____.

A. The imperfect subjunctive

Give the imperfect subjunctive of the verbs given.

1. ...que ellos _____ (asistir)
2. ...que tú _____ (ser)
3. ...que nosotros _____ (devolver)
4. ...que Estela _____ (ir)
5. ...que yo _____ (recoger)
6. ...que Roberto _____ (poder)
7. ...que Ud. _____ (querer)
8. ...que Uds. _____ (dar)
9. ...que Luis y yo _____ (hacer)
10. ...que las niñas _____ (traer)

B. Uses of the imperfect subjunctive

Rephrase the following sentences according to the new beginnings.

1. Yo tuve que trabajar.
   No era verdad que yo...
2. Nosotros pusimos el dinero en el banco.
   Ella quería que nosotros...
3. Tú fuiste al correo.
   Tu papá te dijo que...
4. Ellos hicieron las diligencias.
   La Sra. Rojas quería que ellos...
5. Ud. llevó el paquete.
   Yo quería que Ud...
6. Uds. hablaron con el jefe.
   Nosotros esperábamos que Uds...
7. María estuvo enferma.
   Yo sentí mucho que María...
8. Esteban perdió la billetera.
   Yo temía que Esteban...

C. *If* clauses

Complete the following sentences, using the Spanish equivalent of the words in parentheses.

1. _____, le diré que tú la necesitas. *(If I see her)*
2. _____, no haría eso. *(If I were you)*
3. _____, iría contigo. *(If she had time)*
4. _____, podré comprar las cortinas. *(If he gives me the money)*
5. _____, llegaríamos mañana. *(If we went by car)*
6. _____, te va a traer el dinero. *(If she can come)*
7. _____, podríamos ir con ellos, Anita. *(If you wanted to)*
8. Iré al banco _____. *(if they go with me)*

D. Vocabulario

Complete the following sentences, using words learned in **Lección 20.**

1. Voy a poner el dinero en la _____.
2. Te voy a _____ el dinero que te pedí _____ la semana pasada.
3. Voy a escribir un _____ para mi clase de historia.
4. No tengo dinero para comprar el coche. Voy a pedir un _____.
5. ¿Tienes tu _____ de cheques?
6. Ellos _____ a la Universidad de Salamanca.
7. Tengo un _____ de cartas para _____ al correo.

Appendix A

Spanish Pronunciation

Vowels

There are five distinct vowels in Spanish: **a, e, i, o,** and **u.** Each vowel has only one basic, constant sound. The pronunciation of each vowel is constant, clear, and brief. The length of the sound is practically the same whether it is produced in a stressed or unstressed syllable.[1]

While producing the sounds of the English stressed vowels that most closely resemble the Spanish ones, the speaker changes the position of the tongue, lips, and lower jaw, so that the vowel actually starts as one sound and then *glides* into another. In Spanish, however, the tongue, lips, and jaw keep a constant position during the production of the sound.

> **English:** ban*a*na **Spanish:** ban*a*na

The stress falls on the same vowel and syllable in both Spanish and English, but the English stressed *a* is longer than the Spanish stressed **a.**

> **English:** ban*a*na **Spanish:** ban*a*na

Note also that the English stressed *a* has a sound different from the other *a*'s in the word, while the Spanish **a** sound remains constant.

a in Spanish sounds similar to the English *a* in the word *father*.

alta	casa	palma	Ana
cama	Panamá	alma	apagar

e is pronounced like the English *e* in the word *eight*.

mes	entre	este	deje
ese	encender	teme	prender

i has a sound similar to the English *ee* in the word *see*.

fin	ir	sí	sin	dividir	Trini	difícil

o is similar to the English *o* in the word *no*, but without the glide.

toco	como	poco	roto
corto	corro	solo	loco

---

[1] In a stressed syllable, the prominence of the vowel is indicated by its loudness.

u is pronounced like the English *oo* sound in the word *shoot,* or the *ue* sound in the word *Sue.*

su	Lulú	Úrsula	cultura
un	luna	sucursal	Uruguay

Diphthongs and Triphthongs

When unstressed **i** or **u** falls next to another vowel in a syllable, it unites with that vowel to form what is called a *diphthong.* Both vowels are pronounced as one syllable. Their sounds do not change; they are only pronounced more rapidly and with a glide. For example:

tra**i**ga	Lid**ia**	tre**i**nta	s**ie**te	**oi**go	ad**iós**
Aurora	ag**ua**	b**ue**no	antig**uo**	c**iu**dad	L**ui**s

A *triphthong* is the union of three vowels: a stressed vowel between two unstressed ones (**i** or **u**) in the same syllable. For example: Parag**uay,** estud**iéis.**

NOTE: Stressed **i** and **u** do not form diphthongs with other vowels, except in the combinations **iu** and **ui.** For example, r**í**-o, sa-**bí**-ais.

In syllabication, diphthongs and triphthongs are considered a single vowel; their components cannot be separated.

Consonants

p Spanish **p** is pronounced in a manner similar to the English *p* sound, but without the puff of air that follows after the English sound is produced.

pesca	pude	puedo	parte	papá
postre	piña	puente	Paco	

k The Spanish **k** sound, represented by the letters **k; c** before **a, o, u,** or a consonant (except **h**); and **qu** (before **e** and **i**), is similar to the English *k* sound, but without the puff of air.

casa	comer	cuna	clima	acción	que
quinto	queso	aunque	kiosko	kilómetro	

t Spanish **t** is produced by touching the back of the upper front teeth with the tip of the tongue. It has no puff of air as in the English *t.*

todo	antes	corto	Guatemala	diente
resto	tonto	roto	tanque	

d The Spanish consonant **d** has two different sounds depending on its position. At the beginning of an utterance and after **n** or **l**, the tip of the tongue presses the back of the upper front teeth.

día	domo	dice	dolor	dar
anda	Aldo	caldo	el deseo	un domicilio

In all other positions the sound of **d** is similar to the *th* sound in the English word *they*, but softer.

medida	todo	nada	nadie	medio
puedo	moda	quedo	nudo	

g The Spanish consonant **g** is similar to the English *g* sound in the word *guy* except before **e** or **i**.

goma	glotón	gallo	gloria	lago	alga
gorrión	garra	guerra	angustia	algo	Dagoberto

j The Spanish sound **j** (or **g** before **e** and **i**) is similar to a strongly exaggerated English *h* sound.

gemir	juez	jarro	gitano	agente
juego	giro	bajo	gente	

b
v There is no difference in sound between Spanish **b** and **v**. Both letters are pronounced alike. At the beginning of an utterance or after **m** or **n**, **b** and **v** have a sound identical to the English *b* sound in the word *boy*.

vivir	beber	vamos	barco	enviar
hambre	batea	bueno	vestido	

When pronounced between vowels, the Spanish **b** and **v** sound is produced by bringing the lips together but not closing them, so that some air may pass through.

sábado	autobús	yo voy	su barco

y
ll In most countries, Spanish **ll** and **y** have a sound similar to the English sound in the word *yes*.

el llavero	trayecto	su yunta	milla
oye	el yeso	mayo	yema
un yelmo	trayectoria	llama	bella

NOTE: When it stands alone or is at the end of a word, Spanish **y** is pronounced like the vowel **i**.

rey	hoy	y	doy	buey
muy	voy	estoy	soy	

r The sound of Spanish **r** is similar to the English *dd* sound in the word *ladder*.

crema	aroma	cara	arena	aro
harina	toro	oro	eres	portero

rr Spanish **rr** and also **r** in an initial position and after **n, l,** or **s** are pronounced with a very strong trill. This trill is produced by bringing the tip of the tongue near the alveolar ridge and letting it vibrate freely while the air passes through the mouth.

rama	carro	Israel	cierra	roto
perro	alrededor	rizo	corre	Enrique

s Spanish **s** is represented in most of the Spanish world by the letters **s, z,** and **c** before **e** or **i**. The sound is very similar to the English sibilant *s* in the word *sink*.

sale	sitio	presidente	signo
salsa	seda	suma	vaso
sobrino	ciudad	cima	canción
zapato	zarza	cerveza	centro

h The letter **h** is silent in Spanish.

hoy	hora	hilo	ahora
humor	huevo	horror	almohada

ch Spanish **ch** is pronounced like the English *ch* in the word *chief*.

hecho	chico	coche	Chile
mucho	muchacho	salchicha	

f Spanish **f** is identical in sound to the English *f*.

difícil	feo	fuego	forma
fácil	fecha	foto	fueron

l Spanish **l** is similar to the English *l* in the word *let*.

dolor	lata	ángel	lago	sueldo
los	pelo	lana	general	fácil

m Spanish **m** is pronounced like the English *m* in the word *mother*.

mano	moda	mucho	muy
mismo	tampoco	multa	cómoda

n In most cases, Spanish **n** has a sound similar to the English *n*.

nada	nunca	ninguno	norte
entra	tiene	sienta	

The sound of Spanish **n** is often affected by the sounds that occur around it. When it appears before **b, v,** or **p,** it is pronounced like an **m.**

tan bueno	toman vino	sin poder
un pobre	comen peras	siguen bebiendo

ñ   Spanish **ñ** is similar to the English *ny* sound in the word *canyon.*

señor	otoño	ñoño	uña
leña	dueño	niños	años

x   Spanish **x** has two pronunciations depending on its position. Between vowels the sound is similar to English *ks.*

examen	exacto	boxeo	éxito
oxidar	oxígeno	existencia	

When it occurs before a consonant, Spanish **x** sounds like *s.*

expresión	explicar	extraer	excusa
expreso	exquisito	extremo	

NOTE: When **x** appears in **México** or in other words of Mexican origin, it is pronounced like the Spanish letter **j.**

Rhythm

Rhythm is the variation of sound intensity that we usually associate with music. Spanish and English each regulate these variations in speech differently, because they have different patterns of syllable length. In Spanish the length of the stressed and unstressed syllables remains almost the same, while in English stressed syllables are considerably longer than unstressed ones. Pronounce the following Spanish words, enunciating each syllable clearly.

es-tu-dian-te	bue-no	Úr-su-la
com-po-si-ción	di-fí-cil	ki-ló-me-tro
po-li-cí-a	Pa-ra-guay	

Because the length of the Spanish syllables remains constant, the greater the number of syllables in a given word or phrase, the longer the phrase will be.

Linking

In spoken Spanish, the different words in a phrase or a sentence are not pronounced as isolated elements but are combined together. This is called *linking*.

Pepe come pan.
Tomás toma leche.
Luis tiene la llave.
la mano de Roberto

Pe-pe-co-me-pan
To-más-to-ma-le-che
Luis-tie-ne-la-lla-ve
la-ma-no-de-Ro-ber-to

1. The final consonant of a word is pronounced together with the initial vowel of the following word.

Carlos anda
un ángel
el otoño
unos estudios interesantes

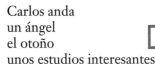

Car-lo-san-da
u-nán-gel
e-lo-to-ño
u-no-ses-tu-dio-sin-te-re-san-

2. A diphthong is formed between the final vowel of a word and the initial vowel of the following word. A triphthong is formed when there is a combination of three vowels (see rules for the formation of diphthongs and triphthongs on page 300).

su hermana
tu escopeta
Roberto y Luis
negocio importante
lluvia y nieve
ardua empresa

suher-ma-na
tues-co-pe-ta
Ro-ber-toy-Luis
ne-go-cioim-por-tan-te
llu-viay-nie-ve
ar-duaem-pre-sa

3. When the final vowel of a word and the initial vowel of the following word are identical, they are pronounced slightly longer than one vowel.

A-na*l*-can-za   Ana alcanza   tie-ne-so   tiene eso
l*o*l-vi-do   lo olvido   Ad*a*-tien-de   Ada atiende

The same rule applies when two identical vowels appear within a word.

cr*e*s   crees
T*e*-rán   Teherán
c*o*r-di-na-ción   coordinación

4. When the final consonant of a word and the initial consonant of the following word are the same, they are pronounced as one consonant with slightly longer than normal duration.

e-*l*a-do   el lado   tie-ne-*s*ed   tienes sed
Car-lo-*s*al-ta   Carlos salta

Intonation

Intonation is the rise and fall of pitch in the delivery of a phrase or a sentence. In general, Spanish pitch tends to change less than English, giving the impression that the language is less emphatic.

As a rule, the intonation for normal statements in Spanish starts in a low tone, raises to a higher one on the first stressed syllable, maintains that tone until the last stressed syllable, and then goes back to the initial low tone, with still another drop at the very end.

Tu amigo viene mañana.   José come pan.
Ada está en casa.   Carlos toma café.

Syllable Formation in Spanish

General rules for dividing words into syllables are as follows.

Vowels

1. A vowel or a vowel combination can constitute a syllable.

   a-lum-no   a-bue-la   Eu-ro-pa

2. Diphthongs and triphthongs are considered single vowels and cannot be divided.

   bai-le   puen-te   Dia-na   es-tu-diáis   an-ti-guo

3. Two strong vowels (**a, e, o**) do not form a diphthong and are separated into two syllables.

   em-ple-ar   vol-te-ar   lo-a

4. A written accent on a weak vowel (**i** or **u**) breaks the diphthong, thus the vowels are separated into two syllables.

   trí-o   dú-o   Ma-rí-a

Consonants

1. A single consonant forms a syllable with the vowel that follows it.

   po-der   ma-no   mi-nu-to

2. When two consonants appear between two vowels, they are separated into two syllables.

   al-fa-be-to   cam-pe-ón   me-ter-se   mo-les-tia

   EXCEPTION: When a consonant cluster composed of **b, c, d, f, g, p,** or **t** with **l** or **r** appears between two vowels, the cluster joins the following vowel: **so-bre, o-tros, ca-ble, te-lé-gra-fo.**

3. When three consonants appear between two vowels, only the last one goes with the following vowel.

   ins-pec-tor   trans-por-te   trans-for-mar

   EXCEPTION: When there is a cluster of three consonants in the combinations described in rule 2, the first consonant joins the preceding vowel and the cluster joins the following vowel: **es-cri-bir, ex-tran-je-ro, im-plo-rar, es-tre-cho.**

Accentuation

In Spanish, all words are stressed according to specific rules. Words that do not follow the rules must have a written accent to indicate the change of stress. The basic rules for accentuation are as follows.

1. Words ending in a vowel, **n,** or **s** are stressed on the next-to-the-last syllable.

hi-jo	**ca**-lle	**me**-sa	fa-**mo**-sos
flo-**re**-cen	**pla**-ya	**ve**-ces	

2. Words ending in a consonant, except **n** or **s,** are stressed on the last syllable.

ma-**yor**	a-**mor**	tro-pi-**cal**
na-**riz**	re-**loj**	co-rre-**dor**

3. All words that do not follow these rules must have the written accent.

ca-**fé**	**lá**-piz	**mú**-si-ca	sa-**lón**
án-gel	**lí**-qui-do	fran-**cés**	**Víc**-tor
sim-**pá**-ti-co	rin-**cón**	a-**zú**-car	**dár**-se-lo
sa-**lió**	**dé**-bil	e-**xá**-me-nes	**dí**-me-lo

4. Pronouns and adverbs of interrogation and exclamation have a written accent to distinguish them from relative pronouns.

—¿**Qué** comes?   *"What are you eating?"*
—La pera que él no comió.   *"The pear that he did not eat."*

—¿**Quién** está ahí?   *"Who is there?"*
—El hombre a quien tú   *"The man whom you called."*
   llamaste.

—¿**Dónde** está?   *"Where is he?"*
—En el lugar donde trabaja.   *"At the place where he works."*

5. Words that have the same spelling but different meanings take a written accent to differentiate one from the other.

el	*the*	él	*he, him*	te	*you*	té	*tea*
mi	*my*	mí	*me*	si	*if*	sí	*yes*
tu	*your*	tú	*you*	mas	*but*	más	*more*

Verbs

Regular Verbs
Model -ar, -er, -ir *verbs*

INFINITIVE		
amar (*to love*)	**comer** (*to eat*)	**vivir** (*to live*)

GERUND		
amando (*loving*)	**comiendo** (*eating*)	**viviendo** (*living*)

PAST PARTICIPLE		
amado (*loved*)	**comido** (*eaten*)	**vivido** (*lived*)

Simple Tenses

Indicative Mood

PRESENT		
(*I love*)	(*I eat*)	(*I live*)
am**o**	com**o**	viv**o**
am**as**	com**es**	viv**es**
am**a**	com**e**	viv**e**
am**amos**	com**emos**	viv**imos**
am**áis**[1]	com**éis**	viv**ís**
am**an**	com**en**	viv**en**

IMPERFECT		
(*I used to love*)	(*I used to eat*)	(*I used to live*)
am**aba**	com**ía**	viv**ía**
am**abas**	com**ías**	viv**ías**
am**aba**	com**ía**	viv**ía**
am**ábamos**	com**íamos**	viv**íamos**
am**abais**	com**íais**	viv**íais**
am**aban**	com**ían**	viv**ían**

---

[1] **Vosotros amáis:** The **vosotros** form of the verb is used primarily in Spain. This form has not been used in this text.

PRETERIT

(I loved)	(I ate)	(I lived)
amé	comí	viví
amaste	comiste	viviste
amó	comió	vivió
amamos	comimos	vivimos
amasteis	comisteis	vivisteis
amaron	comieron	vivieron

FUTURE

(I will love)	(I will eat)	(I will live)
amaré	comeré	viviré
amarás	comerás	vivirás
amará	comerá	vivirá
amaremos	comeremos	viviremos
amaréis	comeréis	viviréis
amarán	comerán	vivirán

CONDITIONAL

(I would love)	(I would eat)	(I would live)
amaría	comería	viviría
amarías	comerías	vivirías
amaría	comería	viviría
amaríamos	comeríamos	viviríamos
amaríais	comeríais	viviríais
amarían	comerían	vivirían

Subjunctive Mood

PRESENT

([that] I [may] love)	([that] I [may] eat)	([that] I [may] live)
ame	coma	viva
ames	comas	vivas
ame	coma	viva
amemos	comamos	vivamos
améis	comáis	viváis
amen	coman	vivan

IMPERFECT (two forms: **-ra, -se**)

([that] I [might] love)	([that] I [might] eat)	([that] I [might] live)
amara(-ase)	comiera(-iese)	viviera(-iese)
amaras(-ases)	comieras(-ieses)	vivieras(-ieses)
amara(-ase)	comiera(-iese)	viviera(-iese)
amáramos (-ásemos)	comiéramos (-iésemos)	viviéramos (-iésemos)
amarais(-aseis)	comierais(-ieseis)	vivierais(-ieseis)
amaran(-asen)	comieran(-iesen)	vivieran(-iesen)

Imperative Mood (Command Forms)

(love)	*(eat)*	*(live)*
am**a** (tú)	com**e** (tú)	viv**e** (tú)
am**e** (Ud.)	com**a** (Ud.)	viv**a** (Ud.)
am**emos** (nosotros)	com**amos** (nosotros)	viv**amos** (nosotros)
am**ad** (vosotros)	com**ed** (vosotros)	viv**id** (vosotros)
am**en** (Uds.)	com**an** (Uds.)	viv**an** (Uds.)

Compound Tenses

PERFECT INFINITIVE

haber amado	**haber comido**	**haber vivido**

PERFECT PARTICIPLE

habiendo amado	**habiendo comido**	**habiendo vivido**

Indicative Mood

PRESENT PERFECT

(I have loved)	*(I have eaten)*	*(I have lived)*
he amado	he comido	he vivido
has amado	has comido	has vivido
ha amado	ha comido	ha vivido
hemos amado	hemos comido	hemos vivido
habéis amado	habéis comido	habéis vivido
han amado	han comido	han vivido

PLUPERFECT

(I had loved)	*(I had eaten)*	*(I had lived)*
había amado	había comido	había vivido
habías amado	habías comido	habías vivido
había amado	había comido	había vivido
habíamos amado	habíamos comido	habíamos vivido
habíais amado	habíais comido	habíais vivido
habían amado	habían comido	habían vivido

FUTURE PERFECT

(I will have loved)	*(I will have eaten)*	*(I will have lived)*
habré amado	habré comido	habré vivido
habrás amado	habrás comido	habrás vivido
habrá amado	habrá comido	habrá vivido
habremos amado	habremos comido	habremos vivido
habréis amado	habréis comido	habréis vivido
habrán amado	habrán comido	habrán vivido

CONDITIONAL PERFECT

(I would have loved)	*(I would have eaten)*	*(I would have lived)*
habría amado	habría comido	habría vivido
habrías amado	habrías comido	habrías vivido
habría amado	habría comido	habría vivido
habríamos amado	habríamos comido	habríamos vivido
habríais amado	habríais comido	habríais vivido
habrían amado	habrían comido	habrían vivido

Subjunctive Mood

PRESENT PERFECT

([that] I [may] have loved)	*([that] I [may] have eaten)*	*([that] I [may] have lived)*
haya amado	haya comido	haya vivido
hayas amado	hayas comido	hayas vivido
haya amado	haya comido	haya vivido
hayamos amado	hayamos comido	hayamos vivido
hayáis amado	hayáis comido	hayáis vivido
hayan amado	hayan comido	hayan vivido

PLUPERFECT

(two forms: **-ra, -se**)

([that] I [might] have loved)	*([that] I [might] have eaten)*	*([that] I [might] have lived)*
hubiera(-iese) amado	hubiera(-iese) comido	hubiera(-iese) vivido
hubieras(-ieses) amado	hubieras(-ieses) comido	hubieras(-ieses) vivido
hubiera(-iese) amado	hubiera(-iese) comido	hubiera(-iese) vivido
hubiéramos(-iésemos) amado	hubiéramos(-iésemos) comido	hubiéramos(-iésemos) vivido
hubierais(-ieseis) amado	hubierais(-ieseis) comido	hubierais(-ieseis) vivido
hubieran(-iesen) amado	hubieran(-iesen) comido	hubieran(-iesen) vivido

Stem-Changing Verbs

The -ar *and* -er *stem-changing verbs*

Stem-changing verbs are those that have a change in the root of the verb. Verbs that end in **-ar** and **-er** change the stressed vowel **e** to **ie**, and the stressed **o** to **ue**. These changes occur in all persons, except the first and second persons plural of the present indicative, present subjunctive, and command.

INFINITIVE	PRESENT INDICATIVE	IMPERATIVE	PRESENT SUBJUNCTIVE
cerrar	cierro	—	cierre
(to close)	cierras	cierra	cierres
	cierra	(Ud.) cierre	cierre
	cerramos	cerremos	cerremos
	cerráis	cerrad	cerréis
	cierran	(Uds.) cierren	cierren
perder	pierdo	—	pierda
(to lose)	pierdes	pierde	pierdas
	pierde	(Ud.) pierda	pierda
	perdemos	perdamos	perdamos
	perdéis	perded	perdáis
	pierden	(Uds.) pierdan	pierdan
contar	cuento	—	cuente
(to count,	cuentas	cuenta	cuentes
to tell)	cuenta	(Ud.) cuente	cuente
	contamos	contemos	contemos
	contáis	contad	contéis
	cuentan	(Uds.) cuenten	cuenten
volver	vuelvo	—	vuelva
(to return)	vuelves	vuelve	vuelvas
	vuelve	(Ud.) vuelva	vuelva
	volvemos	volvamos	volvamos
	volvéis	volved	volváis
	vuelven	(Uds.) vuelvan	vuelvan

Verbs that follow the same pattern include the following.

acertar to guess right	**entender** to understand
acordarse to remember	**llover** to rain
acostar(se) to go to bed	**mostrar** to show
almorzar to have lunch	**mover** to move
atravesar to go through	**negar** to deny
cegar to blind	**nevar** to snow
cocer to cook	**pensar** to think, to plan
colgar to hang	**probar** to prove, to taste
comenzar to begin	**recordar** to remember
confesar to confess	**resolver** to decide on
costar to cost	**rogar** to beg
demostrar to demonstrate, to show	**sentar(se)** to sit down
	soler to be in the habit of
despertar(se) to wake up	**soñar** to dream
empezar to begin	**tender** to stretch, to unfold
encender to light, to turn on	**torcer** to twist
encontrar to find	

The -ir stem-changing verbs

There are two types of stem-changing verbs that end in **-ir:** one type changes stressed **e** to **ie** in some tenses and to **i** in others, and stressed **o** to **ue** or **u;** the second type always changes stressed **e** to **i** in the irregular forms of the verb.

Type I   **e:ie**   or   **i**
         -ir:
                    o:ue   or   **u**

These changes occur as follows.

Present Indicative: all persons except the first and second plural change **e** to **ie** and **o** to **ue.** *Preterit:* third person, singular and plural, changes **e** to **i** and **o** to **u.** *Present Subjunctive:* all persons change **e** to **ie** and **o** to **ue,** except the first and second persons plural, which change **e** to **i** and **o** to **u.** *Imperfect Subjunctive:* all persons change **e** to **i** and **o** to **u.** *Imperative:* all persons except the second person plural change **e** to **ie** and **o** to **ue;** first person plural changes **e** to **i** and **o** to **u.** *Present Participle:* changes **e** to **i** and **o** to **u.**

	Indicative		Imperative	Subjunctive	
INFINITIVE	PRESENT	PRETERIT		PRESENT	IMPERFECT
sentir	siento	sentí	—	sienta	sintiera(-iese)
(to feel)	sientes	sentiste	siente	sientas	sintieras
	siente	sintió	(Ud.) sienta	sienta	sintiera
PRESENT	sentimos	sentimos	sintamos	sintamos	sintiéramos
PARTICIPLE	sentís	sentisteis	sentid	sintáis	sintierais
sintiendo	sienten	sintieron	(Uds.) sientan	sientan	sintieran
dormir	duermo	dormí	—	duerma	durmiera(-iese)
(to sleep)	duermes	dormiste	duerme	duermas	durmieras
	duerme	durmió	(Ud.) duerma	duerma	durmiera
PRESENT	dormimos	dormimos	durmamos	durmamos	durmiéramos
PARTICIPLE	dormís	dormisteis	dormid	durmáis	durmierais
durmiendo	duermen	durmieron	(Uds.) duerman	duerman	durmieran

Other verbs that follow the same pattern include the following.

advertir   to warn
arrepentir(se)   to repent
consentir   to consent, to pamper
convertir(se)   to turn into
discernir   to discern
divertir(se)   to amuse oneself

herir   to wound, to hurt
mentir   to lie
morir   to die
preferir   to prefer
referir   to refer
sugerir   to suggest

Type II   -ir: e:i

The verbs in this second category are irregular in the same tenses as those of the first type. The only difference is that they only have one change: **e:i** in all irregular persons.

	Indicative		Imperative	Subjunctive	
INFINITIVE	PRESENT	PRETERIT		PRESENT	IMPERFECT
pedir	pido	pedí	—	pida	pidiera(-iese)
(to ask for,	pides	pediste	pide	pidas	pidieras
to request)	pide	pidió	(Ud.) pida	pida	pidiera
PRESENT	pedimos	pedimos	pidamos	pidamos	pidiéramos
PARTICIPLE	pedís	pedisteis	pedid	pidáis	pidierais
pidiendo	piden	pidieron	(Uds.) pidan	pidan	pidieran

Verbs that follow this pattern include the following.

competir to compete	**reír(se)** to laugh
concebir to conceive	**reñir** to fight
despedir(se) to say good-bye	**repetir** to repeat
elegir to choose	**seguir** to follow
impedir to prevent	**servir** to serve
perseguir to pursue	**vestir(se)** to dress

Orthographic-Changing Verbs

Some verbs undergo a change in the spelling of the stem in certain tenses, in order to maintain the original sound of the final consonant. The most common verbs of this type are those with the consonants **g** and **c**. Remember that **g** and **c** have a soft sound in front of **e** or **i**, and have a hard sound in front of **a**, **o**, or **u**. In order to maintain the soft sound in front of **a**, **o**, and **u**, **g** and **c** change to **j** and **z**, respectively. And in order to maintain the hard sound of **g** and **c** in front of **e** and **i**, **u** is added to the **g** (**gu**) and **c** changes to **qu**.

The following important verbs undergo spelling changes in the tenses listed below.

1. Verbs ending in **-gar** change **g** to **gu** before **e** in the first person of the preterit and in all persons of the present subjunctive.

   pagar (*to pay*)
   Preterit: pa**gué**, pagaste, pagó, etc.
   Pres. Subj.: pa**gue**, pa**gue**s, pa**gue**, pa**gue**mos, pa**gué**is, pa**gue**n

   Verbs that follow the same pattern: **colgar, jugar, llegar, navegar, negar, regar, rogar.**

2. Verbs ending in **-ger** and **-gir** change **g** to **j** before **o** and **a** in the first person of the present indicative and in all persons of the present subjunctive.

   proteger (*to protect*)
   Pres. Ind.:   prote**j**o, proteges, protege, etc.
   Pres. Subj.: prote**j**a, prote**j**as, prote**j**a, prote**j**amos, prote**j**áis, prote**j**an

   Verbs that follow the same pattern: **coger, corregir, dirigir, elegir, escoger, exigir, recoger.**

3. Verbs ending in **-guar** change **gu** to **gü** before **e** in the first person of the preterit and in all persons of the present subjunctive.

averiguar (*to find out*)
Preterit:　averigüé, averiguaste, averiguó, etc.
Pres. Subj.:　averigüe, averigües, averigüe, averigüemos,
　　　　　　averigüéis, averigüen

The verb **apaciguar** follows the same pattern.

4. Verbs ending in **-guir** change **gu** to **g** before **o** and **a** in the first person of the present indicative and in all persons of the present subjunctive.

conseguir (*to get*)
Pres. Ind.:　consigo, consigues, consigue, etc.
Pres. Subj.:　consiga, consigas, consiga, consigamos, consigáis,
　　　　　　consigan

Verbs that follow the same pattern: **distinguir, perseguir, proseguir, seguir.**

5. Verbs ending in **-car** change **c** to **qu** before **e** in the first person of the preterit and in all persons of the present subjunctive.

tocar (*to touch, to play* [*a musical instrument*])
Preterit:　toqué, tocaste, tocó, etc.
Pres. Subj.:　toque, toques, toque, toquemos, toquéis, toquen

Verbs that follow the same pattern: **atacar, buscar, comunicar, explicar, indicar, pescar, sacar.**

6. Verbs ending in **-cer** and **-cir** preceded by a consonant change **c** to **z** before **o** and **a** in the first person of the present indicative and in all persons of the present subjunctive.

torcer (*to twist*)
Pres. Ind.:　tuerzo, tuerces, tuerce, etc.
Pres. Subj.:　tuerza, tuerzas, tuerza, torzamos, torzáis, tuerzan

Verbs that follow the same pattern: **convencer, esparcir, vencer.**

7. Verbs ending in **-cer** and **-cir** preceded by a vowel change **c** to **zc** before **o** and **a** in the first person of the present indicative and in all persons of the present subjunctive.

conocer (*to know, to be acquainted with*)
Pres. Ind.:　conozco, conoces, conoce, etc.
Pres. Subj.:　conozca, conozcas, conozca, conozcamos,
　　　　　　conozcáis, conozcan

Verbs that follow the same pattern: **agradecer, aparecer, carecer, entristecer, establecer, lucir, nacer, obedecer, ofrecer, padecer, parecer, pertenecer, reconocer, relucir.**

8. Verbs ending in **-zar** change **z** to **c** before **e** in the first person of the preterit and in all persons of the present subjunctive.

rezar (*to pray*)
Preterit: recé, rezaste, rezó, etc.
Pres. Subj.: rece, reces, rece, recemos, recéis, recen

Verbs that follow the same pattern: **abrazar, alcanzar, almorzar, comenzar, cruzar, empezar, forzar, gozar.**

9. Verbs ending in **-eer** change the unstressed **i** to **y** between vowels in the third person singular and plural of the preterit, in all persons of the imperfect subjunctive, and in the present participle.

creer (*to believe*)
Preterit: creí, creíste, creyó, creímos, creísteis, creyeron
Imp. Subj.: creyera(ese), creyeras, creyera, creyéramos, creyerais, creyeran
Pres. Part.: creyendo

Leer and **poseer** follow the same pattern.

10. Verbs ending in **-uir** change the unstressed **i** to **y** between vowels (except **-quir,** which has the silent **u**) in the following tenses and persons.

huir (*to escape, to flee*)
Pres. Part.: huyendo
Past Part.: huido
Pres. Ind.: huyo, huyes, huye, huimos, huís, huyen
Preterit: huí, huiste, huyó, huimos, huisteis, huyeron
Imperative: huye, huya, huyamos, huid, huyan
Pres. Subj.: huya, huyas, huya, huyamos, huyáis, huyan
Imp. Subj.: huyera(ese), huyeras, huyera, huyéramos, huyerais, huyeran

Verbs that follow the same pattern: **atribuir, concluir, constituir, construir, contribuir, destituir, destruir, disminuir, distribuir, excluir, incluir, influir, instruir, restituir, sustituir.**

11. Verbs ending in **-eír** lose one **e** in the third person singular and plural of the preterit, in all persons of the imperfect subjunctive, and in the present participle.

reír(se) (*to laugh*)
Preterit: reí, reíste, rió, reímos, reísteis, rieron
Imp. Subj.: riera(ese), rieras, riera, riéramos, rierais, rieran
Pres. Part.: riendo

Freír and **sonreír** follow the same pattern.

12. Verbs ending in **-iar** add a written accent to the **i**, except in the first and second persons plural of the present indicative and subjunctive.

fiar(se) (*to trust*)
Pres. Ind.:   fío, fías, fía, fiamos, fiáis, fían
Pres. Subj.:   fíe, fíes, fíe, fiemos, fiéis, fíen

Verbs that follow the same pattern: **ampliar, criar, desviar, enfriar, enviar, esquiar, guiar, telegrafiar, vaciar, variar.**

13. Verbs ending in **-uar** (except **-guar**) add a written accent to the **u**, except in the first and second persons plural of the present indicative and subjunctive.

actuar (*to act*)
Pres. Ind.:   actúo, actúas, actúa, actuamos, actuáis, actúan
Pres. Subj.:   actúe, actúes, actúe, actuemos, actuéis, actúen

Verbs that follow the same pattern: **acentuar, continuar, efectuar, exceptuar, graduar, habituar, insinuar, situar.**

14. Verbs ending in **-ñir** remove the **i** of the diphthongs **ie** and **ió** in the third person singular and plural of the preterit and in all persons of the imperfect subjunctive. They also change the **e** of the stem to **i** in the same persons.

teñir (*to dye*)
Preterit: teñí, teñiste, **tiñó,** teñimos, teñisteis, **tiñeron**
Imp. Subj.:   tiñera(ese), tiñeras, tiñera, tiñéramos, tiñerais, tiñeran

Verbs that follow the same pattern: **ceñir, constreñir, desteñir, estreñir, reñir.**

Some Common Irregular Verbs

Only those tenses with irregular forms are given below.

adquirir (*to acquire*)
Pres. Ind.:   adquiero, adquieres, adquiere, adquirimos, adquirís, adquieren
Pres. Subj.:   adquiera, adquieras, adquiera, adquiramos, adquiráis, adquieran
Imperative: adquiere, adquiera, adquiramos, adquirid, adquieran

andar (*to walk*)
Preterit: anduve, anduviste, anduvo, anduvimos, anduvisteis, anduvieron
Imp. Subj.:   anduviera (anduviese), anduvieras, anduviera, anduviéramos, anduvierais, anduvieran

avergonzarse (*to be ashamed, to be embarrassed*)
Pres. Ind.:   me avergüenzo, te avergüenzas, se avergüenza, nos
                avergonzamos, os avergonzáis, se avergüenzan
Pres. Subj.:   me avergüence, te avergüences, se avergüence, nos
                avergoncemos, os avergoncéis, se avergüencen
Imperative: avergüénzate, avergüéncese, avergoncémonos,
                avergonzaos, avergüéncense

caber (*to fit, to have enough room*)
Pres. Ind.:   quepo, cabes, cabe, cabemos, cabéis, caben
Preterit: cupe, cupiste, cupo, cupimos, cupisteis, cupieron
Future: cabré, cabrás, cabrá, cabremos, cabréis, cabrán
Conditional: cabría, cabrías, cabría, cabríamos, cabríais, cabrían
Imperative: cabe, quepa, quepamos, cabed, quepan
Pres. Subj.:   quepa, quepas, quepa, quepamos, quepáis, quepan
Imp. Subj.:   cupiera (cupiese), cupieras, cupiera, cupiéramos, cu-
                pierais, cupieran

caer (*to fall*)
Pres. Ind.:   caigo, caes, cae, caemos, caéis, caen
Preterit: caí, caíste, cayó, caímos, caísteis, cayeron
Imperative: cae, caiga, caigamos, caed, caigan
Pres. Subj.:   caiga, caigas, caiga, caigamos, caigáis, caigan
Imp. Subj.:   cayera (cayese), cayeras, cayera, cayéramos, cayerais,
                cayeran
Past Part.:   caído

conducir (*to guide, to drive*)
Pres. Ind.:   conduzco, conduces, conduce, conducimos, conducís,
                conducen
Preterit: conduje, condujiste, condujo, condujimos, condujisteis,
                condujeron
Imperative: conduce, conduzca, conduzcamos, conducid,
                conduzcan
Pres. Subj.:   conduzca, conduzcas, conduzca, conduzcamos,
                conduzcáis, conduzcan
Imp. Subj.:   condujera (condujese), condujeras, condujera,
                condujéramos, condujerais, condujeran

                (All verbs ending in **-ducir** follow this pattern.)

convenir (*to agree*) See **venir.**

dar (*to give*)
Pres. Ind.:   doy, das, da, damos, dais, dan
Preterit: di, diste, dio, dimos, disteis, dieron
Imperative: da, dé, demos, dad, den
Pres. Subj.:   dé, des, dé, demos, deis, den
Imp. Subj.:   diera (diese), dieras, diera, diéramos, dierais, dieran

decir (*to say, to tell*)
Pres. Ind.:   digo, dices, dice, decimos, decís, dicen
Preterit: dije, dijiste, dijo, dijimos, dijisteis, dijeron
Future: diré, dirás, dirá, diremos, diréis, dirán
Conditional: diría, dirías, diría, diríamos, diríais, dirían
Imperative: di, diga, digamos, decid, digan
Pres. Subj.: diga, digas, diga, digamos, digáis, digan
Imp. Subj.: dijera (dijese), dijeras, dijera, dijéramos, dijerais, dijeran
Pres. Part.: diciendo
Past Part.: dicho

detener (*to stop, to hold, to arrest*) See **tener.**

entretener (*to entertain, to amuse*) See **tener.**

errar (*to err, to miss*)
Pres. Ind.:   yerro, yerras, yerra, erramos, erráis, yerran
Imperative: yerra, yerre, erremos, errad, yerren
Pres. Subj.: yerre, yerres, yerre, erremos, erréis, yerren

estar (*to be*)
Pres. Ind.:   estoy, estás, está, estamos, estáis, están
Preterit: estuve, estuviste, estuvo, estuvimos, estuvisteis,
              estuvieron
Imperative: está, esté, estemos, estad, estén
Pres. Subj.: esté, estés, esté, estemos, estéis, estén
Imp. Subj.: estuviera (estuviese), estuvieras, estuviera,
              estuviéramos, estuvierais, estuvieran

haber (*to have*)
Pres. Ind.:   he, has, ha, hemos, habéis, han
Preterit: hube, hubiste, hubo, hubimos, hubisteis, hubieron
Future: habré, habrás, habrá, habremos, habréis, habrán
Conditional: habría, habrías, habría, habríamos, habríais, habrían
Imperative: he, haya, hayamos, habed, hayan
Pres. Subj.: haya, hayas, haya, hayamos, hayáis, hayan
Imp. Subj.: hubiera (hubiese), hubieras, hubiera, hubiéramos,
              hubierais, hubieran

hacer (*to do, to make*)
Pres. Ind.:   hago, haces, hace, hacemos, hacéis, hacen
Preterit: hice, hiciste, hizo, hicimos, hicisteis, hicieron
Future: haré, harás, hará, haremos, haréis, harán
Conditional: haría, harías, haría, haríamos, haríais, harían
Imperative: haz, haga, hagamos, haced, hagan
Pres. Subj.: haga, hagas, haga, hagamos, hagáis, hagan
Imp. Subj.: hiciera (hiciese), hicieras, hiciera, hiciéramos, hicierais,
              hicieran
Past Part.: hecho

imponer (*to impose, to deposit*) See **poner.**

introducir (*to introduce, to insert, to gain access*) See **conducir.**

ir (*to go*)
Pres. Ind.:   voy, vas, va, vamos, vais, van
Imp. Ind.:   iba, ibas, iba, íbamos, ibais, iban
Preterit: fui, fuiste, fue, fuimos, fuisteis, fueron
Imperative: ve, vaya, vayamos, id, vayan
Pres. Subj.: vaya, vayas, vaya, vayamos, vayáis, vayan
Imp. Subj.:   fuera (fuese), fueras, fuera, fuéramos, fuerais, fueran

jugar (*to play*)
Pres. Ind.:   juego, juegas, juega, jugamos, jugáis, juegan
Imperative: juega, juegue, juguemos, jugad, jueguen
Pres. Subj.: juegue, juegues, juegue, juguemos, juguéis, jueguen

obtener (*to obtain*) See **tener.**

oír (*to hear*)
Pres. Ind.:   oigo, oyes, oye, oímos, oís, oyen
Preterit: oí, oíste, oyó, oímos, oísteis, oyeron
Imperative: oye, oiga, oigamos, oíd, oigan
Pres. Subj.: oiga, oigas, oiga, oigamos, oigáis, oigan
Imp. Subj.:   oyera (oyese), oyeras, oyera, oyéramos, oyerais, oyeran
Pres. Part.: oyendo
Past Part.:   oído

oler (*to smell*)
Pres. Ind.:   huelo, hueles, huele, olemos, oléis, huelen
Imperative: huele, huela, olamos, oled, huelan
Pres. Subj.: huela, huelas, huela, olamos, oláis, huelan

poder (*to be able*)
Pres. Ind.:   puedo, puedes, puede, podemos, podéis, pueden
Preterit: pude, pudiste, pudo, pudimos, pudisteis, pudieron
Future: podré, podrás, podrá, podremos, podréis, podrán
Conditional: podría, podrías, podría, podríamos, podríais, podrían
Imperative: puede, pueda, podamos, poded, puedan
Pres. Subj.: pueda, puedas, pueda, podamos, podáis, puedan
Imp. Subj.:   pudiera (pudiese), pudieras, pudiera, pudiéramos, pudierais, pudieran
Pres. Part.: pudiendo

poner (*to place, to put*)
Pres. Ind.:   pongo, pones, pone, ponemos, ponéis, ponen
Preterit: puse, pusiste, puso, pusimos, pusisteis, pusieron
Future: pondré, pondrás, pondrá, pondremos, pondréis, pondrán
Conditional: pondría, pondrías, pondría, pondríamos, pondríais, pondrían

Imperative: pon, ponga, pongamos, poned, pongan
Pres. Subj.: ponga, pongas, ponga, pongamos, pongáis, pongan
Imp. Subj.: pusiera (pusiese), pusieras, pusiera, pusiéramos, pusierais, pusieran
Past Part.: puesto

querer (*to want, to wish, to like*)
Pres. Ind.: quiero, quieres, quiere, queremos, queréis, quieren
Preterit: quise, quisiste, quiso, quisimos, quisisteis, quisieron
Future: querré, querrás, querrá, querremos, querréis, querrán
Conditional: querría, querrías, querría, querríamos, querríais, querrían
Imperative: quiere, quiera, queramos, quered, quieran
Pres. Subj.: quiera, quieras, quiera, queramos, queráis, quieran
Imp. Subj.: quisiera (quisiese), quisieras, quisiera, quisiéramos, quisierais, quisieran

resolver (*to decide on*)
Past Part.: resuelto

saber (*to know*)
Pres. Ind.: sé, sabes, sabe, sabemos, sabéis, saben
Preterit: supe, supiste, supo, supimos, supisteis, supieron
Future: sabré, sabrás, sabrá, sabremos, sabréis, sabrán
Conditional: sabría, sabrías, sabría, sabríamos, sabríais, sabrían
Imperative: sabe, sepa, sepamos, sabed, sepan
Pres. Subj.: sepa, sepas, sepa, sepamos, sepáis, sepan
Imp. Subj.: supiera (supiese), supieras, supiera, supiéramos, supierais, supieran

salir (*to leave, to go out*)
Pres. Ind.: salgo, sales, sale, salimos, salís, salen
Future: saldré, saldrás, saldrá, saldremos, saldréis, saldrán
Conditional: saldría, saldrías, saldría, saldríamos, saldríais, saldrían
Imperative: sal, salga, salgamos, salid, salgan
Pres. Subj.: salga, salgas, salga, salgamos, salgáis, salgan

ser (*to be*)
Pres. Ind.: soy, eres, es, somos, sois, son
Imp. Ind.: era, eras, era, éramos, erais, eran
Preterit: fui, fuiste, fue, fuimos, fuisteis, fueron
Imperative: sé, sea, seamos, sed, sean
Pres. Subj.: sea, seas, sea, seamos, seáis, sean
Imp. Subj.: fuera (fuese), fueras, fuera, fuéramos, fuerais, fueran

suponer (*to assume*) See **poner.**

tener (*to have*)
Pres. Ind.: tengo, tienes, tiene, tenemos, tenéis, tienen
Preterit: tuve, tuviste, tuvo, tuvimos, tuvisteis, tuvieron

Future: tendré, tendrás, tendrá, tendremos, tendréis, tendrán
Conditional: tendría, tendrías, tendría, tendríamos, tendríais,
                 tendrían
Imperative: ten, tenga, tengamos, tened, tengan
Pres. Subj.:   tenga, tengas, tenga, tengamos, tengáis, tengan
Imp. Subj.:   tuviera (tuviese), tuvieras, tuviera, tuviéramos, tu-
                 vierais, tuvieran

traducir (*to translate*) See **conducir.**

traer (*to bring*)
Pres. Ind.:   traigo, traes, trae, traemos, traéis, traen
Preterit: traje, trajiste, trajo, trajimos, trajisteis, trajeron
Imperative: trae, traiga, traigamos, traed, traigan
Pres. Subj.:   traiga, traigas, traiga, traigamos, traigáis, traigan
Imp. Subj.:   trajera (trajese), trajeras, trajera, trajéramos, trajerais,
                 trajeran
Pres. Part.:   trayendo
Past Part.:   traído

valer (*to be worth*)
Pres. Ind.:   valgo, vales, vale, valemos, valéis, valen
Future: valdré, valdrás, valdrá, valdremos, valdréis, valdrán
Conditional: valdría, valdrías, valdría, valdríamos, valdríais, valdrían
Imperative: vale, valga, valgamos, valed, valgan
Pres. Subj.:   valga, valgas, valga, valgamos, valgáis, valgan

venir (*to come*)
Pres. Ind.:   vengo, vienes, viene, venimos, venís, vienen
Preterit: vine, viniste, vino, vinimos, vinisteis, vinieron
Future: vendré, vendrás, vendrá, vendremos, vendréis, vendrán
Conditional: vendría, vendrías, vendría, vendríamos, vendríais,
                 vendrían
Imperative: ven, venga, vengamos, venid, vengan
Pres. Subj.:   venga, vengas, venga, vengamos, vengáis, vengan
Imp. Subj.:   viniera (viniese), vinieras, viniera, viniéramos,
                 vinierais, vinieran
Pres. Part.:   viniendo

ver (*to see*)
Pres. Ind.:   veo, ves, ve, vemos, veis, ven
Imp. Ind.:   veía, veías, veía, veíamos, veíais, veían
Preterit: vi, viste, vio, vimos, visteis, vieron
Imperative: ve, vea, veamos, ved, vean
Pres. Subj.:   vea, veas, vea, veamos, veáis, vean
Imp. Subj.:   viera (viese), vieras, viera, viéramos, vierais, vieran
Past. Part.:   visto

volver (*to return*)
Past Part.:   vuelto

Careers and Occupations

accountant **contador(a)**

actor **actor**

actress **actriz**

administrator **administrador(a)**

agent **agente**

architect **arquitecto(a)**

artisan **artesano(a)**

artist **artista**

baker **panadero(a)**

bank officer **empleado(a) ban-cario(a)**

bank teller **cajero(a)**

banker **banquero(a)**

barber **barbero(a)**

bartender **barman, cantinero(a)**

bill collector **cobrador(a)**

bookkeeper **tenedor(a) de libros**

brickmason (bricklayer) **albañil**

butcher **carnicero(a)**

buyer **comprador(a)**

camera operator **camarógrafo(a)**

carpenter **carpintero(a)**

cashier **cajero(a)**

chiropractor **quiropráctico(a)**

clerk **dependiente(a)** *(store)*, **oficinista** *(office)*

computer operator **computista**

construction worker **obrero(a) de la construcción**

constructor **constructor(a)**

contractor **contratista**

cook **cocinero(a)**

copilot **copiloto(a)**

counselor **consejero(a)**

dancer **bailarín(ina)**

decorator **decorador(a)**

dental hygienist **higienista dental**

dentist **dentista**

designer **diseñador(a)**

detective **detective**

dietician **especialista en dietética**

diplomat **diplomático(a)**

director **director(a)**

dockworker **obrero(a) portuario(a)**

doctor **doctor(a), médico(a)**

draftsman **dibujante**

dressmaker **modista**

driver **conductor(a)**

economist **economista**

editor **editor(a)**

electrician **electricista**

engineer **ingeniero(a)**

engineering technician **ingeniero(a) técnico(a)**

eye doctor **oculista**

farmer **agricultor(a)**

fashion designer **diseñador(a) de alta costura**

fire fighter **bombero(a)**

fisherman **pescador(a)**

flight attendant **auxiliar de vuelo**

foreman **capataz, encargado(a)**

funeral director **empresario(a) de pompas fúnebres**

garbage collector **basurero(a)**

gardener **jardinero(a)**

guard **guardia**

guide **guía**

hairdresser **peluquero(a)**

housekeeper **mayordomo, ama de llaves**

inspector **inspector(a)**
instructor **instructor(a)**
insurance agent **agente
de seguros**
interior designer
diseñador(a) de interiores
interpreter **intérprete**
investigator **investigador(a)**
janitor **conserje**
jeweler **joyero(a)**
journalist **periodista**
judge **juez(a)**
lawyer **abogado(a)**
librarian **bibliotecario(a)**
machinist **maquinista**
maid **criada**
mail carrier **cartero(a)**
manager **gerente**
mechanic **mecánico(a)**
midwife **comadrón(ona),
partero(a)**
miner **minero(a)**
model **modelo**
musician **músico(a)**
nurse **enfermero(a)**
optician **óptico(a)**
optometrist **optometrista**
painter **pintor(a)**
paramedic **paramédico(a)**
pharmacist **farmacéutico(a)**
photographer **fotógrafo(a)**
physical therapist **terapista
físico(a)**
physician **médico(a)**
pilot **piloto** *(masc., fem.),*
aviador(a)
plumber **plomero(a)**
police officer **policía**
printer **impresor(a)**
psychologist **psicólogo(a)**
public relations agent **agente
de relaciones públicas**
real estate agent **agente de bie-
nes raíces**
receptionist **recepcionista**
reporter **reportero(a),
periodista**

sailor **marinero(a)**
sales representative
vendedor(a)
scientist **científico(a)**
secretary **secretario(a)**
security guard **guardia**
social worker **trabajador(a) social**
sociologist **sociólogo(a)**
soldier **soldado, militar**
stenographer **estenógrafo(a)**
stockbroker **bolsista**
student **estudiante**
supervisor **supervisor(a)**
surgeon **cirujano(a)**
systems analyst **analista de sis-
temas**
tailor **sastre**
taxi driver **chófer de taxi,
taxista**
teacher **maestro(a)** *(elem.
school),* **profesor(a)** *(high
school and college)*
technician **técnico(a)**
telephone operator
telefonista
television and radio announcer
locutor(a)
television and radio technician
**técnico(a) de radio y
televisión**
teller **cajero(a)**
therapist **terapista**
travel agent **agente de viajes**
truck driver **camionero(a)**
typist **mecanógrafo(a),
dactilógrafo(a)**
undertaker **director(a) de
pompas fúnebres**
veterinarian **veterinario(a)**
waiter **mozo, camarero**
waitress **camarera**
watchmaker **relojero(a)**
worker **obrero(a)**
writer **escritor(a)**

Answer Key to *¿Cuánto sabe usted ahora?* Sections

Lección 1

A. 1. hablan / hablamos 2. trabajas / trabajo 3. toman / deseo / desea 4. necesitan / necesita / necesita 5. estudia / estudio

B. 1. —¿Ellos pagan la cuenta? / —No, ellos no pagan la cuenta. 2. —¿A qué hora deseas estudiar, Anita? / —Yo no deseo estudiar hoy.

C. 1. champán francés 2. mantel blanco / servilletas rojas 3. un muchacho (chico) muy guapo

D. 1. por la mañana / a las ocho y media de la mañana / Son las siete menos cuarto.

E. 1. mil quinientos setenta y ocho 2. once mil setecientos cincuenta 3. veintitrés mil trescientos ochenta 4. cuarenta y ocho mil seiscientos sesenta 5. cuatrocientos veinte mil doscientos

F. 1. hora 2. noche 3. alemana 4. inglés / francés 5. guapo 6. Cuántos 7. solamente (sólo) 8. tinto 9. servilletas 10. cuchara 11. deseo 12. cuenta

Lección 2

A. 1. los pollos asados 2. la papa frita 3. las muchachas mexicanas 4. las mujeres francesas 5. la leche fría

B. 1. beben / bebemos 2. escribe / escribimos 3. viven / vive / vive 4. comes / como 5. abren 6. lee / Leo

C. 1. —¿Ella es la hermana de Sergio? —No, es la prima de Mario. 2. —¿Ud. necesita la dirección de Luisa, Srta. Fuentes? / —No, yo necesito el número de teléfono de María.

D. 1. No, nosotros no necesitamos nuestros libros. 2. No, nuestra profesora no es de Venezuela. 3. No, yo no vivo con mi madre. 4. No, nuestros amigos no son de Colombia. 5. No, el profesor no necesita su coche hoy.

E. 1. —¿A quién llama Ud., Sr. Viñas? / —A mi sobrina.
2. —¿Ud. lleva a la hija de la Sra. Mena a la universidad, Srta. Soto? / —No, llevo al hijo del Sr. Villalba.

F. 1. leche   2. botella   3. beber   4. frito   5. amiga
6. malo   7. de quién   8. bueno

Lección 3

A. 1. Yo voy a la universidad los lunes.   2. Nosotros no damos nuestro número de teléfono.   3. Los chicos están en la cafetería ahora.   4. ¿Tú vas a la fiesta de Nora?   5. Elena da solamente cinco dólares.   6. Yo estoy cansado y enfermo.

B. 1. Nosotros vamos a comer pollo frito.   2. Yo voy a estar en el hotel a las seis.   3. Mi amiga va a esperar a su mamá.
4. Ellos van a viajar con Alberto.   5. Mi papá va a visitar al señor Mejía.

C. 1. ¿De dónde es Teresa y dónde está ahora? ¿Ella es casada o soltera?   2. ¿Qué día es hoy? ¿Dónde es la fiesta de Ana?
3. ¿Estás cansado, Carlos?   4. ¿Eva es la amiga o la novia de Mario? ¿Ella es francesa o inglesa?

D. 1. al / de la / a la   2. a los / del / al / de la   3. al / de la
4. a las / del

E. 1. h   2. l   3. a   4. k   5. c   6. b   7. e   8. g   9. d
10. f   11. j   12. i

Lección 4

A. 1. Yo vengo a la universidad con Mirta porque no tengo coche.   2. Nosotras venimos a la universidad con Mirta porque no tenemos coche.   3. Los chicos vienen a la universidad con Mirta porque no tienen coche.   4. Tú vienes a la universidad con Mirta porque no tienes coche.

B. 1. Yo tengo (mucho) calor.   2. Nosotros tenemos (mucho) frío.   3. Carlos tiene (mucho) miedo.   4. Marisa tiene (mucha) hambre.   5. Luis y Beto tienen (mucha) prisa.
6. Yo tengo (mucha) sed.   7. Tú tienes (mucho) sueño.
8. Liliana tiene diez años (de edad).

C. 1. —¿Tú eres tan alta como tu hermana, Anita? / —No, ella es mucho más alta que yo. Ella es la más alta de la familia.
2. —¿Su casa es grande, Sr. Varela? / Sí, pero no tiene tantos cuartos (tantas habitaciones) como la casa de tus abuelos, Rosita.

D. 1. a. Marisol es la mayor de las tres. b. Amelia es la menor de las tres. 2. a. El hotel Azteca es el mejor. b. El hotel Sandoval es el peor.

E. 1. gerente 2. llega 3. más 4. barato 5. la biblioteca 6. creo 7. grande 8. solo 9. la llave 10. valijas

Lección 5

A. 1. quieres / prefiero 2. empiezan / empezamos 3. pierde 4. entiende / entiendo 5. comienzan

B. 1. los lunes 2. la cena 3. la escuela / la iglesia 4. el próximo viernes (el viernes próximo) 5. la cárcel 6. la educación 7. el champán

C. 1. Yo estoy leyendo y él está durmiendo. 2. Ella está trabajando y ellos están estudiando. 3. ¿Tú estás comiendo pollo? 4. Nosotros estamos esperando al profesor. 5. ¿Uds. están bebiendo vino o cerveza?

D. 1. primer 2. Junio 3. noveno 4. Marzo 5. segundo 6. Abril 7. décimo 8. Mayo 9. octavo 10. séptimo

E. 1. iglesia 2. cárcel 3. piso 4. cerrar 5. perder 6. desayuno 7. ¡Ya lo creo!

Lección 6

A. (*Possibilities; answers may vary.*) 1. (Yo) vuelvo a mi casa a las cinco y media. 2. Cuando (nosotros) vamos a México, volamos. 3. Sí, (nosotros) recordamos los verbos irregulares. 4. (Yo) duermo ocho horas. 5. No, (nosotros) no podemos ir a la playa.

B. 1. Ellos recuerdan algo. 2. Hay alguien en el cuarto. 3. Yo quiero volar también. 4. Recibimos algunos regalos. 5. Siempre tiene fiestas en su casa.

C. 1. ¿(Ud.) puede (Tú puedes) venir conmigo? 2. ¿(Ud.) va (Tú vas) a trabajar con ellos? 3. El dinero es para ti, Anita. 4. El regalo no es para mí. Es para ella. 5. No, Paco, (yo) no puedo ir contigo.

D. 1. Yo las espero. 2. Uds. van a comprarlo. 3. Nosotros no queremos visitarte. 4. Ella la lee. 5. ¿Ud. me llama? 6. Él los escribe. 7. Carlos va a visitarnos. 8. Nosotros no lo esperamos.

E. 1. vista / mar   2. almuerzan   3. colchón   4. cuesta
5. lugares   6. alcohólicas   7. duerme   8. oficina / correos

Lección 7

A. (*Possibilities; answers may vary.*) 1. (Nosotros) servimos
sopa.   2. (Yo) pido Coca-Cola para beber.   3. No, (yo) no
digo mi edad.   4. Sí, (yo) sigo en la universidad.   5. Sí,
(nosotros) siempre pedimos postre.

B. 1. conduzco   2. salgo   3. pongo   4. traduzco
5. conozco   6. traigo   7. hago   8. veo   9. sé

C. 1. (Yo) conozco a su (tu) hijo.   2. (Él) no sabe francés.
3. ¿Sabe (Ud.) nadar, Srta. Vera?   4. ¿Conoce (Ud.) (Conoces)
al agente de viajes?   5. ¿Conocen los estudiantes las novelas
de Cervantes?

D. 1. Me va a dar dinero.   2. Le doy una revista.   3. Nos
habla en español.   4. Les voy a decir que es tarde.   5. Les
pregunto la dirección de la oficina.   6. Le estamos escribiendo
a nuestro padre.   7. Le escribo los lunes.   8. Le doy la
información al agente de viajes.   9. Te hablo en inglés.
10. No me compran nada.

E. 1. agencia   2. nadar   3. memoria   4. reservación
5. pasaportes   6. cancelar   7. queda / avenida

Lección 8

A. 1. (Yo) pregunto dónde vive.   2. Rosa pide las entradas.
3. (Nosotros) preguntamos la hora.   4. Los niños piden las
pelotas.   5. (Tú) pides la raqueta.   6. El entrenador pregunta
tu edad.

B. 1. me gustan   2. te hace falta   3. le duele   4. nos hace
falta   5. Le gusta   6. le hacen falta   7. me duelen   8. nos
gusta

C. 1. estas / aquéllas   2. este / ése   3. estos / aquéllos
4. esa / ésta   5. eso

D. 1. ¿El dinero? (Yo) se lo doy mañana, Sr. Peña.   2. (Yo) sé
que necesitas mi libro, Anita, pero (yo) no puedo prestártelo
(no te lo puedo prestar).   3. (Yo) necesito (Me hace falta) mi
mochila. ¿Puede (Ud.) traérmela, Srta. López?   4. ¿Las
plumas? (Ella) nos las trae.   5. Cuando él necesita (le hacen
falta) patines, su madre se los compra.

E. 1. deportiva   2. quién   3. pelota / raqueta   4. bolsas
5. entradas   6. duele   7. campaña   8. hacen

Lección 9

A. 1. No, no son mías.   2. No, no son de ella.   3. No, no
es mío.   4. No, no es nuestra.   5. No, no es de ellos.
6. No, no son míos.   7. No, no es nuestra.   8. No, no es
de Uds.

B. 1. (Yo) me levanto a las siete, me baño, me visto y salgo a
las siete y media.   2. ¿A qué hora se despiertan los niños?
3. (Ella) no quiere sentarse.   4. (Él) se afeita todos los días.
5. ¿(Tú) te acuerdas de tus maestros, Carlitos?
6. (Ellos / Ellas) siempre se están quejando.   7. Primero (ella)
acuesta a los niños, y después (ella) se acuesta.   8. ¿Quiere
(Ud.) probarse estos pantalones, señorita?   9. ¿Dónde van a
poner (Uds.) el dinero, señoras?   10. Los estudiantes siempre
se duermen en esta clase.

C. 1. Abra   2. Hablen   3. Traiga   4. Vengan   5. cierre
6. Doblen   7. Siga   8. Den   9. Estén   10. sean
11. vaya   12. Vuelva   13. Sirva   14. Pongan
15. Escriban

D. 1. Dígales mi dirección, Sr. Mena.   2. ¿El vestido?
No me lo traiga ahora, Srta. Ruiz.   3. No se lo diga a mi
peluquero(a), por favor.   4. Traigan las bebidas, señores.
Tráiganlas a la terraza.   5. No se levante, Sra. Miño.
6. ¿El té? Tráigaselo a las cuatro de la tarde, Sr. Vargas.

E. 1. afeitar   2. peluquería / lavarme / pelo   3. tintorería
4. tarjeta de crédito   5. izquierda   6. mismo   7. acostar
8. derecho

Lección 10

A. 1. Ayer ella entró en la cafetería y comió tallarines.
2. Ayer María le escribió a su suegra.   3. El viernes pasado
ella me prestó su abrigo.   4. El año pasado ellos fueron los
mejores estudiantes.   5. El sábado pasado ellos te esperaron
cerca del supermercado.   6. El verano pasado mi hijo fue
a Cuba.   7. Ayer por la mañana le di el impermeable.
8. El lunes pasado nosotros decidimos comprar la aspiradora.
9. Anoche le pregunté la hora.   10. Anoche tú no pagaste por
la ropa.   11. El jueves pasado fuimos los primeros.   12. Ayer
me dieron muchos problemas.   13. Anoche mi suegro no be-
bió café.   14. Ayer yo no fui a esquiar.   15. La semana pasada
te dimos el suéter.

B. 1. por   2. por   3. por   4. para   5. por / para   6. por
7. Para   8. por   9. para / por

C. 1. Hace (Hay) mucho viento hoy.   2. Aquí hace mucho
frío en (el) invierno.   3. ¿Hace mucho calor en (el) verano en
Cuba?   4. ¿Qué tiempo hace hoy?   5. ¿Hace sol o está
nublado?   6. No hay vuelos por la niebla.   7. ¿Ud. prefiere
(Tú prefieres) el otoño o la primavera?

D. 1. abrigo (suéter)   2. límite   3. impermeable   4. salsa
5. lavadora   6. prepara (cocina)   7. criada   8. tiempo

Lección 11

A. 1. —¿Cuánto tiempo hace que (Uds.) trabajan en San Juan? /
—Hace cinco años que (nosotros) trabajamos en San Juan.
2. —¿Cuánto tiempo hace que (ellos) esperan? / —Hace tres
horas que (ellos) esperan.   3. —¿Cuánto tiempo hace que (ella)
estudia español? / —Hace dos años que (ella) estudia español.

B. 1. Ayer María no estuvo en la clase.   2. Anoche no
pudieron venir.   3. El mes pasado puse el dinero en el banco.
4. El domingo pasado no hiciste nada.   5. Ayer ella vino con
Juan.   6. El lunes pasado no quisimos venir a clase.
7. Anoche yo no dije nada.   8. Ayer trajimos la tostadora.
9. Anoche yo conduje mi coche.   10. Ayer ellos tradujeron
las lecciones.

C. 1. Ayer ella eligió la secadora.   2. Anoche Marta
no durmió bien.   3. Ayer no le pedí nada.   4. La semana
pasada ella te mintió.   5. El sábado pasado ellos sirvieron los
refrescos.   6. Ayer no lo repetí.   7. Anoche ella siguió
estudiando.   8. El lunes pasado tú no conseguiste nada.

D. 1. Ven acá, por favor.   2. Habla con la profesora.
3. Dime tu dirección.   4. Lávate las manos.   5. Ponte el
abrigo.   6. Tráenos el arroz con pollo.   7. Compra los
libros.   8. Hazme un favor.   9. Apaga la luz.   10. Ve de
compras hoy.   11. Sal temprano.   12. Aféitate aquí.
13. Ten paciencia.   14. Sé buena.   15. Come con nosotros.

E. 1. No se lo digas (a él).   2. No salgas ahora.   3. No te
levantes.   4. No traigas el postre ahora.   5. No bebas (tomes)
el café.   6. No les hables.   7. No vayas a la tienda.   8. ¿Ese
vestido? ¡No te lo pongas!   9. No hagas eso.

F. 1. compras   2. apaga   3. arroz   4. trabajos
5. liquidación (venta)   6. media   7. caminar   8. nunca
9. despedir   10. vez

Lección 12

A. 1. Nosotros llegamos al aeropuerto a las seis y media.
2. Mi cuñada está en casa.   3. Ellos están en la joyería.
4. La fiesta es a las doce.   5. ¿Raúl está en la clase?

B. 1. Vivíamos en Alaska.   2. Hablaba alemán.   3. (Siempre) veía a mi abuela.   4. Poníamos el dinero en el Banco Nacional.   5. Se acostaban a las nueve.   6. Iba a la universidad.
7. Compraba arroz.   9. Enseñaba español.

C. 1. estábamos comiendo   2. estabas haciendo   3. estaba escribiendo   4. estaba hablando   5. estaban comprando
6. estaba leyendo   7. estaban estudiando   8. estaba trabajando

D. 1. (Nosotros) nos acostamos a las once anoche.   2. (Ella) escribía a máquina cuando la vi.   3. (Nosotros) íbamos a Lima todos los veranos.   4. Eran las diez y media cuando (yo) llamé a mi cuñada.   5. (Ella) dijo que quería leer.

E. 1. traje   2. catálogo   3. quedarnos / todo   4. máquina
5. encontrarme   6. vacaciones   7. juntos (juntas)
8. aeropuerto   9. zapatos   10. comercial / vidrieras (escaparates)

Lección 13

A. 1. conocía / conocí   2. sabíamos / supimos   3. quiso
4. quería / supe

B. 1. (a) Hace tres meses que nosotros llegamos a California.
(b) Nosotros llegamos a California hace tres meses.   2. (a) Hace dos horas que el chico tomó café.   (b) El chico tomó café hace dos horas.   3. (a) Hace dos días que ellos terminaron la lección.   (b) Ellos terminaron la lección hace dos días.
4. (a) Hace veinte años que ella vino a esta ciudad.   (b) Ella vino a esta ciudad hace veinte años.   5. (a) Hace dos días que tú viste a tu nieta.   (b) Tú viste a tu nieta hace dos días.

C. (*Possibilities; answers may vary.*)   1. En los Estados Unidos se hablan inglés y español.   2. Se dice *colchón*.   3. La oficina de correos se cierra a las tres.   4. Mi nombre se escribe...
5. Las bibliotecas se abren a las diez.

D. 1. ¿Qué es un impermeable?   2. ¿Cuál es su (tu) dirección?   3. ¿Qué es una biblioteca?   4. ¿Cuál es su (tu) número de teléfono?   5. ¿Cuáles son sus ideas sobre esto?

E. 1. mueblería   2. portugués   3. ascensor   4. galería
5. oro   6. mecánica   7. chaqueta   8. nieta   9. sortija
10. talla

Lección 14

A. 2. recibido   3. volver   4. usado   5. escrito   6. ir
7. aprendido   8. abrir   9. cubierto   10. comido   11. ver
12. hecho   13. sido   14. decir   15. cerrado   16. morir
17. romper   18. dormido   19. estado   20. poner

B. 1. El libro está escrito en inglés.   2. La ventana está rota.
3. La puerta está abierta.   4. ¿Están cerrados los bancos?
5. La mesa está cubierta.

C. 1. he venido   2. Han terminado   3. hemos hablado
4. ha dicho   5. has escrito   6. hemos hecho / hemos tenido
7. ha abierto   8. ha puesto   9. han comido   10. han roto

D. 1. (Yo) ya había traído la batería (el acumulador).
2. (Ellos, Ellas) no habían llamado al empleado (a la empleada).
3. (Ellos, Ellas) habían roto las ventanas.   4. (Él) ya había
visto al profesor (a la profesora).   5. ¿Había cubierto (Ud.) las
mesas, Srta. Peña?

E. 1. servicio / gasolina   2. acumulador   3. vacío   4. goma
(llanta) / pinchada   5. automovilístico   6. aceite   7. cerrada
8. repuesto

Lección 15

A. 1. irán   2. vendrá   3. pagarán   4. llevarás   5. será
6. pondrás   7. manejarán   8. revisará   9. harán
10. alquilaré

B. 1. iríamos   2. venderían   3. habría   4. serviría
5. trabajarías   6. Pondría   7. preferirían   8. Seguirían
9. Te levantarías

C. 1. (Nosotros) no llegaremos a la universidad a las seis.
2. ¿Llevaste (tú) a tu perro al veterinario, María?   3. Después
(nosotros) viajaremos en avión.   4. (Ella) está en la agencia de
alquiler de automóviles.   5. ¿De qué están hablando (ellos,
ellas)?

D. 1. agencia   2. peligrosas   3. mecánicos / automáticos
4. depositar   5. plata   6. revisar (chequear)   7. falta
8. examen

Lección 16

A. 1. cerremos   2. vayan   3. abras   4. recomiende
5. salga (se vaya)   6. vuelva (regrese)   7. quieran
8. entienda   9. tengamos   10. pongan   11. traigas
12. den   13. esté   14. sea   15. sepan

B. 1. —¿Quieres ir al hospital conmigo, Anita? / —No puedo.
Alberto quiere que vaya a la estación de trenes con él.

2. —¿Qué quieres hacer este fin de semana, Pedro? / —No sé...
¿Qué me sugieres que haga? / —Te sugiero que estudies.

3. —¿Necesita Ud. que yo le traiga el horario de trenes, Srta.
Rojas? / —Sí, y le ruego que venga esta tarde, Sr. Varela. /
—¿A qué hora quiere que esté en su casa? / —A las dos.

4. —Voy a pedirle que compre los boletos. / —Yo prefiero
comprarlos esta tarde.

C. 1. dificilísimo(a)   2. lentísima   3. buenísimas   4. altísimo
5. larguísimo   6. rapidísimo   7. inteligentísimos(as)
8. facilísimos(as)

D. 1. antes   2. descuento / ciento   3. asiento   4. rápido
(expreso)   5. estación   6. niego

Lección 17

A. 1. —Espero conseguir la beca. / —Temo que no pueda(s)
conseguirla porque sus (tus) notas no son muy buenas.

2. —Me alegro de estar aquí contigo, Anita. / —Espero que
puedas ir a la fiesta conmigo esta noche, Carlos.

3. —Temo que no podamos matricularnos en la clase de física. /
—Siento que no tengan el dinero, chicas...

4. —Esperamos tomar una clase de literatura. / —Nos
alegramos de que quieran tomar literatura.

B. 1. matricularse   2. pueda   3. sacar   4. den   5. sea
6. firmar   7. tomar   8. tenga

C. 1. especialmente   2. recientemente   3. lenta y
claramente   4. generalmente   5. fácilmente

D. 1. calculadora   2. parcial / final   3. alegro / notas
4. matrícula   5. ser   6. necesario   7. física
8. consejero(a)

Lección 18

A. 1. —La Dra. Soto dice que (ella) puede cuidar a mis pacientes. / —Estoy seguro(a) de que puede.

2. —No creo que el médico esté en su consultorio. / —Entonces tengo que llamar a su casa.

3. —Dudo que el Sr. Soto pueda llevar a su esposa a la sala de emergencia. / —¿Puede llevarla su hija? / —No creo que esté en casa.

4. —¡(Yo) estoy seguro(a) de que ella necesita muletas! / —Es verdad que le duele la pierna, pero no es verdad que necesite muletas...

B. 1. que sea de México.   2. que pueda llevarlo a la sala de rayos X.   3. que hable español.   4. que sepa poner inyecciones.   5. que cuida a mis hijos.

C. 1. Carmencita   2. arbolito   3. niñitos   4. cafecito 5. camioncito   6. favorcito   7. piernitas   8. bracito 9. hermanita   10. nochecita

D. 1. ambulancia   2. muletas   3. sala   4. consultorio 5. radiografía   6. poner   7. enyesar   8. momento

Lección 19

A. 1. venga su abogado(a)   2. me trae   3. baje la fiebre 4. sepa   5. los (las) lleven   6. llega   7. tomes   8. tenga fiebre

B. 1. haya llegado   2. hayan vuelto   3. haya ido   4. hayas dicho   5. hayamos hecho   6. haya preferido   7. haya abierto   8. hayan puesto

C. 1. hayamos hecho el trabajo.   2. haya estado enfermo. 3. hayan muerto muchos.   4. haya ido a México.   5. le hayas escrito una carta.   6. ellos hayan hablado con la enfermera. 7. no hayan visto a sus pacientes.   8. que Ana y yo hayamos ido a su consultorio.

D. 1. pasajeros   2. termómetro   3. autopista   4. jarabe 5. antes   6. dieta

Lección 20

A. 1. asistieran   2. fueras   3. devolviéramos   4. fuera 5. recogiera   6. pudiera   7. quisiera   8. dieran 9. hiciéramos   10. trajeran

B. 1. tuviera que trabajar.   2. pusiéramos el dinero en el banco.   3. fueras al correo.   4. hicieran las diligencias.
5. llevara el paquete.   6. hablaran con el jefe.   7. estuviera enferma.   8. perdiera la billetera.

C. 1. Si la veo   2. Si yo fuera Ud. (tú)   3. Si ella tuviera tiempo   4. Si él me da el dinero   5. Si fuéramos en coche
6. Si ella puede venir   7. Si tú quisieras   8. si ellos van conmigo

D. 1. billetera   2. devolver / prestado   3. informe
4. préstamo   5. talonario   6. asisten   7. montón / echar

Vocabularies

The number following each vocabulary item indicates the lesson in which it first appears.

The following abbreviations are used.

adj.	adjective	*Méx.*	México
f.	feminine noun	*pl.*	plural
fam.	familiar	*pron.*	pronoun
form.	formal	*sing.*	singular
m.	masculine noun		

Spanish-English

A

a   to, 3; at, 1; in, 15
— **casa**   home, 6
— **la derecha**   to the right, 9
— **la izquierda**   to the left, 9
— **menos que**   unless, 19
— **menudo**   often, 2
¿— **qué hora... ?**   at what time?, 1
¿— **quién?**   to whom?, 2
abierto(a)   open
abogado(a) (*m., f.*)   lawyer, 17
abrigo (*m.*)   coat, 10
abril   April, PI
abrir   to open, 2
abuela (*f.*)   grandmother, 3
abuelo (*m.*)   grandfather, 3
aburrido(a)   boring, bored, 11
acabar de (+ *inf.*)   to have just (done something), 13
accidente (*m.*)   accident, 11
aceite (*m.*)   oil, 14
aconsejar   to advise, 16
acordarse (o:ue) (de)   to remember, 9
acostar (o:ue)   to put to bed, 9
acostarse   to go to bed, to lie down, 9

acumulador (*m.*)   battery, 14
adiós   good-bye, PI
¿adónde?   where to?, 3
aeropuerto (*m.*)   airport, 12
afeitarse   to shave (oneself), 9
agencia (*f.*)   agency
— **de alquiler de automóviles** (*f.*)   car rental agency, 15
— **de viajes** (*f.*)   travel agency, 7
agente de viajes (*m., f.*)   travel agent, 7
agosto   August, PI
ahora   now, 3
— **mismo**   right now, 9
aire acondicionado (*m.*)   air conditioning, 4
alberca (*f.*)   swimming pool (*Méx.*), 4
alcohólico(a)   alcoholic, 6
alegrarse (de)   to be glad, 17
alemán (alemana)   German, 1
algo   something, anything, 6
alguien   someone, anyone, 6
algún   any, some, 6
alguna vez   ever, 6
algunas veces   sometimes, 6

boleto (*m.*)   ticket, 16
bolsa de dormir (*f.*)
   sleeping bag, 8
bonito(a)   pretty, 3
bote (*m.*)   can (*Méx.*), 10
botella (*f.*)   bottle, 2
botiquín (*m.*)   medicine
   cabinet, 9
buenas noches   good
   evening (good night), PI
buenas tardes   good
   afternoon, PI
bueno(a)   good, 2; kind, 16
buenos días   good morning
   (good day), PI
buscar   to look for, to pick
   up, to get, 16

C

caballo (*m.*)   horse, 8
cabeza (*f.*)   head, 8
café   brown, PI; (*m.*) coffee, 2
cafetera (*f.*)   coffeepot, 11
cafetería (*f.*)   cafeteria, 1
cajero(a) (*m., f.*)   cashier, 15
   — **automático**   automatic
      teller machine (ATM), 15
calculadora (*f.*)   calculator, 17
caliente   hot, 2
calle (*f.*)   street, PI
cama (*f.*)   bed, 6
camarero(a) (*m., f.*)   waiter,
   waitress, 2
cambiar   to change, 14
   — **un cheque**   to cash a
      check, 15
caminar   to walk, 11
camisón (*m.*)   nightgown, 13
cancelar   to cancel, 7
cansado(a)   tired, 3
cárcel (*f.*)   jail, 5
carne (*f.*)   meat, 7
caro(a)   expensive, 4
carro (*m.*)   car, automobile, 3
carta (*f.*)   letter, 6
cartera (*f.*)   purse, 12

casa (*f.*)   house, PII
casado(a)   married, PI
casi   almost, 14
   — **nunca**   hardly ever, 11
catálogo (*m.*)   catalogue, 12
catorce   fourteen, PI
cena (*f.*)   dinner, 5
centro comercial (*m.*)
   mall, 12
cepillo (*m.*)   brush, 9
cerca de   near to, 6
cero   zero, PI
cerrado(a)   closed, 14
cerrar (e:ie)   to close, 5
cerveza (*f.*)   beer, 1
champán (*m.*)   champagne, 1
champú (*m.*)   shampoo, 9
chaqueta (*f.*)   jacket, 13
cheque (*m.*)   check, 6
chequear   to check, 15
chica (*f.*)   girl, young
   woman, 2
chico (*m.*)   boy, young man, 2
chocar   to collide, 19
chocolate (*m.*)   chocolate, 2
cien, ciento   one hundred, PII
cinco   five, PI
cincuenta   fifty, PII
cine (*m.*)   movie theater,
   movies, 5
cirugía (*f.*)   surgery, 19
cirujano(a) (*m., f.*)   surgeon, 19
ciudad (*f.*)   city, PI
claro(a)   clear, 17
clase (*f.*)   class, 4
clima (*m.*)   climate, PII
club (*m.*)   club, 3
   — **automovilístico** (*m.*)
      auto club, 14
cobija (*f.*)   blanket, 6
cobrar   to charge, 15
cocina (*f.*)   kitchen, 10
cocinar   to cook, 10
cocinero(a) (*m., f.*)   cook, 11
coche (*m.*)   car, automobile, 3
colchón (*m.*)   mattress, 6
collar (*m.*)   necklace, 13

comenzar (e:ie)   to begin, to start, 5
comer   to eat, 2
comida (*f.*)   meal, food, 1
como   since, 20
¿cómo?   how?, 3
  ¿— es?   what is he (she, it) like?, 3
  ¿— está usted?   how are you?, PI
  ¿— se dice... ?   how do you say. . . ?, 6
comprar   to buy, 5
computadora (*f.*)   computer, 12
con   with, 2
  ¿— quién?   with whom?, 2
  — tal que   provided that, 19
  — vista al mar   with an ocean view, 6
concierto (*m.*)   concert, 5
conducir   to drive, 7
conferencia (*f.*)   lecture, 17
confirmar   to confirm, 7
conocer   to know, to be familiar with, 7; to meet (for the first time), 13
conseguir (e:i)   to obtain, to get, 7
consejero(a) (*m., f.*)   adviser, 17
consulado (*m.*)   consulate, 20
consultorio (*m.*)   doctor's office, 18
contrato (*m.*)   contract, 17
conversación (*f.*)   conversation, PII
conviene   it is advisable, 17
corbata (*f.*)   tie, 13
correo (*m.*)   post office, 20
cortar   to cut, 9
cortina (*f.*)   curtain, 20
corto(a)   short, 9
cosa (*f.*)   thing, 11
costar (o:ue)   to cost, 6
crédito (*m.*)   credit, 20

creer   to think, to believe, 4
criado(a) (*m., f.*)   servant, 10
¿cuál(es)?   what?, which (one)?, 3
cuando   when, 19
¿cuándo?   when?, 4
¿cuánto(a)?   how much?, 5
  — antes   as soon as possible, 16
  ¿— tiempo hace que... ?   how long ago . . . ?, 14
  ¿— tiempo?   how long?, 11
¿cuántos(as)?   how many?, 1
cuarenta   forty, PII
cuarto (*m.*)   room, 4
cuarto(a) (*adj.*)   fourth, 5
cuatro   four, PI
cubrir   to cover, 14
cuchara (*f.*)   spoon, 1
cuenta (*f.*)   bill, check, 1; account, 15
cuidadoso(a)   careful, 17
cuidar   to take care, 18
cuñada (*f.*)   sister-in-law, 3
cuñado (*m.*)   brother-in-law, 3

D

dar   to give, 3
de   of, from, PII
  — cambios mecánicos   a car with a standard shift, 15
  ¿— dónde es... ?   where is . . . from?, PII
  — memoria   by heart, 7
  — nada   you're welcome, PI
  ¿— quién?   whose?, 2
  — vez en cuando   once in a while, 12
debajo (de)   underneath, 11
deber (+ *inf.*)   must, to have to, should, 2
decidir   to decide, 2
décimo(a)   tenth, 5

decir (e:i) to say, 5; to tell, 6
decisión (*f.*) decision, PII
dentista (*m., f.*) dentist, 18
depositar to deposit, 15
desayunar to have
breakfast, 5
desayuno (*m.*) breakfast, 5
descuento (*m.*) discount, 16
desear to want, to wish, 1
despedirse (e:i) to say
good-bye, 11
despertarse (e:ie) to wake
up, 9
después later, 6; afterwards,
15
devolver (o:ue) to return
(something), to give back, 20
día (*m.*) day, PII
diario (*m.*) newspaper, 6
diciembre December, PI
diecinueve nineteen, PI
dieciocho eighteen, PI
dieciséis sixteen, PI
diecisiete seventeen, PI
diez ten, PI
difícil difficult, 16
diligencia (*f.*) errand, 20
dinero (*m.*) money, PII
dirección (*f.*) address, PI
divertirse (e:ie) to have a
good time, 11
divorciado(a) divorced, PI
doblar to turn, 9
doce twelve, PI
doctor(a) (*m., f.*) M.D.,
doctor, PII
dólar (*m.*) dollar, 3
doler (o:ue) to hurt, to
ache, 8
dolor (*m.*) pain, 18
domicilio (*m.*) address, PI
domingo (*m.*) Sunday, PI
¿dónde? where?, PII
dormir (o:ue) to sleep, 5
dormirse (o:ue) to fall
asleep, 9
dormitorio (*m.*) bedroom, 9

dos two, PI
doscientos two hundred,
PII
dudar to doubt, 18
dueño(a) (*m., f.*) owner, 4

E

echar al correo to mail, 20
edad (*f.*) age, PI
educación (*f.*) education, 5
el the (*m.*), PII
él he, 1; him, 6
elegante elegant, 13
elegir (e:i) to choose, to
select, 11
ella she, 1; her, 6
ellas they (*f.*), 1; them (*f.*), 6
ellos they (*m.*), 1; them
(*m.*), 6
embajada (*f.*) embassy, 7
emergencia (*f.*)
emergency, 18
empezar (e:ie) to begin, to
start, 5
empleado(a) (*m., f.*) clerk,
attendant, 14
en in, at, 1; inside, over, 15
— **casa** at home, 12
— **caso de que** in case, 19
— **cuanto** as soon as, 19
— **esa época** in those
days, 12
— **este momento** at this
moment, 18
— **seguida** right away, 14
encontrarse (o:ue) (con)
to meet (for an
appointment), 12
enero January, PI
enfermero(a) (*m., f.*) nurse,
PI
enfermo(a) sick, 3
ensalada (*f.*) salad, 7
enseñar to teach, 11
entender (e:ie) to
understand, 5

entonces   then, in that case, 7
entrada (*f.*)   ticket (for an event), 8
entrar   to enter, to come in, 10
entrenador(a) (*m.*, *f.*) trainer, coach, 8
entrevista (*f.*)   interview, 20
enviar   to send, 8
enyesar   to put a cast on, 18
escalera (*f.*)   stairs, 13
  — mecánica (*f.*) escalator, 13
escaparate (*m.*)   store window, 12
escoba (*f.*)   broom, 10
escribir   to write, 2
  — a máquina   to type, 12
escuela (*f.*)   school, 5
ese(os), esa(as) (*adj.*)   that, those (nearby), 8
ése(os), ésa(as) (*pron.*)   that (one), those (nearby), 8
eso (*neuter pron.*)   that, 8
espaguetis (*m. pl.*) spaghetti, 10
España   Spain, 7
español (*m.*)   Spanish (language), PII
español(a)   Spanish, 1
especial   special, 17
espejo (*m.*)   mirror, 9
esperar   to wait (for), 3; to hope, 16
esposa (*f.*)   wife, 4
esposo (*m.*)   husband, 4
esquiar   to ski, 8
esquíes (*m. pl.*)   skis, 8
esquís (*m. pl.*)   skis, 8
esta noche   tonight, 5
está nublado   it's cloudy, 10
estación de servicio (*f.*)   gas station, 14
estación de trenes (*f.*)   train station, 16
estado civil (*m.*)   marital status, PI

Estados Unidos (*m. pl.*) United States, 3
estampilla (*f.*)   stamp, 6
estar   to be, 3
este(a)   this, 6
este(os), esta(s) (*adj.*)   this, these, 8
éste(os), ésta(s) (*pron.*)   this (one), these, 8
esto (*neuter pron.*)   this, 8
estudiante (*m.*, *f.*)   student, 3
estudiar   to study, 1
examen (*m.*)   exam, 15
  — final (*m.*)   final exam, 17
  — parcial (*m.*)   midterm exam, 17
excursión (*f.*)   excursion, 6
extranjero(a)   foreign, 7

F

fácil   easy, 16
falso(a)   false
familia (*f.*)   family, 3
farmacia (*f.*)   pharmacy, 6
favor (*m.*)   favor, 11
febrero   February, PI
fecha (*f.*)   date, PI
  — de nacimiento (*f.*) date of birth, PI
feliz   happy, 1
femenino(a)   feminine, PI
ferretería (*f.*)   hardware store, 13
fiebre (*f.*)   fever, 19
fiesta (*f.*)   party, 2
fin de semana (*m.*) weekend, 16
firmar   to sign, 17
física (*f.*)   physics, 17
folleto turístico (*m.*)   tourist brochure, 7
fotocopia (*f.*)   photocopy, 20
fracturarse   to break (a bone), 18

francés (*m.*)   French (language), 1
francés (francesa)   French, 1
frazada (*f.*)   blanket, 6
fregadero (*m.*)   sink, 11
freno (*m.*)   brake, 14
frío(a)   cold, 2
frito(a)   fried, 2
funcionar   to work, to function, 13

G

galería de arte (*f.*)   art gallery, 13
gasolina (*f.*)   gasoline, 14
gasolinera (*f.*)   gas station, 14
general   general, 17
generalmente   generally, 9
gente (*f.*)   people
gerente (*m., f.*)   manager, 4
gimnasio (*m.*)   gym, 4
goma (*f.*)   tire, 14
— **pinchada** (*f.*)   flat tire, 14
gracias   thank you, PI
grande   big, large, 1
gris   gray, PI
grúa (*f.*)   tow truck, 14
guapo(a)   handsome, 1
guía (*m., f.*)   guide, 6
gustar   to like, to be pleasing, 8
gusto   pleasure, PI
   el — **es mío**   the pleasure is mine, PI

H

habitación   (*f.*) room, 4
hablar   to speak, to talk, 1
hacer   to do; to make, 5
— **buen (mal) tiempo**   to be good (bad) weather, 10
— **(mucho) calor**   to be (very) hot, 10
— **diligencias**   to do errands, 20

— **ejercicio**   to exercise, 19
— **falta**   to need, to lack, 8
— **(mucho) frío**   to be (very) cold, 10
— **sol**   to be sunny, 10
— **(mucho) viento**   to be (very) windy, 10
hasta   until, 15
— **luego**   I'll see you later, PI
— **mañana**   I'll see you tomorrow, PI
— **que**   until, 19
hay   there is, there are, PII
hay que (+ *inf.*)   one must, 6
helado(a)   frozen, iced, 7
hermana (*f.*)   sister, 3
hermano (*m.*)   brother, 3
hermoso(a)   beautiful, 15
hija (*f.*)   daughter, 2
hijo (*m.*)   son, 2
hijos (*m. pl.*)   children (son[s] and daughter[s]), 2
hola   hi, hello, PI
hombre (*m.*)   man, PII
hora (*f.*)   hour, 4
horario (*m.*)   schedule, 16
horrible   horrible, 19
hospital (*m.*)   hospital, 3
hotel (*m.*)   hotel, 3
hoy   today, PI
huevo (*m.*)   egg, 2

I

idea (*f.*)   idea, PII
idioma (*m.*)   language, PII
iglesia (*f.*)   church, 5
impaciente   impatient, 9
impermeable (*m.*)   raincoat, 10
importante   important, 5
imposible   impossible, 14
información (*f.*)   information, 7
informe (*m.*)   report, 20

inglés (*m.*)   English (language), 1
inglés (inglesa)   English, 1
inteligente   intelligent, 1
interesante   interesting, 11
invierno (*m.*)   winter, 10
invitado(a) (*m., f.*)   guest, 11
inyección (*f.*)   shot, injection, 18
ir   to go, 3
  — **a esquiar**   to go skiing, 8
  — **a pie**   to walk, to go on foot, 11
  — **caminando**   to walk, to go on foot, 11
  — **de compras**   to go shopping, 11
  — **de vacaciones**   to go on vacation, 12
irse   to leave, to go away, 9
italiano (*m.*)   Italian (language), 1
itinerario (*m.*)   schedule, 16

J

jabón (*m.*)   soap, 5
jamás   never, 6
jarabe (*m.*)   syrup, 19
jefe(a) (*m., f.*)   boss, chief, 20
joyería (*f.*)   jewelry store, 12
jueves (*m.*)   Thursday, PI
jugar (u:ue)   to play (a game or sport), 8
julio   July, PI
junio   June, PI
junta (*f.*)   meeting, 11
juntos(as)   together, 12

L

la   the (*f.*), PII; her, it (*f.*), you (*form. f.*), 7
lámpara (*f.*)   lamp, PII
lápiz (*m.*)   pencil, PII
largo(a)   long, 16

las (*f. pl.*)   the, PII; them, you (*f.*), 7
lata (*f.*)   can, 10
lavadora (*f.*)   washing machine, 10
lavar(se)   to wash (oneself), 9
lavarse la cabeza   to wash one's hair, 9
le   (to) her, (to) him, (to) you (*form.*), 8
lección (*f.*)   lesson, PII
leche (*f.*)   milk, 2
leer   to read, 2
lengua (*f.*)   language, PII
lento(a)   slow, 16
levantar   to lift, to raise, 9
levantarse   to get up, 9
libertad (*f.*)   liberty, PII
librería (*f.*)   bookstore, 6
libro (*m.*)   book, PII
licuadora (*f.*)   blender, 11
límite (*m.*)   limit, 10
  — **de velocidad** (*m.*)   speed limit, 10
limpiar   to clean, 10
limpiaparabrisas (*m.*)   windshield wiper, 14
liquidación (*f.*)   sale, 11
listo(a)   ready, 14
literatura (*f.*)   literature, 17
llamar   to call, 2
llamarse   to be named, 9
llanta (*f.*)   tire, 14
llave (*f.*)   key, 4
llegar   to arrive, 4
llenar   to fill, 14
llevar   to take (something or someone to someplace), 2
llover (o:ue)   to rain, 10
lluvia (*f.*)   rain, 10
lo   him, it (*m.*), you (*form. m.*), 7
  — **siento**   I'm sorry, PI
los   the (*m. pl.*), PII; them (*m.*), you (*m. pl.*), 7
los (las) dos   both, 10

lugar (*m.*)   place, 13
— **de interés** (*m.*)   place of
   interest, 6
— **de nacimiento** (*m.*)
   place of birth, PI
— **donde trabaja** (*m.*)
   place of work, PI
lunes (*m.*)   Monday, PI
luz (*f.*)   light, PII

M

madera (*f.*)   wood, 3
madre (*f.*)   mom, mother, 3
mal   badly, 4
maleta (*f.*)   suitcase, 4
malo(a)   bad, 2
mamá (*f.*)   mom, mother, 3
mandar   to send, 8; to
   order, 16
manejar   to drive, 7
mano (*f.*)   hand, PII
manta (*f.*)   blanket, 6
mantel (*m.*)   tablecloth, 1
mañana (*f.*)   morning, 1
mañana   tomorrow, 3
máquina de afeitar (*f.*)
   razor, 9
máquina de escribir (*f.*)
   typewriter, 12
mar (*m.*)   ocean, 6
marca (*f.*)   brand, 11
mareado(a)   dizzy, 16
marrón   brown, PI
martes (*m.*)   Tuesday, PI
marzo   March, PI
más   more, 4
— **tarde**   later, 6
masculino(a)   masculine, PI
matrícula (*f.*)   tuition, 17
matricularse   to register, 17
mayo (*m.*)   May, PI
mayor   older; bigger, 4
me   me, 7; (to) me, 8; (to)
   myself, 9
— **gusta...**   I like . . . , PI

mecánico(a) (*m., f.*)
   mechanic, 14
media hora   half an hour,
   11
mediano(a)   medium, 13
medianoche (*f.*)   midnight, 9
médico(a) (*m., f.*)   M.D.,
   doctor, PII
mejor   better, 4; best
menor   younger; smaller, 4
menos   to, until (with time),
   1; less, fewer, 4
mentir (e:ie)   to lie, 11
menú (*m.*)   menu, 2
mercado (*m.*)   market, 4
mes (*m.*)   month, 5
mesa (*f.*)   table, PII
metal (*m.*)   metal, 3
mexicano(a)   Mexican, 1
mi (*adj.*)   my, 3
mí (*pron.*)   me, 6
miércoles (*m.*)   Wednesday,
   PI
mil   thousand, 1
milla (*f.*)   mile, 10
mirar   to look at, 12
— **vidrieras**   to window
   shop, 12
mío(a) (*adj.*)   my, of mine, 9
mío(a) (*pron.*)   mine, 9
mochila (*f.*)   backpack, 8
moda (*f.*)   fashion, 13
momento (*m.*)   moment, 9
montar a caballo   to ride a
   horse, 8
montar en bicicleta   to ride
   a bicycle, 8
morado(a)   purple, PI
morir (o:ue)   to die, 11
moto (*f.*)   motorcycle, 15
motocicleta (*f.*)
   motorcycle, 15
motor (*m.*)   engine, 15
mozo (*m.*)   waiter, 2
muchacha (*f.*)   girl, young
   woman, 1

muchacho (*m.*)   boy, young man, 1
muchas gracias   thank you very much, PI
mucho   a lot, very much, 1
— **gusto**   it's a pleasure to meet you, PI
mueblería (*f.*)   furniture store, 13
mujer (*f.*)   woman, PII
muleta (*f.*)   crutch,   18
museo (*m.*)   museum, 2
muy   very, 3

N

nacionalidad (*f.*)   nationality, PI
nada   nothing, 6
nadar   to swim, 7
nadie   nobody, no one, 6
Navidad (*f.*)   Christmas, 18
necesario(a)   necessary, 17
necesitar   to need, 1
negar (e:ie)   to deny, 16
negro(a)   black, PI
neumático (*m.*)   tire, 14
nevar (e:ie)   to snow, 10
ni... ni   neither . . . nor, 6
niebla (*f.*)   fog, 10
nieta (*f.*)   granddaughter, 13
nieto (*m.*)   grandson, 13
ningún   none, not any, 6
ninguno(a)   none, not any, 6
niño(a) (*m., f.*)   child, kid, 8
noche (*f.*)   evening, 1
nombre (*m.*)   name, PI
norteamericano(a)   North American (from the U.S.), PI
nos   us, 7; (to) us, 8; (to) ourselves, 9
nosotros(as)   we, 1; us, 6
nota (*f.*)   grade, 17
novela (*f.*)   novel, 7
noveno(a)   ninth, 5
noventa   ninety, PII
novia (*f.*)   girlfriend, 3

noviembre   November, PI
novio (*m.*)   boyfriend, 3
nublado(a)   cloudy, 10
nuestro(a) (*adj.*)   our, 3
nuestro(s), nuestra(s) (*pron.*) ours, 9
nueve   nine, PI
nuevo(a)   new, 12
número (*m.*)   number, PI
— **de la licencia para conducir (manejar)** (*m.*) driver's license number, PI
— **de seguro social** (*m.*) social security number, PI
— **de teléfono** (*m.*)   phone number, PI
nunca   never, 6

O

o   or, 2
o... o   either . . . or, 6
ochenta   eighty, PII
ocho   eight, PI
octavo(a)   eighth, 5
octubre   October, PI
oculista (*m., f.*)   eye doctor, 19
ocupación (*f.*)   occupation, PI
ocupado(a)   busy, 16
oficina (*f.*)   office, 5
— **de correos** (*f.*)   post office, 6
— **de turismo** (*f.*)   tourist office, 7
ojalá   if only . . . , I hope, 17
ómnibus (*m.*)   bus, 2
once   eleven, PI
operación (*f.*)   surgery, 19
opuesto(a)   opposite
oro (*m.*)   gold, 13
otoño (*m.*)   fall, 10
otra vez   again, 11
otro(a)   other, another, 4

P

paciencia (*f.*)   patience, 11
paciente (*m., f.*)   patient, 18
padre (*m.*)   dad, father, 3
padres (*m. pl.*)   parents, 3
pagar   to pay (for), 1
página deportiva (*f.*)   sports
   page, 8
país (*m.*)   country, 7
panadería (*f.*)   bakery, 13
pantalón (*m.*)   pants, 9
pantalones (*m. pl.*)   pants, 9
papa (*f.*)   potato, 2
papá (*m.*)   dad, father, 3
paquete (*m.*)   package, 20
par (*m.*)   pair, 12
para   to, in order to, 5; for, 6;
   by, 10
   — que   in order that, 19
   ¿— quién?   for whom?, 8
parabrisas (*m.*)   windshield, 14
paraguas (*m. sing.*)
   umbrella, 10
paramédico(a) (*m., f.*)
   paramedic, 18
parar   to stop
parque (*m.*)   park, 9
partido (*m.*)   game, match, 8
pasado(a)   past, last, 10
pasaje (*m.*)   ticket, 7
pasajero(a) (*m., f.*)
   passenger, 19
pasaporte (*m.*)   passport, 7
pasar   to happen, 18
pasar (por)   to go by, 10
pase   come in, PI
pastel (*m.*)   pie, 2
pastilla (*f.*)   pill, 19
patata (*f.*)   potato (*Spain*), 2
patines (*m. pl.*)   skates, 8
pedir (e:i)   to ask, 5; to
   request, to order, 6
   — prestado   to borrow,
   20
peine (*m.*)   comb, 9
peligroso(a)   dangerous, 15

pelo (*m.*)   hair, 9
pelota (*f.*)   ball, 8
peluquería (*f.*)   beauty salon,
   beauty parlor, 9
peluquero(a) (*m., f.*)   hair
   dresser, 9
pensión (*f.*)   boarding house, 4
peor   worse, 4
pequeño(a)   small, little
   (size), 4
perder (e:ie)   to lose, 5
perfume (*m.*)   perfume, 9
periódico (*m.*)   newspaper, 6
pero   but, 1
perro (*m.*)   dog, 15
persona (*f.*)   person, 13
pescado (*m.*)   fish, 2
peso (*m.*)   weight, 19
pie (*m.*)   foot, 8
pierna (*f.*)   leg, 18
pieza de repuesto (*f.*)   spare
   part, 14
piscina (*f.*)   swimming pool, 4
piso (*m.*)   floor (story), 5;
   (surface), 11
plata (*f.*)   silver, 15
playa (*f.*)   beach, 6
pluma (*f.*)   pen, PII
poco(a)   little (quantity), 4
poder (o:ue)   to be able, 6
poema (*m.*)   poem, PII
pollo (*m.*)   chicken, 2
poner   to put, to place, 7
   — una inyección   to give a
   shot, 18
ponerse   to put on, 9
   — a dieta   to go on a diet,
   19
por   around, along, by, for,
   through, 10
   — ciento   percent, 16
   — favor   please, PI
   — hora   per hour, 10
   — noche   per night, 6
   ¿— qué?   why?, 3
   — suerte   luckily, 13
   — teléfono   on the phone

porque because, 3

portugués (*m.*) Portuguese (language), 13

posible possible, 17

postre (*m.*) dessert, 7

precio (*m.*) price, 15

preferir (e:ie) to prefer, 5

preguntar to ask a question, 8

preocuparse to worry, 20

preparar to prepare, 10

presidente(a) (*m., f.*) president, 8

préstamo (*m.*) loan, 20

prestar to lend, 8

primavera (*f.*) spring, 5

primero(a) first, 5

primo(a) (*m., f.*) cousin, 3

probable probable, 17

probablemente probably, 15

probador (*m.*) fitting room, 12

probar (o:ue) to try, to taste, 9

probarse (o:ue) to try on, 9

problema (*m.*) problem, PII

profesión (*f.*) profession, 3

profesor(a) (*m., f.*) professor, teacher, instructor, PI

programa (*m.*) program, PII

progreso (*m.*) progress, PII

pronto soon, 17

próximo(a) next, 5

pueblo (*m.*) town, 6

puerta (*f.*) door, PII

— **de atrás** (*f.*) back door, 10

pues well, 12

Q

que than, that, 4; which, 8

— **viene** next, 6

¿qué? what?, 1

¿— **tal?** how's it going?, PI

¿— **tiempo hace hoy?** what's the weather like today?, 10

¿— **hora es?** what time is it?, 1

quedar to be located, 7

quedarse to stay, to remain, 12

querer (e:ie) to want, 5

querido(a) dear, 9

¿quién(es)? who?, whom?, 2

química (*f.*) chemistry, 17

quince fifteen, PI

quinto(a) fifth, 5

quitar to take away, to remove, 9

quitarse to take off (e.g., one's clothing), 9

R

radiografía (*f.*) X-ray, 18

rápido (*m.*) express train, 16

¡rápido! quick!, 11

rápido(a) fast, 16

raqueta de tenis (*f.*) tennis racket, 8

recibir to receive, 2

reciente recent, 17

recientemente recently, 14

recoger to pick up, 20

recomendar (e:ie) to recommend, 16

recordar (o:ue) to remember, 6

refresco (*m.*) soft drink, soda, 1

regalar to give (a present), 8

regalo (*m.*) present, gift, 6

reloj (*m.*) clock, watch, 15

remolcador (*m.*) tow truck, 14

repetir (e:i) to repeat, 7

requisito (*m.*) requirement, 17

reservación (*f.*)   reservation, 7
reservar   to reserve, 16
restaurante (*m.*)   restaurant, 1
resultado (*m.*)   result, 19
reunión (*f.*)   meeting, 11
revisar   to check, 15
revista (*f.*)   magazine, 5
rogar (o:ue)   to beg, 16
rojo(a)   red, P1
romper   to break, 14
romperse   to break (i.e.,
   a bone), 18
ropa (*f.*)   clothes, clothing, 10
rosado(a)   pink, PI

S

sábado (*m.*)   Saturday, PI
saber   to know how, to know
   a fact, 7
sacar una nota   to get a
   grade, 17
sala (*f.*)   ward, room, 18
   — de emergencia (*f.*)
      emergency room, 18
   — de rayos X (*f.*)   X-ray
      room, 18
salir   to go out, to leave, 7
salsa (*f.*)   sauce, 10
se   (to) himself, (to) herself,
   (to) yourself (*form.*,), (to)
   yourselves, (to) themselves, 9
   — dice   one says, 6
secadora (*f.*)   dryer, 11
secretario(a) (*m., f.*)
   secretary, PII
seguir (e:i)   to continue, to
   follow, 7
   — derecho   to continue
      straight ahead, 9
según   according to, 11
segundo(a)   second, 5
seguro(a)   sure, 18
seis   six, PI
sello (*m.*)   stamp, 6

semana (*f.*)   week, 5
sentar (e:ie)   to sit, 9
sentarse (e:ie)   to sit down, 9
sentir (e:ie)   to regret, to be
   sorry, 17
sentirse (e:ie)   to feel, 12
señor   Mr., sir, gentleman, PI
señora   Mrs., madam, lady, PI
señorita   Miss, young lady, PI
separado(a)   separated, PI
septiembre   September, PI
séptimo(a)   seventh, 5
ser   to be, PII
   — difícil   it's unlikely, 17
   — importante   it is
      important, 17
   — imposible   it is
      impossible, 17
   — (una) lástima   it is a
      pity, 17
   — mejor   it is better, 17
   — necesario   it is
      necessary, 17
   — seguro   it is certain,
      17
servilleta (*f.*)   napkin, 1
servir (e:i)   to serve, 5
sesenta   sixty, PII
setenta   seventy, PII
sexo (*m.*)   sex, PI
sexto(a)   sixth, 5
si   if, 8
sí   yes, 1
siempre   always, 2
siete   seven, PI
silla (*f.*)   chair, PII
sin falta   without fail, 15
sin que   without, 19
sistema (*m.*)   system, PII
sobre   about, 13
sobrevivir   to survive, 19
sobrina (*f.*)   niece, 3
sobrino (*m.*)   nephew, 3
solamente   only, 1
solo(a)   alone, 4

sólo only, 1
soltero(a) single, PI
sombrero (*m.*) hat, 12
sopa (*f.*) soup, 7
sortija (*f.*) ring, 13
su (*adj.*) his, her, its, your
  (*form.*), their, 3
suegra (*f.*) mother-in-law, 3
suegro (*m.*) father-in-law, 3
suerte (*f.*) luck, 7
suéter (*m.*) sweater, 10
sugerir (e:ie) to suggest, 16
sumamente extremely,
  highly, 16
supermercado (*m.*)
  supermarket, 10
supervisor(a) (*m., f.*)
  supervisor, 4
suyo(s), suya(s) (*pron.*)
  yours (*form.*), his, hers,
  theirs, 9

T

talla (*f.*) size, 13
tallarines (*m. pl.*) spaghetti, 10
taller (*m.*) repair shop, 14
talonario de cheques (*m.*)
  checkbook, 20
también also, too, 4
tampoco neither, 6
tan as, 4
  — pronto como as soon
    as, 19
  — ... como as . . . as, 4
tanque (*m.*) tank, 14
tarde (*f.*) afternoon, 1
tarde late, 2
tarjeta (*f.*) card, 9
  — de crédito (*f.*) credit
    card, 9
taxi (*m.*) taxi, 2
te you (*fam.*), 7; (to) you, 8;
  (to) yourself, 9
  ¿— gusta? do you
    like . . . ?, PI
té (*m.*) tea, 2

teatro (*m.*) theater, 5
teléfono (*m.*) telephone, PII
telegrama (*m.*) telegram, PII
televisión (*f.*) television, PII
temer to fear, 17
temprano early, 2
tenedor (*m.*) fork, 1
tener to have, 4
  — ... años (de edad) to be
    . . . years old, 5
  — calor to be hot, 5
  — cuidado to be careful, 5
  — frío to be cold, 5
  — hambre to be hungry, 5
  — miedo to be afraid, 5
  — paciencia to be patient,
    11
  — prisa to be in a hurry, 5
  — que (+ *inf.*) to have to, 4
  — razón to be right, 5
  — sed to be thirsty, 5
  — sueño to be sleepy, 5
tenis (*m.*) tennis, 8
tercero(a) third, 5
terminar to finish, 15
termómetro (*m.*)
  thermometer, 19
terraza (*m.*) terrace, 9
testamento (*m.*) will, 19
ti (*fam. sing.*) you, 6
tía (*f.*) aunt, 3
tiempo (*m.*) time, 18
tienda (*f.*) store, 4
  — de campaña (*f.*) tent, 8
timbre (*m.*) stamp (*Méx.*), 6
tintorería (*f.*) dry cleaners, 9
tío (*m.*) uncle, 3
tipo (*m.*) type, 13
toalla (*f.*) towel, 5
tobillo (*m.*) ankle, 18
todavía yet, 9
todo(a) all, 11
  — el día all day long, 12
todos(as) every, 11
  — los días every day, 18
tomar to drink, 1; to take
  (i.e., the bus), 2

tome asiento sit down (take a seat), PI
tomate (*m.*) tomato, 10
torcerse (o:ue) to twist, 18
tos (*f.*) cough
tostadora (*f.*) toaster, 11
trabajar to work, 1
trabajos de la casa (*m. pl.*) household chores, 11
traducir to translate, 7
traer to bring, 5
traje (*m.*) suit, outfit, 13
— **de baño** (*m.*) bathing suit, 12
trece thirteen, PI
treinta thirty, PI
tren (*m.*) train, 15
tres three, PI
tu (*adj.*) your (*fam.*), 3
tú you (*fam.*), 1
tuyo(s), tuya(s) (*pron.*) yours (*fam. sing.*), 9

U

últimamente lately, 14
un(a) one, PI; a, an, PII
un montón de a lot of, 20
universidad (*f.*) university, PII
uno one, PI
unos(as) some, PII
usar to use, to wear, 13
usted you (*form. sing.*), 1
ustedes you (*pl.*) 1

V

vacaciones (*f. pl.*) vacation, 5
vacío(a) empty, 14
valija (*f.*) suitcase, 4
varios(as) several, various, 13
veinte twenty, PI
veinticinco twenty-five, PI
veinticuatro twenty-four, PI
veintidós twenty-two, PI
veintinueve twenty-nine, PI
veintiocho twenty-eight, PI

veintiséis twenty-six, PI
veintisiete twenty-seven, PI
veintitrés twenty-three, PI
veintiuno twenty-one, PI
velocidad (*f.*) velocity, speed, 10
vender to sell, 13
venir to come, 4
venta (*f.*) sale, 11
ventana (*f.*) window, 9
ver to see, 7
verano (*m.*) summer, 10
verdad (*f.*) truth, 7
verdadero(a) true
verde green, PI
vestido (*m.*) dress, 9
vestirse (e:i) to get dressed, 9
veterinario(a) (*m., f.*) veterinarian, 15
vez (*f.*) time (occasion), 15
viajar to travel, 3
viaje (*m.*) trip, 7
vidriera (*f.*) store window, 12
viernes (*m.*) Friday, PI
vino (*m.*) wine, 1
— **tinto** red wine, 1
visitar to visit, 2
viudo(a) (*m., f.*) widowed, PI
vivir to live, 2
volar (o:ue) to fly, 6
volver (o:ue) to return, to come (go) back, 6
vuelo (*m.*) flight, 7

Y

y and, 1
ya already
— **lo creo** I'll say, 5
yo I, 1

Z

zapatería (*f.*) shoe store, 12
zapato (*m.*) shoe, 12

English-Spanish

A

a un(a), PI
a lot mucho, 1; **a lot of** un montón de, 20
about sobre, 13
accident accidente *(m.)*, 11
according to según, 11
account cuenta *(f.)*, 15
ache doler (o:ue), 8
address dirección *(f.)*, domicilio *(m.)*, PI
advise aconsejar, 16
adviser consejero(a) *(m., f.)*, 17
afternoon tarde *(f.)*, 1
afterwards después, 15
again otra vez, 11
age edad *(f.)*, PI
air conditioning aire acondicionado *(m.)*, 4
airplane avión *(m.)*, 7
airport aeropuerto *(m.)*, 12
alcoholic alcohólico(a), 6
all todo(a), 11
  —**day long** todo el día, 12
almost casi, 14
alone solo(a), 4
along por, 10
already ya
also también, 4
always siempre, 2
ambulance ambulancia *(f.)*, 18
American americano(a), 20
an un(a), PI
ankle tobillo *(m.)*, 18
another otro(a), 4
any algún, alguno(a), algunos(as), 6
anyone alguien, 6
anything algo, 6
April abril, PI

Argentinian argentino(a) *(m., f.)*, 3
around por, 10
arrive llegar, 4
art gallery galería de arte *(f.)*, 13
as tan, 4
  —**soon as** en cuanto, tan pronto como, 19
  —**soon as possible** cuanto antes, 16
  —**. . . as** tan... como, 4
ask pedir (e:i), 5; preguntar, 8
aspirin aspirina *(f.)*, 8
assistant ayudante *(m., f.)*, 19
at a, en, 1
  —**home** en casa, 12
  —**this moment** en este momento, 18
  —**what time?** ¿a qué hora...?, 1
attend asistir, 20
  —**to** atender (e:ie), 9
August agosto, PI
aunt tía *(f.)*, 3
auto club club automovilístico *(m.)*, 14
automatic automático(a), 15
  —**teller machine (ATM)** cajero automático*(m.)*, 15
automobile auto *(m.)*, carro *(m.)*, coche *(m.)*, 3
autumn otoño *(m.)*, 10
avenue avenida *(f.)*, 7

B

back door puerta de atrás *(f.)*, 10
backpack mochila *(f.)*, 8
bad malo(a), 2
badly mal, 4
baked asado(a), 2

bakery   panadería, *(f.)*, 13
ball   pelota *(f.)*, 8
bank   banco *(m.)*, 6
basketball   básquetbol *(m.)*, 8
bathe *(oneself)*   bañar(se), 9
bathing suit   traje de baño
   (m.), 12
bathroom   baño *(m.)*, 9
battery   acumulador *(m.)*,
   batería *(f.)*, 14
be   ser, PII; estar, 3
   — . . . years old   tener...
      años (de edad), 5
   —able   poder (o:ue), 6
   —afraid   tener miedo, 5
   —careful   tener cuidado, 5
   —cold   tener frío, 5; hacer
      frío, 10
   —familiar with   conocer, 7
   —glad   alegrarse (de), 17
   —good (bad) weather
      hacer buen (mal)
      tiempo, 10
   —hot   tener calor, 5; hacer
      calor, 10
   —hungry   tener hambre, 5
   —in a hurry   tener prisa, 5
   —located   quedar, 7
   —named   llamarse, 9
   —patient   tener
      paciencia, 11
   —pleasing   gustar, 8
   —right   tener razón, 5
   —sleepy   tener sueño, 5
   —sorry   sentir (e:ie), 17
   —thirsty   tener sed, 5
   —(very) windy   hacer
      (mucho) viento, 10
beach   playa *(f.)*, 6
beautiful   hermoso(a), 15;
   bello(a), 16
beauty salon   peluquería
   (f.), 9
because   porque, 3
bed   cama *(f.)*, 6
bedroom   dormitorio *(m.)*, 9
beer   cerveza *(f.)*, 1

before   antes de, 9; antes de
   que, 19
beg   rogar (o:ue), 16
begin   comenzar (e:ie),
   empezar (e:ie), 5
believe   creer, 4
best   mejor
better   mejor, 4
bicycle   bicicleta *(f.)*, 8
big   grande, 1
bill   cuenta *(f.)*, 1
black   negro, PI
blanket   cobija *(f.)*, frazada
   (f.), manta *(f.)*, 6
blender   licuadora *(f.)*, 11
blue   azul, PI
boarding house   pensión
   (f.), 4
book   libro *(m.)*, PII
bookstore   librería *(f.)*, 6
bored   aburrido(a), 11
boring   aburrido(a), 11
borrow   pedir prestado, 20
boss   jefe(a) *(m., f.)*, 20
both   los (las) dos, 10
bottle   botella *(f.)*, 2
boy   chico *(m.)*, muchacho
   (m.), 1
boyfriend   novio *(m.)*, 3
brake   freno *(m.)*, 14
brand   marca *(f.)*, 11
break   romper, 14
   —a bone   fracturarse,
      romperse, 18
breakfast   desayuno *(m.)*, 5
bring   traer, 5
broom   escoba *(f.)*, 10
brother   hermano *(m.)*, 3
brother-in-law   cuñado
   (m.), 3
brown   café, marrón, PI
brush   cepillo *(m.)*, 9
bus   autobús *(m.)*, ómnibus
   (m), 2
busy   ocupado(a), 16
but   pero, 1
buy   comprar, 5

by para, por, 10
—**heart** de memoria, 7

C

cafeteria cafetería (f.), 1
calculator calculadora (f.), 17
call llamar, 2
can bote (m.) (Méx.),
   lata (f.), 10
cancel cancelar, 7
car auto (m.), automóvil (m.),
   carro (m.), coche (m.), 3
   —**rental agency** agencia
   de alquiler de automóviles
   (f.), 15
card tarjeta (f.), 9
careful cuidadoso(a), 17
cash a check cambiar un
   cheque, 15
cashier cajero(a) (m., f.), 15
catalogue catálogo (m.), 12
chair silla (f.), PII
champagne champán (m.), 1
change cambiar, 14
charge cobrar, 15
check (restaurant) cuenta
   (f.), 1; (bank) cheque (m.),
   6; chequear, revisar, 15
checkbook talonario de
   cheques (m.), 20
chemistry química (f.), 17
chicken pollo (m.), 2
   —**with rice** arroz con
   pollo, 11
chief jefe(a) (m., f.), 20
child niño(a) (m., f.), 8
**children (son[s] and
   daughter[s])**
   hijos (m. pl.), 2
chocolate chocolate (m.), 2
choose elegir (e:i), 11
Christmas Navidad (f.), 18
church iglesia (f.), 5
city ciudad (f.), PI
class clase (f.), 4

clean limpiar, 10
clear claro(a), 17
clerk empleado(a) (m., f.),
   14
climate clima (m.), PII
clock reloj (m.), 15
close cerrar (e:ie), 5
closed cerrado(a), 14
clothes ropa (f.), 10
clothing ropa (f.), 10
cloudy nublado(a), 10
club club (m.), 3
coach entrenador(a) (m., f.), 8
coat abrigo (m.), 10
coffee café (m.), 2
coffeepot cafetera (f.), 11
cold frío(a), 2
collide chocar, 19
comb peine (m.), 9
come venir, 4
   —**back** volver (o:ue), 6
   —**in** pase, PI; entrar, 10
computer computadora
   (f.), 12
concert concierto (m.), 5
confirm confirmar, 7
consulate consulado
   (m.), 20
continue seguir (e:i), 7
   —**straight ahead** seguir
   derecho, 9
contract contrato (m.), 17
conversation conversación
   (f.), PII
cook cocinar, 10; cocinero(a)
   (m., f.), 11
cost costar (o:ue), 6
cousin primo(a) (m., f.), 3
country país (m.), 7
cover cubrir, 14
credit crédito (m.), 20
   —**card** tarjeta de crédito
   (f.), 9
crutch muleta (f.), 18
curtain cortina (f.), 20
cut cortar, 9

D

dad papá, 3
dangerous peligroso(a), 15
date fecha *(f.)*, PI
—**of birth** fecha de nacimiento *(f.)*, PI
daughter hija *(f.)*, 2
day día *(m.)*, PII
—**before yesterday** anteayer, 12
dear querido(a), 9
December diciembre, PI
decide decidir, 2
decision decisión *(f.)*, PII
decrease bajar, 19
dentist dentista *(m., f.)*, 18
deny negar (e:ie), 16
deposit depositar, 15
dessert postre *(m.)*, 7
die morir (o:ue), 11
difficult difícil, 16
dinner cena *(f.)*, 5
discount descuento *(m.)*, 16
divorced divorciado(a), PI
dizzy mareado(a), 16
do hacer, 5
—**errands** hacer diligencias, 20
do you like . . . ? ¿te gusta . . . ?, PI
doctor's office consultorio *(m.)*, 18
doctor doctor(a) *(m., f.)*, médico(a) *(m., f.)*, PII
dog perro *(m.)*, 15
dollar dólar *(m.)*, 3
door puerta *(f.)*, PII
doubt dudar, 18
dress vestido *(m.)*, 9
drink tomar, 1; bebida *(f.)*, beber, 2
drive conducir, manejar, 7
driver's license number número de la licencia para conducir (manejar) *(m.)*, PI

dry cleaners tintorería *(f.)*, 9
dryer secadora *(f.)*, 11

E

early temprano, 2
earrings aretes *(m. pl.)*, 13
easy fácil, 16
eat comer, 2
education educación *(f.)*, 5
egg huevo *(m.)*, 2
eight ocho, PI
eighteen dieciocho, PI
eighth octavo(a), 5
eighty ochenta, PII
either . . . or o... o, 6
elegant elegante, 13
elevator ascensor *(m.)*, 13
eleven once, PI
embassy embajada *(f.)*, 7
emergency room sala de emergencia *(f.)*, 18
emergency emergencia *(f.)*, 18
empty vacío(a), 14
engagement ring anillo de compromiso *(m.)*, 13
engine motor *(m.)*, 15
English *(language)* inglés *(m.)*, 1
English inglés(esa), 1
enter entrar, 10
errand diligencia *(f.)*, 20
escalator escalera mecánica, 13
evening noche *(f.)*, 1
ever alguna vez, 6
every todos(as), 11
—**day** todos los días, 18
exam examen *(m.)*, 15
excursion excursión *(f.)*, 6
exercise hacer ejercicio, 19
expensive caro(a), 4
express train rápido *(m.)*, expreso *(m.)*, 16
extremely sumamente, 16

eye doctor   oculista
  (m., f.), 19

F

fall   otoño *(f.)*, 10
fall asleep   dormirse (o:ue), 9
family   familia *(f.)*, 3
fashion   moda *(f.)*, 13
fast   rápido(a), 16
father   padre, papá *(m.)*, 3
father-in-law   suegro *(m.)*, 3
favor   favor *(m.)*, 11
fear   temer, 17
February   febrero, PI
feel   sentirse (e:ie), 12
feminine   femenino(a), PI
fever   fiebre *(f.)*, 19
fewer   menos, 4
fifteen   quince, PI
fifth   quinto(a), 5
fifty   cincuenta, PII
fill   llenar, 14
final exam   examen final
  (m.), 17
fine   bien, PI
finish   terminar, 15
first   primero(a), 5
fish   pescado *(m.)*, 2
fitting room   probador *(m.)*,
  12
five   cinco, PI
fix   arreglar, 14
flat tire   goma pinchada *(f.)*,
  14
flight   vuelo *(m.)*, 7
floor *(story)*   piso *(m.)*, 5;
  (surface), 11
fly   volar (o:ue), 6
fog   niebla *(f.)*, 10
follow   seguir (e:i), 7
food   comida *(f.)*, 1
foot   pie *(m.)*, 8
for   para, 6; por, 10
  —whom   ¿para quién?, 8
foreign   extranjero(a), 7

fork   tenedor *(m.)*, 1
forty   cuarenta, PII
four   cuatro, PI
fourteen   catorce, PI
fourth   cuarto(a), 5
freeway   autopista *(f.)*, 19
French *(language)*   francés
  (f.), 1
French   francés (francesa), 1
Friday   viernes, PI
fried   frito(a), 2
friend   amigo(a) *(m., f.)*, 2
friendship   amistad *(f.)*, PII
from   de, PII
frozen   helado(a), 7
function   funcionar, 13
furniture store   mueblería
  (f.), 13

G

game *(match)*   partido *(m.)*, 8
garbage   basura *(f.)*, 11
gas station   estación de
  servicio *(f.)*, gasolinera
  (f.), 14
gasoline   gasolina *(f.)*, 14
general   general, 17
generally   generalmente, 9
gentleman   señor, PI
German   alemán (alemana), 1
get   conseguir (e:i), 7; buscar,
  16
  —a grade   sacar una
    nota, 17
  —dressed   vestirse (e:i), 9
  —up   levantarse, 9
gift   regalo, 6
girl   chica *(f.)*, muchacha
  (f.), 1
girlfriend   novia *(f.)*, 3
give   dar, 3
  —a present   regalar, 8
  —a shot   poner una
    inyección, 18
  —back   devolver (o:ue), 20

go ir, 3
—**away** irse, 9
—**by** pasar (por), 10
—**down** bajar, 19
—**on a diet** ponerse a dieta, 19
—**on foot** ir a pie, 11
—**on vacation** ir de vacaciones, 12
—**out** salir, 7
—**shopping** ir de compras, 11
—**skiing** ir a esquiar, 8
—**to bed** acostarse (o:ue), 9
gold oro *(m.)*, 13
good bueno(a), 2
—**afternoon** buenas tardes, PI
—**evening** *(good night)* buenas noches, PI
—**morning** buenos días, PI
goodbye adiós, PI
grade nota *(f.)*, 17
granddaughter nieta *(f.)*, 13
grandfather abuelo *(m.)*, 3
grandmother abuela *(f.)*, 3
grandson nieto *(m.)*, 13
gray gris, PI
green verde, PI
guest invitado(a) *(m., f.)*, 11
guide guía *(m.)*, 6
gym gimnasio *(m.)*, 4

H

hair pelo *(m.)*, 9
—**dresser** peluquero(a) *(m., f.)*, 9
half an hour media hora, 11
hand mano *(f.)*, PII
handsome guapo(a), 1
happen pasar, 18
happy feliz, 1
hardly ever casi nunca, 11

hardware store ferretería *(f.)*, 13
hat sombrero *(m.)*, 12
have tener, 4
—**a good time** divertirse (e:ie), 11
—**breakfast** desayunar, 5
—**just** *(done something)* acabar de (+ *inf.*), 13
—**lunch** almorzar (o:ue), 6
—**to** deber (+ *inf.*), 2; tener que (+ *inf.*), 4
he él, 1
head cabeza *(f.)*, 8
hello hola, PI
help ayudar, 10
her su, 3; ella, 6; la, 7; le, 8
here aquí, 2
hers suyo(s), suya(s), 9
herself se, 9
highly sumamente, 16
him él, 6; lo, 7; le, 8
himself se, 9
his su, 3; suyo(s), suya(s), 9
hope esperar, 16
horrible horrible, 19
horse caballo *(m.)*, 8
hospital hospital *(m.)*, 3
hot caliente, 2
hotel hotel *(m.)*, 3
hour hora *(f.)*, 4
house casa *(f.)*, PII
household chores trabajos de la casa *(m. pl.)*, 11
how? ¿cómo?, 3
—**are you?** ¿cómo está usted?, PI
—**do you say . . . ?** ¿cómo se dice... ?, 6
—**long ago . . . ?** ¿cuánto tiempo hace que... ?, 14
—**long?** ¿cuánto tiempo?, 11
—**many?** ¿cuántos(as)?, 1
—**much?** ¿cuánto(a)?, 5

little   poco(a) (*quantity*), pequeño(a) (*size*), 4
live   vivir, 2
loan   préstamo (*m.*), 20
long   largo(a), 16
look at   mirar, 12
look for   buscar, 16
lose   perder (e:ie), 5
love   amor (*m.*)
luck   suerte (*f.*), 7
luckily   por suerte, 13
lunch   almuerzo (*m.*), 5

M

madam   señora, PI
magazine   revista (*f.*), 5
maiden name   apellido de soltera (*m.*), PI
mail   echar al correo, 20
make   hacer, 5
mall   centro comercial (*m.*), 12
man   hombre (*m.*), PII
manager   gerente (*m., f.*), 4
March   marzo, PI
marital status   estado civil (*m.*), PI
market   mercado (*m.*), 4
married   casado(a), PI
masculine   masculino, PI
mattress   colchón (*m.*), 6
May   mayo, PI
me   mí, 6; me, 7
meal   comida (*f.*), 1
meat   carne (*f.*), 7
mechanic   mecánico(a) (*m., f.*), 14
medicine cabinet   botiquín (*m.*), 9
medium   mediano(a), 13
meet   (*for an appointment*) encontrarse (o:ue), 12; (*for the first time*) conocer, 13
meeting   junta (*f.*), reunión (*f.*), 11
menu   menú (*m.*), 2

metal   metal (*m.*), 3
Mexican   mexicano(a), 1
midnight   medianoche (*f.*), 9
midterm exam   examen parcial (*m.*), 17
mile   milla (*f.*), 10
milk   leche (*f.*), 2
mine   mío(a), 9
mirror   espejo (*m.*), 9
mom   mamá, 3
moment   momento (*m.*), 9
Monday   lunes, PI
money   dinero (*m.*), PII
month   mes (*m.*), 5
more   más, 4
morning   mañana (*f.*), 1
mother   madre (*f.*), 3
mother-in-law   suegra (*f.*), 3
motorcycle   moto (*f.*), 15; motocicleta (*f.*), 15
movie theater   cine (*m.*), 5
movies   cine (*m.*), 5
Mr.   señor, PI
Mrs.   señora, PI
much   mucho, 2
museum   museo (*m.*), 2
must   deber (+ *inf.*), 2
my   mi, 3; mío(a), 9
myself   me, 9

N

name   nombre (*m.*), PI
napkin   servilleta (*f.*), 1
nationality   nacionalidad (*f.*), PI
near to   cerca de, 6
necessary   necesario(a), 17
necklace   collar (*m.*), 13
need   necesitar, 1
neither   tampoco, 6
neither . . . nor   ni... ni, 6
nephew   sobrino (*m.*), 3
never   jamás, 6; nunca, 6
new   nuevo(a), 12
newspaper   diario (*m.*), periódico (*m.*), 6

next próximo(a), 5; que
viene, 6
niece sobrina (f.), 3
nightgown camisón (m.), 13
nine nueve, PI
nineteen diecinueve, PI
ninety noventa, PII
ninth noveno(a), 5
niño(a) (m., f.) child, 8
no one nadie, 6
nobody nadie, 6
none ninguno(a), ningún, 6
North American (from the
U.S.) norteamericano(a), PI
not any ningún, ninguno(a), 6
not very well no muy bien,
PI
nothing nada, 6
novel novela (f.), 7
November noviembre, PI
now ahora, 3
number número (m.), PI
nurse enfermero(a) (m., f.),
PI

O

obtain conseguir (e:i), 7
occupation ocupación (f.), PI
ocean mar (m.), 6
October octubre, PI
of de, PII
of mine mío(a) (adj.), 9
office oficina (f.), 5
often a menudo, 2
oil aceite (m.), 14
older mayor, 4
once in a while de vez en
cuando, 12
one uno, un(a), PI
one hundred cien, ciento,
PII
one must hay que (+ inf.), 6
one says se dice, 6
only solamente, 2
open abrir, 2; abierto(a), 14
or o, 2

orange anaranjado, PI
order mandar, 16;
pedir (e:i), 6
other otro(a), 4
our nuestro(a) (adj.), 3
ours nuestro(s), nuestra(s), 9
ourselves nos, 9
over there allá, 8
owner dueño(a) (m., f.), 4

P

package paquete (m.), 20
pain dolor (m.), 18
pair par (m.), 12
pants pantalón (m.);
pantalones (m. pl.), 9
paramedic paramédico(a)
(m., f.), 18
parents padres (m.), 3
park parque (m.), 9
party fiesta (f.), 2
passenger pasajero(a)
(m., f.), 19
passport pasaporte (m.), 7
past y (with time expressions),
1; pasado(a), 10
patience paciencia (f.), 11
patient paciente (m., f.), 18
pay (for) pagar, 1
pen pluma (f.), PII
pencil lápiz (m.), PII
people gente (f.)
percent por ciento, 16
per hour por hora, 10
per night por noche, 6
percent por ciento, 16
perfume perfume (m.), 9
person persona (f.), 13
pharmacy farmacia (f.), 6
phone number número de
teléfono, PI
photocopy fotocopia (f.), 20
physics física (f.), 17
pick up buscar, 16;
recoger, 20
pie pastel (m.), 2

pill pastilla *(f.)*, 19
pink rosado, PI
place poner, 7; lugar *(m.)*, 13
—**of birth** lugar de
  nacimiento, PI
—**of interest** lugar de
  interés, 6
—**of work** lugar donde
  trabaja, PI
play *(a game or sport)*
  jugar (u:ue), 8
please por favor, PI
poem poema *(m.)*, PII
Portuguese *(language)*
  portugués *(m.)*, 13
possible posible, 17
post office oficina de
  correos *(f.)*, 6; correo
  (m.), 20
potato papa *(f.)*, patata *(f.)*, 2
prefer preferir (e:ie), 5
prepare preparar, 10
present regalo *(m.)*, 6
president presidente(a)
  (m., f.), 8
pretty bonito(a), 3
price precio *(m.)*, 15
probable probable, 17
probably probablemente, 15
problem problema *(m.)*, PII
profession profesión *(f.)*, 3
program programa *(m.)*, PII
progress progreso *(m.)*, PII
provided that con tal que, 19
purple morado, PI
purse cartera *(f.)*, 12
put poner, 7
—**a cast on** enyesar, 18
—**on** ponerse, 9
—**to bed** acostar (o:ue), 9

R

rain llover (o:ue); lluvia
  (f.), 10
raincoat impermeable
  (m.), 10

raise levantar, 9
razor máquina de afeitar
  (f.), 9
read leer, 2
ready listo(a), 14
receive recibir, 2
recent reciente, 17
recently recientemente,
  14
recommend recomendar
  (e:ie), 16
red rojo, PI
red wine vino tinto *(m.)*, 1
register matricularse, 17
regret sentir (e:ie), 17
remain quedarse, 12
remember recordar (o:ue),
  6; acordarse (o:ue) (de), 9
remove quitar, 9
rent alquilar, 15
repair shop taller *(m.)*, 14
repeat repetir (e:i), 17
report informe *(m.)*, 20
request pedir (e:i), 6
requirement requisito
  (m.), 17
reservation reservación
  (f.), 7
reserve reservar, 16
restaurant restaurante
  (m.), 1
result resultado *(m.)*, 19
return volver (o:ue), 6;
  (something) devolver
  (o:ue), 20
rice arroz *(m.)*, 11
ride a bicycle montar en
  bicicleta, 8
ride a horse montar a
  caballo, 8
right away en seguida, 14
right now ahora mismo, 9
ring anillo *(m.)*, sortija
  (f.), 13
roasted asado(a), 2
room cuarto *(m.)*, habitación
  (f.), 4

S

salad   ensalada (f.), 7
sale   liquidación (f.), venta
   (f.), 11
Saturday   sábado, PI
sauce   salsa (f.), 10
say   decir (e:i), 5
   —goodbye   despedirse
   (e:i), 11
schedule   horario (m.),
   itinerario (m.), 16
scholarship   beca (f.), 17
school   escuela (f.), 5
seat   asiento (m.), 16
second   segundo(a), 5
secretary   secretario(a)
   (m., f.), PII
see   ver, 7
select   elegir (e:i), 11
sell   vender, 13
send   mandar, enviar, 8
separated   separado(a), PI
September   septiembre, PI
servant   criado(a) (m., f.), 10
serve   servir (e:i), 5
seven   siete, PI
seventeen   diecisiete, PI
seventh   séptimo(a), 5
seventy   setenta, PII
several   varios(as), 13
sex   sexo, PI
shampoo   champú (m.), 9
shave (oneself)   afeitar(se), 9
she   ella, 1
ship   barco (m.), 15
shoe   zapato (m.), 12
   —store   zapatería (f.), 12
short   corto(a), 9
shot   inyección (f.), 18
should   deber (+ inf.), 2
sick   enfermo(a), 3
sign   firmar, 17
silver   plata (f.), 15
since   como, 20
single   soltero(a), PI

sink   fregadero (m.), 11
sir   señor, PI
sister   hermana (f.), 3
sister-in-law   cuñada (f.), 3
sit   sentar (e:ie), 9
   —down   sentarse (e:ie), 9
   —down (take a seat)
   tome asiento, PI
six   seis, PI
sixteen   dieciséis, PI
sixth   sexto(a), 5
sixty   sesenta, PII
size   talla (f.), 13
skates   patines (m. pl.), 8
ski   esquiar, 8
skis   esquíes (m. pl.), esquís
   (m. pl.), 8
sleep   dormir (o:ue), 5
sleeping bag   bolsa de
   dormir (f.), 8
slow   lento(a), 16
small   pequeño(a), 4
smaller   menor, 4
snow   nevar (e:ie), 10
soap   jabón (m.), 5
social security number
   número de seguro social
   (m.), PI
soda   refresco (m.), 1
soft drink   refresco (m.), 1
some   unos(as), PII;
   algunos(as) (pl.), algún,
   alguno(a), 6
someone   alguien, 6
something   algo, 6
sometimes   algunas veces, 6
son   hijo (m.), 2
soon   pronto, 17
soup   sopa (f.), 7
spaghetti   espaguetis (m. pl.),
   tallarines (m. pl.), 10
Spanish (language)   español
   (m.), PII
Spanish   español(a), 1
spare part   pieza de repuesto
   (f.), 14

speak hablar, 1
special especial, 17
speed limit límite de
velocidad *(m.)*, 10
speed velocidad *(f.)*, 10
spoon cuchara *(f.)*, 1
sports page página
deportiva *(f.)*, 8
spring primavera *(f.)*, 5
stairs escalera *(f.)*, 13
stamp timbre *(m.) (Méx.)*,
estampilla *(f.)*, sello *(m.)*, 6
start comenzar (e:ie),
empezar (e:ie), 5
stay quedarse, 12
stop parar
store tienda *(f.)*, 4
—**window** escaparate *(m.)*,
vidriera *(f.)*, 12
street calle *(f.)*, PI
student estudiante *(m., f.)*, 3
study estudiar, 1
suggest sugerir (e:ie), 16
suit traje *(m.)*, 13
suitcase maleta *(f.)*, valija
(f.), 4
summer verano *(m.)*, 10
Sunday domingo, PI
supermarket supermercado
(m.), 10
supervisor supervisor(a)
(m., f.), 4
sure seguro(a), 18
surgeon cirujano(a)
(m., f.), 19
surgery cirugía *(f.)*,
operación *(f.)*, 19
surname apellido *(m.)*, PI
survive sobrevivir, 19
sweater suéter *(m.)*, 10
sweep barrer, 10
swim nadar, 7
swimming pool alberca *(f.)*
(Méx.), piscina *(f.)*, 4
syrup jarabe *(m.)*, 19
system sistema *(m.)*, PII

T

table mesa *(f.)*, PII
tablecloth mantel *(m.)*, 1
take tomar, 2; *(something or
someone to someplace)* llevar, 2
—**away** quitar, 9
—**care** cuidar, 18
take off *(i.e., one's clothing)*
quitarse, 9
talk hablar, 1
tall alto(a), 3
tank tanque *(m.)*, 14
taste probar (o:ue), 9
taxi taxi *(m.)*, 2
tea té, 2
teach enseñar, 11
teacher profesor(a)
(m., f.), PI
telegram telegrama *(m.)*, PII
telephone teléfono *(m.)*, PII
television televisión *(f.)*, PII
tell decir (e:i), 6
ten diez, PI
tennis tenis *(m.)*, 8
—**racquet** raqueta de tenis
(f.), 8
tent tienda de campaña *(f.)*, 8
tenth décimo(a), 5
terrace terraza *(m.)*, 9
test *(analysis)* análisis *(m.)*, 19
than que, 4
thank you gracias, PI
that aquel, aquella *(adj.)*, 8;
aquello *(neuter pron.)*, 8; ese,
esa *(adj.)*, 8; eso *(neuter
pron.)*, 8; que, 4
that (one) aquél, aquélla
(pron.), 8; ése, ésa *(pron.)*, 8
the el, la, las, los, PII
the pleasure is mine el
gusto es mío, PI
theater teatro *(m.)*, 5
their su *(adj.)*, 3
theirs suyo(s), suya(s) *(pron.)*, 9
them ellas, ellos, 6; las, los, 7;

twenty-two   veintidós, PI
twist   torcerse, 18
two   dos, PI
two hundred   doscientos, PII
type   escribir a máquina, 12;
  tipo *(m.)*, 13
typewriter   máquina de
  escribir *(f.)*, 12

U

umbrella   paraguas
  (m. sing.), 10
uncle   tío *(m.)*, 3
underneath   debajo (de), 11
understand   entender (e:ie), 5
United States   Estados
  Unidos, 3
university   universidad *(f.)*,
  PII
unless   a menos que, 19
until   hasta, 15; hasta que, 19
us   nos, 7; nosotros(as), 6
use   usar, 13

V

vacation   vacaciones *(f. pl.)*, 5
vacuum cleaner   aspiradora
  (f.), 10
various   varios(as), 13
velocity   velocidad *(f.)*, 10
very   muy, 3
  —much   mucho, 1
  —well, and you?   muy
    bien, ¿y usted?, PI
veterinarian   veterinario(a)
  (m., f.), 15
visit   visitar, 2

W

wait   *(for)* esperar, 3; *(on)*
  atender (e:ie), 9
waiter   camarero *(m.)*, mozo
  (m.), 2
waitress   camarera *(f.)*, 2
wake up   despertarse (e:ie), 9

walk   caminar, 11; ir
  caminando, ir a pie, 11
wallet   billetera *(f.)*, 20
want   desear, 1; querer
  (e:ie), 5
ward room   sala *(f.)*, 18
wash   lavar, 9
wash one's hair   lavarse la
  cabeza, 9
washing machine   lavadora
  (f.), 10
watch   reloj *(m.)*, 15
we   nosotros(as), 1
Wednesday   miércoles, PI
week   semana *(f.)*, 5
weekend   fin de semana *(m.)*,
  16
weight   peso *(m.)*, 19
well   bien, PI; pues, 12
what?   ¿qué?, 1; ¿cuál(es)?, 3
  —is he (she, it) like?
    ¿cómo es?, 3
  —time is it?   ¿qué hora
    es?, 1
  **—is the weather like
    today?**   ¿qué tiempo
    hace hoy?, 10
when   ¿cuándo?, 4;
  cuando, 19
where?   ¿dónde?, PII
where is . . . from?   ¿de
  dónde es... ?, PII
where to?   ¿adónde?, 3
which   que, 8
which (one)?   ¿cuál(es)?, 3
white   blanco, PI
who?   ¿quién(es)?, 2
whom?   ¿quién(es)?, 2
whose?   ¿de quién?, 2
why?   ¿por qué?, 3
widowed   viudo(a) *(m., f.)*,
  PI
wife   esposa *(f.)*, 4
will   testamento *(m.)*, 19
window   ventana *(f.)*, 9
  —shop   mirar vidrieras, 12
windshield   parabrisas *(m.)*,

14
—**wiper** limpiaparabrisas
(*m.*), 14
wine vino (*m.*), 1
winter invierno (*m.*), 10
with con, 2
—**whom?** ¿con quién?, 2
without sin que, 19
—**fail** sin falta, 15
woman mujer (*f.*), PII
wood madera (*f.*), 3
work trabajar, 1; (*i.e., a
machine*) funcionar, 13
worry preocuparse, 20
worse peor, 4
write escribir, 2

X

X-ray radiografía (*f.*), 18
—**room** sala de rayos X
(*f.*), 18

Y

year(s) año(s) (*m.*), PI
yellow amarillo, PI
yes sí, 1

yesterday ayer, 10
yet todavía, 9
you tú, usted, ustedes, 1; ti, 6;
te, la, las, lo, los, 7; le, les,
te, 8
young man chico (*m.*),
muchacho (*m.*), 1
young woman chica (*f.*),
muchacha (*f.*), 1
younger menor, 4
your tu (*fam. adj.*), su
(*form. adj.*), 3
yours tuyo(s), tuya(s)
(*fam. pron.*), 9; suyo(s),
suya(s) (*form. pron.*), 9
yourself te, se, 9
yourselves se, 9

Z

zero cero, PI

Index